Learning Waray:

Waray-English and English-Waray Dictionary

Volume 2

Dr. Wilmo C. Orejola

Printed in the United States of America
By BookBaby Bookshop, Pennsaukin, NJ 08110
Published by WCO Books, Pompton Plains, NJ 07444
Email: wilcore@optonline.net

ISBN 978-1-09837-719-9

Library of Congress Control Number: 2021913631

Introduction

This Dictionary (*Purulungan*) of Waray-English and English-Waray words supplements grammar and syntax learning of the Waray language. This compilation of contemporary Waray vocabulary is the most current and comprehensive.

There are more than 4,500 Waray words in nearly 10,000 terms defined in this Dictionary. Spanish-derived Waray words make 12% of borrowed terms, while a few come from English or American.

Binisaya dictionaries date back to the Spanish colonization of the Waray speaking region. Spanish missionaries wrote them as they learned the native language to be able to communicate. Around 1616 Fr. Mateo Sanchez, SJ, wrote the *Vocabulario de la Lengua Bisaya* (Manila: *Colegio de la Sagrada Compaña de Jesus*) in Dagami, Leyte but was not published until 1711. Subsequent dictionaries with accompanying grammar books were written by Fr. Antonio Sanchez de la Rosa, OFM, who published a *Bisaya* grammar book (in 1887) and dictionaries in1886 and 1895. In 1914, he published his work with Antonio Valeriano Alcazar, OFM, *Diccionario Español para las Provincias de Samar y Leyte (Tercera Edicion)*. Manila: Imp. Y Lit. de Santos y Bernal.

Local authors also published dictionaries of the language. Eduardo A. Makabenta, Sr. published his *Binisaya-English Dictionary* and *English-Binisaya Dictionary* (Quezon City: Adbox Book Distributors and Eduardo A. Makabenta, Sr.) in 1979. The second edition of similar work was *Pagpurulungan nga Binisaya (Waray) ha Leyte ug Samar (Binisaya-English English-Binisaya Dictionary)* in 2004. Tomas A. Abuyen's *Dictionary English/Waray-Waray/Tagalog* became available (National Book Store, Quezon City) in 2005.

Many of the dictionaries have been out of print. This compilation relied mainly on relevant contemporary words the author knows as a Waray speaker himself and those provided by his Waray-speaking friends and families.

In the pre-colonial era, the inhabitants of Samar, the Northern part of Leyte, and Biliran Island provinces spoke Austronesian supported by a Visayan script and calligraphy called *badlit*, like the Tagalog *baybayin*. The Spanish supplanted this pre-colonial system of writing with Latin script and a Hispanized version of the dialect.

There is no officially approved orthography for the language. Different writers use differing orthographic styles. Because of this, there has been a wide variation in the spelling of common and practical Waray words. Many follow current orthographic conventions of *Filipino*, the Philippines' national language implemented in the 1987 Constitution. *Filipino* evolved from *Pilipino* – the official *Wikang Pambansa* (National Language) declared by President Manuel L. Quezon in 1939. Pilipino is a standardized Tagalog spoken by residents of the National Capital Region and has become the "second language" of the rest of the country, aside from English.

Waray the Language

Waray (wah-râi), also called *Winaray, Lineyte-Samarnon,* or *Samar-Leyte Binisaya,* is the people's specific language in the region where others speak distinctly different languages. More than 3 million Waray speakers make it the fifth, most-spoken native regional language after Hiligaynon, Ilocano, Cebuano, and Tagalog. Depending on classification methods, there are between 120 and 187 recognized languages and dialects spoken in the whole archipelago.

The standard language is Tacloban City's dialect and its neighboring towns, being the commerce, communication, and education center of the Eastern Visayas region. There are twenty-five dialects and subdialects identified in the area by Jason W. Lobel ("Samar-Leyte," *Concise Encyclopedia of Languages of the World,* Keith Brown and Sarah Ogilvie, eds. Elsevier, Oxford, UK, 2009).

As a Bisayan language, Waray is closely related to Central languages of Ilonggo (Hiligaynon) and Cebuano, and Southern languages of Surigaonon and Butuanon and Northern languages of the Bicolano and Tagalog.

ii

Since Capul Island, off the main Samar Island, is the home of another subgroup Sama Abaknon, the major dividing line of Waray is between Northern Samarenyo and the rest of the Waray region. The Allen, Samar dialect is predominantly Southern Sorsogon mixed with Northern Samarenyo. To the South, there is heavy Cebuano influence and borrowings in the dialects of Abuyog, Leyte, and Culaba, Biliran, while a Waray substratum exists in Baybay, Leyte and Camotes Island. These dialects and subdialects are defined mainly through word variations with minimal phonological and grammatical differences.

Waray is most readily distinguishable from other Central Philippine Languages by the *h* sound for *s*. This change has affected a small number of common grammatical meanings in Samar south of the Sta. Margarita – Matuginao - Las Navas - Gamay line and all of Leyte Waray except the towns of Javier and Abuyog.

The Waray Alphabet (*Surat Winaray*)

As recorded by Spanish missionaries in Samar and Leyte like Fathers Alcina, Ezguerra, and Delgado, before the 18th century, the proto-Austronesian *Binisaya* writings included essentially 16 syllabic characters, which consists of 13 consonants and three vowel phonemes: *a, i,* and *u.* Borrowed letters from the Spanish alphabet in many Waray words have enriched the language since.

The *basic* Waray alphabet derived from the antiquated *Binisaya* has now 15 consonants and four vowel sounds or phonemes.

The 15 consonant phonemes include *b, k, d, g, h, l, m, n, ng, p, r, s, t, w,* and *y.* The Waray alphabet lacks the letters: *c, f, j, q, v, x,* and *z* in English, and these consonants including *ch, ll,* and *ñ* in the Spanish alphabets. This deficiency facilitated Waray speakers to enrich their vocabulary by borrowing Spanish or English words. Such terms' spelling has been modified to avail letters from the *basic* Waray alphabet that would give similar sounds, aptly referred to here as the *practical* Waray alphabet.

The four vowel phonemes are *a, i, o,* and *u.* Borrowings from Spanish and English have resulted in the addition of vowel *e* (eh), resulting in five distinct vowel phonemes. These vowels are recognized in the *practical* Waray alphabet: *a, e, i, o,* and *u.*

In the practical alphabet, combinations of letters that create similar consonant phonemes replace the missing consonant. For instance, using *basic* Waray letters with similar sounds like *k* for *c, p* for *f, b* for *v, s* for *z,* or a combination of *kw* for *q* and *ks* for *x,* etc., as shown in Table 1.

The vowel *u* has a hard and long *oo* sound and distinct from the short and abrupt *o* sound (oh) for vowel *o*. When both *o* and *u* are present in a word, hard *u* comes first before a short, accented *o,* mostly occupying the end syllable. For example, the word *tuod* (*true*) is a more appropriate spelling by enunciation than *tuud,* or *tood,* or *toud.*

The use of vowels in Waray is the source of many nuanced variations in different subdialects. There are no English long *a* (*aye*) and short *e* (*eh*) and *u* (*yu*) phonemes. Waray speakers are hard *ee* and hard *uu* speakers, although they have adopted the softer versions of these vowels. When the letter *e* is present in a Waray word, it is likely a borrowed word.

It is also notable that Waray speakers do not pronounce short *e* (*eh*) at the beginning of a word but conveniently when inside it. For this reason, this Dictionary does not have letter *E* as an alphabetical heading, although the letter is present in many borrowed words. For example, the Spanish *escuela* becomes *iskwelahan,* or English *exam* would be *iksam.*

As illustrated in table 1, the *practical* alphabet represents inclusive phonemic letters lacking in the *basic* Waray alphabet.

Table 1. A comparison of the Alphabets

Waray Alphabet		Foreign Alphabets	
Basic	Practical	Spanish	English
A	A	A	A
B	B	B	B
K	K	C [c]	C [d]
-	Ts [a]	Ch [c]	-
D	D	D	D
-	E [a]	E [c]	E [d]
-	P	F [c]	F [d]
G	G	G	G
H	H	H	H
I	I	I	I
-	Dy [a]	J [c]	J [d]
-	K	-	K
L	L	L	L
-	Y or Ly [a]	Ll [c]	-
M	M	M	M
N	N	N	N
-	Ny [a]	Ñ [c]	-
NG	NG [b]	-	-
O	O	O	O
P	P	P	P
-	Kw [a]	Q [c]	Q [d]
R	R	R	R
S	S	S	S
T	T	T	T
U	U	U	U
-	B	V [c]	V [d]
W	W	-	W
-	Ks [a]	X [c]	X [d]
Y	Y	Y	Y
-	S	Z [c]	Z [d]

Legend:
a - Practical Waray letter to substitute missing *basic Binisaya* letters
b - Waray letter with no equivalent in Spanish and English alphabets
c - Spanish letters absent in the *basic* Waray alphabet
d - English letters absent in the *basic* Waray alphabet

A sampling of the Waray lexeme derived from Spanish and English words are listed in Table 2. It illustrates how the practical alphabet accommodates the phonemic equivalents of such words.

Table 2. How the *practical* Waray alphabet spells some borrowed words.

Spanish words	Practical Waray words
accidente (*accident*)	aksidente
apellido (*surname*)	apelyido
arcangel (*archangel*)	arkanghel
ciudad (*city*)	syudad
chocolate (*chocolate*)	tsokolate
cuaresma (*Lent*)	kwaresma
doña (*honorific for lady*)	donya
escuela (*school*)	iskwelahan
esquina (*corner*)	iskina
familia (*family*)	pamilya
guitarra (*guitar*)	gitara
harina (*flour*)	arina
hechura (*shape*)	hitsura
herbolario (*herbalist*)	arbularyo
jugador (*gambler*)	hugador
llano (*simple, plain*)	yano
llave (*key*)	yabe
investigar (*investigate*)	imbistigar
maquina (*machine*)	makina
marcha (*march*)	martsa
negociante (*businessman*)	negosyante
ojales (*buttonholes*)	ohales
ochenta (*eighty*)	otsenta
pavo (*turkey*)	pabo
perjuicio (*damage*)	piruwisyo
pizarra (*blackboard*)	pisara
querida (*mistress*)	kerida
señal (*signal*)	sinyal
vacio (*empty*)	basiyo
ventana (*window*)	bintana
zapatos (*shoes*)	sapatos
English words	
computer	kompyuter
decision	desisyon
doctor	doktor
keyboard	kibord
mouse	maus
nurse	nars
toothbrush	tutbras
X-ray	iksre
xerox	seroks
xylophone	silopon

A word is composed of a single or more syllables of varying phonemes. It defines a different thought or meaning. Tradition sets specific rules to polish and harmonize the thought process expressed by a group of words and avoid confusion.

There are innumerable possibilities of combinations of the letters of the alphabet to form a word. A word denotes an idea or action, classified into various word classes or parts of Speech. It can transform from one class to another so does its meaning. The process is called *inflection*.

There are basic and systematic methods or rules that allow transforming words from one part of Speech to another and vice-versa and using them freely in sentences. Also, a verb could be inflected in various ways to signify its usage relative to the tense, number, voice, aspect, etc. This part of Waray grammar and syntax is discussed thoroughly in the first volume of this book *Learning Waray: Words and Sentences.*

Guide to Pronunciation

Syllables in each Waray word are distinct and separate when pronounced. Each syllable matters. A combination of available phonemic letters substitutes missing letters in borrowed Spanish or English words.

Typical of the *Binisaya* (*basic* Waray), the pronunciation of words sometimes requires a diacritic accent, an apostrophe, or a hyphen. When placed over a syllable's vowel, a diacritic emphasizes that syllable, which assumes a crescendo sound when enunciated.

An apostrophe usually indicating a missing vowel or syllable in a shortened word, signals that an accent is on the preceding syllable where two consonants come together. When the two vowels come together, a hyphen is used instead.

The apostrophe signals a break in the word's pronunciation especially when two consonants come together as a result. But a break in the pronunciation occurs between the consonants despite an apostrophe. The accented sound falls on the preceding syllable. For example: accented "kalaw'dan" (*sea*), (contraction of the word "kalawuran," where the apostrophe indicates the missing vowel *u*) or no accent "kalawdan" has a break in pronunciation between "law" and "dan."

On the other hand, in the word "mangga" (*mango*), there is no omitted vowel between the g's, but still pronounced with a break between "mang" and "ga." Thus, the use of an apostrophe becomes unnecessary. Apostrophes may have been used for that purpose in other Waray texts but not in this dictionary.

The nasal consonants "ng" and "mga" are common in the Austronesian alphabet. One unfamiliar with the language would ask, "how do you pronounce these consonants without a vowel?" especially at the beginning of a word.

In these instances, consonants coming together, the nasal sound of "ng" muffles the vowel. Convention determines this resulting phoneme. For example, it is common to find words with *n* and *g* together, as in *ng*, the vowel phonemes are "n(a)ga," "n(i)gi," and "n(o)go" or "n(u)gu," or in short "nga," "ngi," "ngo," and "ngu."

Another example is the determiner "mga" which has phonemes "m(a)n(a)ga," in short "manga." It is not necessary to show the silent vowel *a*.

When vowels go together in a word, each vowel phoneme is pronounced distinctly. A hyphen (-) between the vowels accents the dominant vowel, which is usually the first vowel. For example, in words "bitu-on" (*star*) and "kabata-an" (*children*), the accent falls on the syllables "tu-" and "ta-."

Like the apostrophe for contracted words, the use of the hyphen for this purpose as part of the language orthography has been customary but also redundant since the rule is clear that the accented sound falls on the preceding vowel or syllable in case of consonants.

However, diacritic accents play a major role in pronunciation of Waray words specially to indicate the accented syllable of some words like "buó" (*complete*) or "baó" (*turtle*) where the accent falls on the last vowel.

Diacritic accents also are essential in distinguishing words with double meanings. The placement of an acute diacritic determines the meaning of the word. For example, the term "báta" (with a diacritic accent on the first syllable) means a *child*. When the diacritic falls on the last syllable, "batá," the same word means *uncle*. Other examples are the words "dúlong" (*prow of a boat*) and "dulóng" (*to wrestle*), "ámo" (*master*) and "amó" (*monkey*).

Word reduplication is a common language tool. Repeating a word usually emphasizes its meaning. Often, a repeated word designates plurality in number, but it can also mean other things. For instance, the word "buho," which means a hole, when duplicated, becomes "buhubuho," which means "many holes." The word "tawo" means a man, but "tawutawo" does not signify plurality of men. Instead, it means a caricature of a man, a henchman, or a crony. From the word "bato" (*rock*), "batubato" literally means "rocky," but it could also be used in a sentence as a figure of speech, meaning critical issue.

Notably, if the last vowel of the word is "o," the final vowel of the first word changes to "u," that is, "tawo" becomes "tawutawo," or "buho" "buhubuho." Like the vowel *e*, the vowel *o* is a relatively weak vowel since it does not really belong to the original Austronesian vowels.

When two consonants come together between the reduplicated words, a hyphen may not also be necessary as it has been in other Waray orthography. For example, the term "tahap," meaning "suspicion," when reduplicated becomes "tahap-tahap," or "tahaptahap." Both would mean "false" allegations with or without a hyphen.

Note that using hyphens even in the English grammar has evolved, and it has become convenient to discard its usage in compound words, in this case, reduplicated words. Hyphens in word reduplication are also unnecessary.

Dictionary (*Purulungan*)

This book contains English translations of commonly used words and phrases in Waray. While sentence construction in Waray varies widely from that in English, the parts of Speech are similar. To ensure a more constructive comparison, it becomes necessary to provide alternative Waray words where no such equivalents are available, especially word classes or parts of Speech (*mga bahin han Pagyakan*).

Table 3. The parts of Speech in Waray and English and their abbreviations in italics.

Purulungan	Abbrev.	Dictionary	Abbrev.
ngaran	*n.*	noun	*n.*
hangaran	*han.*	pronoun	*pron.*
kangaran	*kan.*	adjective	*adj.*
ági	*a.*	verb	*v.*
kaági	*kaa.*	adverb	*adv.*
sumpay	*s.*	conjunction	*conj.*
katungod	*kat.*	preposition	*prep.*
kahiusa	*kah.*	interjection	*interj.*
tudlok	*tud.*	article	*art.*

Translations are in English, but many of the borrowed words are Spanish derived. Therefore, the equivalents are for both the Spanish term and the modified or acquired Waray lexeme. On the other hand, certain Waray words do not have exact translations, which would require more words in English to describe them.

In the first part of this book, the word entry follows the *basic* Waray alphabet sequentially as follows: *A, B, K, D, G, H, I, L, M, N, NG, O, P, R, S, T, U, W,* and *Y.* Note that there is no *E* heading in the alphabetical list because Waray words do not begin with short *E* sound including Spanish-derived words.

Bold letters identify the Waray word using the practical alphabet. Following the dash is the English word equivalent or its definition with an abbreviation before it, indicating its word classification in English. The original term in italics and its source indicate a borrowed lexeme.

Sample of word entry:

> **apelyido** – *n.* family name, surname, Spanish *apellido*
> **apiki** – *adj.* close, near; *v.* to get close
> **bilib** – *v.* to admire, to impress, to believe in one's qualities or abilities, English *believe*

In the second part of this book, the word entry follows the English alphabet sequentially as follows: *A, B, C, D, E, F, G, H, I, J, K, L, M, N, O, P, Q, R, S, T, U, V, W, X, Y,* and *Z.*

Sample of word entry:

> **land turtle** – *n.* baó, hangag
> **landing place** – *n.* duungan, duruungan, pantalan, landingan - English *landing*
> **language** – *n.* yinaknan, kayakan, purulungan, pinulungan, lingguahi - Spanish *lenguaje*
> **lantern** – *n.* suga, parol - Spanish *farol*
> **laptop** – *n.* laptap - American *laptop*

The English word is in bold letters and following the dash is the Waray word equivalent and for Spanish or English borrowed words, its Waray lexeme. The abbreviation indicates its word classification in Waray.

In many instances, a Waray word as an English definition indicates both as *n.* for ngaran (*noun*) and *a.* for ági (*verb*). Its infinitive form as a verbal, prefixed with *pag* or *pagpa*, is a noun in a sentence, but its stem could be further inflected as a verb.

Sample word entry:

> **destroy** – *n., a.* bungkag, guba, ruba, pagbungkag, pagguba, pagruba
> **detach** – *n., a.* lukba, bulag, paglukba, pagbulag

The characteristic feature of the Austronesian VSO (Verb-Subject-Object) sentence construct makes many inflected derivations from a particular active or passive infinitive of a verb. This feature and the rules of inflection are thoroughly discussed in the first volume of this book *Learning Waray: Words and Sentences.*

Certain Waray words may have different, even opposite meanings, from one dialect to another. The author reserves the right to interpret variations or nuances among dialects that may misrepresent that dialect's essence based on the standard dialect. Some also may have material differences lost in translation.

The author acknowledges the limitation of providing more English vocabulary than Waray words available because of a rich and voluminous contemporary English dictionary. To use this book for its intended purpose in learning to speak and write Waray, one needs to know the English language.

With great interest and good intentions, the author and his language advisors hope that this dictionary of contemporary Waray provides adequate materials to learn the language.

Acknowledgments

The author owes an enormous debt of gratitude to his language advisors Joan Gray Atillo, Wilhelma Orejola, Alejo Yu, Wilfredo Orejola, and my wife Crescencia Orejola for their insightful contributions and input in putting together this Dictionary, to Cedric Orejola and Oliver Orejola in collating data and formatting the manuscript, and to Nadine Demers for the artistic design of the book covers.

Wilmo C. Orejola

Part 1

Waray

to

English

A:a

aada – *pron.*that place; *adv.* there

aadi – *pron.* this place; *adv.* here

aarig – *n.* competition; *v.* to compete

abaka - *n.* banana plant variety used for rope-making, Manila hemp, *Musa textilis*

abadaw – *interj.* expression of surprise or concern, *Alas!*

abaniko – *n.* fan, Spanish *abanico*

abante – *v.* to advance, Spanish *avance*

abat – *v.* to feel

abayan – *n.* float, life vest

abiabi – *v.* to invite, to encourage, to enjoin

abir – *conj.* so that

abiriya – *v.* to stall like motor

abiso – *n.* warning; *v.* to warn, Spanish *aviso*

abitapa – *conj.* as if

abó, agbo - *n.* ashes, soot, gray color

abot – *v.* to arrive, to reach

abri – *v.* to open, Spanish *abrir*

Abril – *n.* April, Spanish *abril*

abrilata – *n.* can opener, Spanish *abrelata*

abtik – *n.* skill, expertise, activity

abukay – *n.* white parrot, cockatoo

abugado – *n.* lawyer, Spanish *abogado*

abugho – *v.* to get jealous

abuhan – *n.* stove

aburido – *adj.* anxious, bored, Spanish *aburrido*

abuyon – *v.* to agree, to conform

abyog – *v.* to swing

akasya – *n.* acacia tree

ako – *pron.* I

akon, ak – *pron.* me, my, mine

aksidente – *n.* accident, Spanish *accidente*; *v.* to get into an accident

ada – *adv.* perhaps

ada takay – *interj.* expression of concurrence or agreement

adlaw – *n.* sun, day

adurno – *n.* decorations; *v.* to decorate, Spanish *adorno*

aga – *n.* morning

agap – *adj.* early

agaron – *n.* boss, master

agaw – *v.* to grab, to snatch

agbay – *v.* to hold hands

aghat – *n.* encouragement, incentive; *v.* to encourage, to prod

ági – *n.* penmanship, tracing, method, verb; *v.* to pass, to flow like water

agí – *v.* to find, to discover

agían, aragian – *n.* passage, road, highway

agikik – *n.* screeching sound

agidaw – *interj.* Alas!, expression of surprise

agidoy, agi – *interj.* Ouch! expression of bodily or emotional pain

agila – *n.* eagle

agod – *adv.* surely, certainly; *conj.* in order to

agoy – *interj.* Ahoy!, expression of exasperation

1

agrabyado – *adj.* insulted, offended, aggrieved, Spanish *agraviar*

agsob – *adv.* often, frequently

agta – *n.* aeta, negrito

agtang – *n.* forehead

agumaa – *n.* small mackerel

agurok – *n.* rumbling and gurgling sound in the intestines, borborygmi

Agusto – *n.* August, Spanish *agosto*

agwanta – *v.* to endure, to sacrifice, Spanish *aguantar*

agwas – *n.* water, public water system, Spanish *agua*

agwason – *n.* poisonous snake

ahinte – *n.* agent, Spanish *agente*

ahos – *n.* garlic, Spanish *ajo*

alad, alasid – *n.* fence

alagad – *n.* servant, follower

alagidagid – *n.* likeness, semblance; *adj.* similar, like

alahas – *n.* jewelry

alamag – *n.* molds; *v.* to become moldy

alamagon – *adj.* moldy

alamre - *n.* wire, Spanish *alambre*

alang – *adv.* surely, certainly

alangalang – *adj.* hesitant, wavering, indecisive; *v.* to hesitate

alapap – *n.* fungal skin infection

alát – *n.* bamboo backpack

alawihaw – *n.* crunchy sour fruit

alayon – *n.* favor, request; *v.* to ask a favor; to request

alburoto – *n.* uproar, disturbance, grumbling, Spanish *alboroto; v.* to grumble, to disturb

alkansiya – *n.* money box, piggy bank, Spanish *alcancia*

alkuba – *n.* ceiling, alcove, Spanish *alcoba*

alibangbang – *n.* butterfly

alibundan – *n.* whirlpool

alikos – *v.* to wind around

alimango – *n.* large grayish, mud crab

alimpapaso – *n.* blood-sucking insect

alimpupuro – *n.* hair whorl

alimuot – *n.* suffocating, confined space

alindanga – *n.* hot, dry weather, scorching heat

alinsuob – *n.* humidity, suffocating heat, sultry weather

alintarakan – *n.* skull

alipuros – *n.* dust devil, tornado

alisngaw – *n.* stench, stifling humid air, humidity

almanaki – *n.* almanac, calendar, Spanish *almanaque*

almiris – *n.* stone or metal mortar, Spanish *almirez*

álo – *n.* embarrassment, morals; *v.* to embarrass

alog – *v.* to fetch water

alop – *n.* stain, empathy; *v.* to stain, to feel sympathy

alpiler – *n.* pin, Spanish *alfiler*

alsa – *v.* to raise, Spanish *alzar*

alta presyon – *n.* high blood pressure, hypertension, Spanish *alta presion*

amakan – *n.* woven bamboo slats used as walls

amasang – *adj.* careless, chaotic, haphazard

amay – *n.* father
ambak – *v.* to leap, to jump
ambisyon – *n.* ambition,
Spanish *ambicion*
ambisyuso – *adj.* ambitious,
Spanish *ambicioso*
ambot – *interj.* am not sure,
expression of denial
amenudo – *n.* a couple's
dance to each partner's style
amerikano – *n.* American
citizen, Spanish *americano*
amihan – *n.* north wind
ámin – *n.* atonement; *v.* to
admit mistakes, to make
amends
amín – *v.* to bless, to be
blessed
ámo – *n.* master; *pron.* which,
that; *adj.* confirmed
amó – *n.* monkey
amóg – *adj.* dirty, filthy,
unsanitary
amon – *pron.* us, our, ours
(excluding listener)
ampo – *v.* to pray
an – *art.* a
anak – *n.* child, son, daughter;
v. to give birth
anak ha gawas – *n.*
stepbrother, stepsister
anahaw – *n.* palm tree with
fan-like leaves, palmetto,
Saribus rotundifolius sp.
anas – *v.* to drift, to be swept
away
anáy – *n.* sow, gestating female
pig
ánay – *n.* termite; *v.* to infest
with termites

andam – *n.* preparation,
readiness; *v.* to prepare, to be
ready
andana – *n.* building floor
andoy – *v.* to sadden, to be
nostalgic
anganangan – *v.* to delay, to
procrastinate
angat – *v.* to raise, to lift
angay – *n.* harmony; *v.* to
oblige, to harmonize; *adj.*
coordinated, similar
angbit – *n.* share; *v.* to partake
angkas – *v.* to ride as passenger
on a bicycle
angkon – *v.* to claim
angkop – *v.* to adopt a child
angga – *n.* nickname, terms of
endearment
anghel – *n.* angel, Spanish
angel
anghit – *n.* armpit odor
angihas – *adj.* uneven,
lopsided; to be lopsided
anglit – *n.* small kettle
angso – *n.* stench of urine
angtod – *n.* burnt smell
anibong – *n.* wild and edible
palm
aningal – *n.* echo; *v.* to echo,
to resonate
aninipot – *n.* firefly
anó – *interj., verb, adj* loose
word to represent any thought
often times comes with
gesticulation; inflected like a
verb, adjective
áno – *pron.* what, which as a
query
anod – *v.* to drift away
antinganting – *n.* talisman,
charm, amulet

antis – *conj.* before, Spanish *antes*

antiyuhos – *n.* eyeglass, Spanish *anteojos*

antos – *n.* suffering; *v.* to suffer

antuman – *adv.* slightly

anyag – *n.* brilliance

anyaw, amyaw – *n.* neighbor

apa – *n.* wafer, ice cream cone

apan – *n.* grasshopper

aparador – *n.* cupboard, Spanish *aparador*

apas – *v.* to catch up, to follow hurriedly, to chase

apaw – *v.* to overflow

apdo – *n.* bile, gall bladder

apektado – *adj.* affected, involved, Spanish *afectar*

apelyido – *n.* family name, surname, Spanish *apellido*

apiki – *adj.* close, near; *v.* to get close

apinas – *adv.* hardly, Spanish *apenas*

apitong – *n.* large tree that gives turpentine-like resin

aplod – *n.* violet color

apog – *n.* calcium powder

apoy – *n.* grandparents, old person

aprak – *v.* to explode, to burst into powder

apras – *v.* to risk, to force ahead, or go against the norm or advice

araba – *n.* complaint; *v.* to complain

arado – *n.* plow; *v.* to plow, Spanish *arado*

aragaw – *n.* competition, rivalry; *v.* to compete, to vie, to fight over something

aragaway – *n.* fight, battle, war; *v.* to fight

aragian – *n.* way, trail, passage

aragmot, amot – *n.* contribution; *v.* to contribute

aragtubang – *n.* face-to-face meeting, confrontation; *v.* to confront, to settle differences

aragway – *n.* quarrel, brawl, riot; *v.* to quarrel, to fight

áram – *n.* knowledge, know-how

arám – *v.* to learn a skill, to study

arampuan – *n.* shrine, altar

aranghita – *n.* tangerine

arbularyo – *n.* herbalist, medicine man, Spanish *herbolario*

arkanghel – *n.* archangel, Spanish *arcangel*

arkitekto – *n.* architect, Spanish *arquitecto*

areglo - *v.* to settle differences, Spanish *arreglar*

arina – *n.* wheat flour, Spanish *harina*

aring – *n.* endearment, romance; *v.* to endear, to express affection

aringaring – *n.* romantic idel talk, shenanigan

aringasa – *n.* noise, commotion

aringit – *adj.* fussy, crabby, irritable, petulant, impetuous; *v.* to whine, to fuss about

ariw – *n.* soot

ariya – *v.* to release, to lower, to haul down, Spanish *arriar*

ariyos – *n.* earrings, Spanish *arreos*

armado – *adj.* armed, Spanish *armado*

armas – *n.* weapon, Spanish *arma*

arasip – *n.* palm flour

aró – *v.* to beg

arog – *v.* to own, to acquire

aroganti – *adj.* arrogant, Spanish *arrogante*

árong – *n.* mole, nevus

arót – *n.* haircut; *v.* to cut hair

arsubispo – *n.* archbishop, Spanish *arzobispo*

artista – *n.* actor, actress, artist, Spanish *artista*

aruga – *n.* care, hospitality, accommodation; *v.* to take care of, to accommodate, to be hospitable

asawa – *n.* spouse, wife

asáy – *adv.* preferably

ásay – *v.* to eat only meat

asdang – *v.* to come face to face, to confront

asero – *n.* steel, Spanish *acero*

asi – *v.* to recognize, to acknowledge

asikaso – *v.* to be responsible

asin – *n.* salt

asintado – *adj.* settled, Spanish *asentado*

aslom – *n.* acidity; grapefruit

asno – *n.* donkey, Spanish *asno*

asó – *n.* smoke

asoge – *n.* mercury, quicksilver, Spanish *azoque*

asosasyon – *n.* association, Spanish *asociacion*

asukar – *n.* sugar, Spanish *azucar*

asul – *adj.* blue, Spanish *azul*

asunto – *n.* case in court, Spanish *asunto*

aswang – *n.* witch

asya – *adj.* correct, right

asyite – *n.* cooking oil, engine oil, Spanish *aceite*

atake – *v.* to attack, Spanish *atacar*

atalabong – *n.* white heron

ataman – *n.* care; *v.* to provide care

atay – *n.* liver

atimangno – *n.* home care; *v.* to provide home care

atipunga – *n.* athlete's foot, fungal infection

atis – *n.* starapple

atitipalo, atipapalo – *n.* butterfly larva, worm that penetrates human ear

ato – *v.* to fight

áton, at – *pron.* us, our, ours (including listener)

atop – *n.* roof

atras – *v.* to back up, Spanish *atras*

atrasado – *adj.* late, behind in time, Spanish *atrasado*

atraso – *n.* setback, arrears, grievances

atsuwete – *n.* annatto seed for red food coloring, Spanish *achiote*

atubáng – *v.* to face the front

atúbang – *prep.* across, in front of

atubangan – *n.* frontage, façade, genitalia; *prep.* in front of

atubangay – *v.* to face each other

atuli – *n.* ear wax

awa – *n.* envy, jealousy; *v.* to envy

awaanon – *adj.* selfish, greedy, envious

awas – *v.* to flow

awat – *v.* to involve, to actively participate

away – *n.* fight, quarrel, squabble; *v.* to fight

awdunon – *adj.* shy, bashful, timid

awil – *v.* to engage, to engross, to retain

awit – *n.* song; *v.* to sing

awód – *n.* embarrassment, shame

awto – *n.* car, American automobile

ayad – *v.* to repair, to fix

ayam – *n.* dog

ayat – *n.* challenge; *v.* to dare, to challenge

áyaw – *v.* to add, to replenish

ayáw – *v.* to prohibit, to refuse, not to do

ayon – *v.* to satisfy, to like

áyos – *n.* order; *v.* to put in order, to arrange

ayós – *interj.* expression of approval, Okay!

ayre – *n.* air, atmosphere, Spanish *aire*

ayskrim – *n.* ice cream, American *ice cream*

ayuda – *n.* help, aid; *v.* to help, to assist, Spanish *ayuda*

B:b

ba – *adv.* interrogative exclamatory word

baa – *interj.* expression of disapproval

bába – *n.* mouth

babá – *v.* to hump, to piggyback

babad – *v.* to soak

babay – *n.* older brother,; *v.* to say goodbye; *interj.* goodbye

babayi – *n.* female

babayínon – *n.* effeminate male, gay; *adj.* effeminate

baboy – *n.* adult pig; *v.* to make a mess

baka – *n.* cow, Spanish *vaca*

bákad – *v.* to unravel, to fray

bakang – *n.* stride; *v.* to stride

bakasyon – *n.* vacation, Spanish *vacacion*

bakhaw – *n.* tropical tree growing in marshland used as firewood

bakhawan – *n.* mangrove, source of firewood

bakho – *v.* to sob silently

bakilid – *n.* slope, *adj.* inclined, lopsided

baklaw – *n.* nose ring of animals

baktas – *v.* to hike, to trek

baktin – *n.* yound pig, piglet

baktinan – *n.* piggery

bakuna – *n.* vaccine; *v.* to vaccinate, Spanish *vacuna*

bakunawa – *n.* eclipse

bakya – *n.* wooden sandal

badbad – *v.* to unravel, to fray

badil – *n.* dynamite fishing; *v.* to fish using dynamite

badlis – *v.* to etch, to write

badlit – *n.* Visayan system of writing, script, or calligraphy

badó – *n.* dress, clothes

baduya – *n.* fried mashed ripe banana

bága – *n.* lung

bagá – *n.* ember, red color; *v.* to burn to embers; *adj.* similar, like, pretentious

bagabaga – *adv.* somewhat, somehow, similarly

bagakay – *n.* thinner variety of bamboo

bagahi – *n.* baggage, Spanish *bagaje*

bágang – *n.* rhinoceros beetle, jet black scarab

bagáng - *n.* molar

bagay – *adj.* similar, coordinated

bágid – *v.* to rub, to scrape

bagis – *n.* straight line; *v.* to etch a straight line, to scratch

bagisbagis – *v.* to wait

bágo – *adj.* new

bagol – *n.* coconut shell; *v.* to pack in coconut shell

bagsak – *v.* to fall, to drop, to crash

bagtak – *v.* to split coconut shell, to hack with a cleaver

bagtik – *v.* to solidify, to thicken as liquid

bagting – *v.* to ring the bell

bagtingan – *n.* bell

bagtinganan – *n.* belfry, bell tower

bagyo – *n.* storm, typhoon

baha – *n.* flood; *v.* to flood

bahag – *n.* loin cloth

bahal – *n.* tangy fresher variety of coconut wine

bahala na – *interj.* expression of fatalistic belief or resignation, come what may

bahalina – *n.* smooth aged variety of coconut wine

bahandi – *n.* wealth, fortune

bahaw – *n.* leftover

bahin – *n.* part, share; *v.* to divide; *conj.* about, in regards to

bahinbahin – *n.* division; *v.* to divide, to distribute

bahó – *n.* odor, fume, Spanish *vaho*

báho – *v.* to smell

bahog – *v.* to mix dish soup on rice

bahol – *adj.* thick, big

bahong – *n.* fermented mussel

baíd – *adj.* sharp, honed as a knife

báid – *v.* to sharpen, to hone sharp tool

bairan – *n.* tool sharpener, hard stone used to sharpen cutting tools

bala – *n.* bullet, Spanish *bala*

balabag – *v.* to cross, to block; *prep.* across

balagon – *n.* vine, liana

balagúnon – *adj.* curly as in hair

balanak – *n.* small mullet fish

balanga – *n.* young corn

balangaw – *n.* rainbow, shingles

baláod – *n.* rules, laws

balat – *n.* sea cucumber

balata – *n.* betrothal, prearranged marriage; *v.* to betroth

baláwang – *n.* waist, loin

balawarte, balwarte – *n.* bulwark, defense, Spanish *baluarte*

7

balay – *n.* house, home; *v.* to build a house
balaybalay, malaybalay – *n.* playhouse, shack
balayi – *n.* parents of son-in-law
balbag – *n.* hard stick, club; *v.* to hit with stick or club
balkon – *n.* balcony, Spanish *balcon*
baldi – *n.* pail, bucket, Spanish *balde*
balhas – *n.* sweat, perspiration; *v.* to sweat, to perspire
balhason – *adj.* sweaty
balhin – *v.* to transfer
bali – *adj.* opposite, reverse
balik – *v.* to return, to reverse course
balikad – *v.* to invert; *adj.* inverse, inside out, reverse
balikawot – *adj.* hook, knotty, gnarly
baliko – *adj.* bent, curved
baligya – *n.* merchandise; *v.* to sell
balimbin, malimbin – *n.* star fruit
balinas – *v.* to slip
balinsasayaw – *n.* swallow, bird
balintong – *n.* forward flip, forward somersault; *v.* to fall forward, to somersault forward
balisa – *v.* to wear in reverse; *adj.* reverse
baliskad – *n.* back flip, backward somersault; *v.* to fall backward, to somersault backward
balitang – *n.* stair step, grade
balitaw, balitgad – *interj.* expression of doubt,

incredulous
balo – *n.* widow, widower
bálod – *n.* turtle doves
balód – *n.* wave
bálon – *n.* provisions; *v.* to bring provisions
balos – *v.* to respond, to repay
balsi – *n.* waltz, Spanish *vals*
baltok – *adj.* smart, intelligent
baluta – *n.* ballot, Spanish *balota*
balúto, barúto – *n.* outrigged dugout canoe, outrigger
balyo – *v.* to exchange, to switch
balyúan, balyuay – *n.* exchange
bana – *n.* spouse, husband
banagan - *n.* lobster, crawfish
banaog – *n.* black coral
banko – *n.* bank, bench, Spanish *banco*
bandira – *n.* banner, flag, Spanish *bandera*
bangad – *n.* backward incline of a boat
bangaran – *n.* aromatic variety of banana
bangaw – *n.* large fly, street kid, thief
bangka – *n.* cockroach
bangkaw – *n.* spear, harpoon; *v.* to throw with a spear
bangga – *v.* to collide, to crash
banggaay – *n.* collision
bangil – *n.* support; *v.* to support, to elevate
bángin – *adv.* perhaps, probably
bangín – *n.* cliff, bluff
bangira – *n.* rack for dishes and pans
bangis – *n.* bravery, courage

bángon – *v.* to wake up, to get up
bangón – *n.* suburb
bangot – *n.* face covering
bangungot – *n.* nightmare, alcoholic pancreatitis; *v.* to have nightmares
bangus – *n.* milkfish
banhaw – *v.* to resurrect
banhod – *n.* numbness
banig – *n.* straw mat
banog – *n.* hawk
banos – *v.* to scrub
bansil – *n.* gold-covered tooth; *v.* to cover tooth with gold
bantad – *n.* movement; *v.* to move, to quicken
bantay – *n.* guard, watchman; *v.* to watch, to guard
bantog – *n.* fame, popularity
bantugan – *adj.* famous, popular
banugbanog, manugbanog – *n.* kite; *v.* to fly a kite
banwa – *n.* grass
banyak – *n.* kick; *v.* to kick
banyaga – *n.* stranger, foreigner
banyera – *n.* bathtub, Spanish *bañera*
banyo – *n.* bathroom, Spanish *baño*
banyos – *n.* medicinal lotion; *v.* to apply ointment or lotion
baó – *n.* land turtle, tortoise
baog – *adj.* sterile, barren, infertile
baol – *n.* trunk, casket
baóng – *n.* caldron
bapor – *n.* ship, steamship, steamboat, Spanish *vapor*
bará – *v.* to block, Spanish *barra*

baráan – *adj.* holy, gracious
baraka – *n.* worry; *v.* to worry
barakasyon – *n.* picnic
barágayaw – *v.* to partake, to distribute shares
baraha – *n.* deck of playing cards, Spanish *baraja*
barahibo – *n.* fuzz, fine hair, feather
barandilya – *n.* balustrade, railing, Spanish *barandilla*
bárang – *v.* to cast spell, to poison
baráng – *n.* spell, curse, poison
barangan – *n.* person who poisons
barangas – *n.* body hair
barangason – *adj.* hirsute, hairy
barangay – *n.* zone, barrio
baras – *n.* sand
barasahan – *n.* library
barasahon – *n.* book, magazine
barason – *adj.* sandy, gritty sensation
barat – *n.* miser; *adj.* greedy
baratilyo – *n.* bargain sale, Spanish *baratillo*
barato – *adj.* cheap, inexpensive, affordable, Spanish *barato*
báraw – *n.* spider
baráw – *v.* to interrupt
barayong – *n.* hard redwood, *Ptecarpus indicus sp.*
barbas – *n.* beard
barbero – *n.* barber, Spanish *barber*
barkada – *n.* gang, gang member
barko – *n.* ship, vessel, Spanish *barco*

9

bári – *v.* to break like a tree branch

barí – *v.* to harvest rice

baribad – *n.* excuse; *v.* to give excuses, to refuse

barikas – *v.* to strip of covering usually by wind

baril – *n.* barrel, Spanish *barril*

barilis – *n.* yellow fin tuna, tuna fish

bariw – *n.* thick woven mat made of *Corypha* fan palm

baró – *v.* to know, to learn

barok – *n.* red bark used to ferment coconut wine

barumbado – *adj.* shabby, wild, uncivilized

baryo – *n.* district, village, Spanish *barrio*

basa – *v.* to read

basag – *adj.* sonorous, garbled voice, hoarse

basahan – *n.* study room

basahon – *n.* reading material, book, magazine

basi – *conj.* so that, based, Spanish *base*

baskit – *n.* interwoven straw container, English *basket*

baskitbol – *n.* basketball; *v.* to play basketball, American *basketball*

baskitbulan – *n.* basketball court

baskog – *n.* tenacity, stiffness

basihan – *n.* basis, reference; *v.* to refer, to base on, Spanish *base*

basiyo – *adj.* empty, vacant, Spanish *vacio; v.* to empty

baso – *n.* drinking glass, Spanish *vaso,* tumbler

basol – *n.* guilt, regret, repentance; *v.* to blame, to repent

basol – *n.* caterpillar

baston – *n.* cane, Spanish *baston*

bastos – *adj.* rude, obscene, profane, ill-mannered, coarse, Spanish *basto*

basuni – *n.* splinter

basura – *n.* trash, waste, garbage, Spanish *basura*

basurahan – *n.* garbage bin, trash can

basya – *v.* to empty, to drain, Spanish *vaciar*

báta – *n.* child; *adj.* young

batá – *n.* uncle

batak – *v.* to throw like stone

batakay – *n.* fight with stones

batad – *n.* broom made of straw

batang – *n.* driftwood, flotsam

batánon – *adj.* young, youthful

batasan – *n.* manners, etiquette, habit

báti - *v.* to listen, to hear, to feel

batikos – *v.* to abuse, to humiliate, to deride

batidor – *n.* beater, Spanish *batidor*

batikulon – *n.* gizzard

bató – *n.* stone, a piece of rock, *v.* to stone

batók – *n.* cough; *v.* to cough

bátok - *n.* nape, back of the neck

batón – *n.* answer, response; *v.* to answer, to respond

báton – *v.* to reach out, to extend hand to help

batos – *n.* henchman, follower, crony, minion

batsi – *n.* road bump, pothole

batsihon – *adj.* bumpy

batúbarani – *n.* magnet

batúbato – *adj.* rocky

batulang – *n.* large basket

batwan – *n.* hard sour fruit

batya – *n.* wash basin, tub

bawas – *v.* to subtract, to take away

bawbaw – *prep.* above, upon, over

bawi – *v.* to retrieve, to take back

baya – *v.* to leave, to abandon

bayád – *n.* payment

báyad – *v.* to pay

bayaw – *n.* brother-in-law

baybay – *n.* seashore, beach

baybayin – *n.* Tagalog system of writing, script, or calligraphy

bayhon – *n.* face

baynte – *num.* twenty, Spanish *veinte*

bayó – *n.* wooden pestle used with matching mortar (lusong) to husk rice; *v.* to pound, to husk rice

bayod – *n.* millipede

báyog – *v.* to shake

bayong – *n.* large straw bag

bayot – *n.* gay, male homosexual

bayrus – *n.* virus, English *virus*

baysay – *n.* beauty

baywang – *n.* loin, waist

bebi – *n.* baby, English *baby*

bendisyon – *n.* blessing, benediction; *v.* to bless, Spanish *bendicion*

benepisyo – *n.* benefits, Spanish *beneficio*

biaw – *adj.* stagnant; *v.* to stagnate

Bibliya – *n.* Bible, Spanish *Biblia*

bikag – *n.* mumps

biko – *n.* sweet rice with coconut milk delicacy; *v.* to cook this delicacy

bikog – *n.* cramps; *v.* to get cramps

bìdo – *n.* sorrow, sadness

bigit – *adj.* upset, mad, disturbed

bigote – *n.* mustache, Spanish *bigote*

bigting – *v.* to amputate

bihag – *n.* captive; *v.* to capture

bihon – *n.* rice noodle

bihod – *n.* fish eggs, roe

bilád – *adj.* flirtatious

bílad – *v.* to get attention, to flirt

bilanghoy – *n.* cassava

bilib – *v.* to admire, to believe one's qualities, American *believe*

bilin – *v.* to remain, to leave somebody behind

biling – *v.* to find, to look for

bilyar – *n.* billiard, American *billiard*

bilyaran – *n.* billiard hall

binatá – *n.* housemaid

binatasan – *n.* tradition, customs

bingwit – *v.* to snatch

binlad – *n.* sun-drying harvested rice

bintana - *n.* window, Spanish *ventana*

bintilador – *n.* electric fan, Spanish *ventilador*

11

bintol – *n.* fish trap; *v.* to catch fish with this contraption

bintulawo – *adj.* listing to one side as a boat

binukbok – *n.* rice flour

binungtuan – *n.* abandoned village

bira – *v.* to shout, to sing off key, Spanish *berra,* to start an engine

birde – *n.* green, Spanish *verde*

birhen – *n.* virgin, Spanish *virgin*

birik – *v.* to turn around

birikbirik – *v.* to spin

birikis – *v.* to twist; *adj.* twisted, distorted

birilingon, biril'ngon – *adj.* rare, uncommon

birtde - *n.* birthday, English *birthday*

biruksot – *v.* to crouch

birtod – *n.* charm, spellbinding power, virtue, Spanish *virtud*

bisagra – *n.* hinge, Spanish *bisagra*

bisan – *conj.* although, even though

bisanla, bisla – *conj.* even though

bisibis – *v.* to water plants

bisikleta – *n.* bike, bicycle, Spanish *bicicleta*

bisita – *n.* visitor, guest; *v.* to visit, Spanish *visita*

biskwit – *n.* bisquit, English *bisquit*

bisog – *n.* resolve; *v.* to undertake with resolve

bistida – *n.* costume, Spanish *vestido*

bisto – *v.* to see, to discover, Spanish *vista*

bisyo – *n.* vice, bad habit, Spanish *vicio*

bitamina – *n.* vitamin, Spanish *vitamina*

bitay – *v.* to hang, to execute by hanging

bitbit – *v.* to hold, to carry, to take

bitíis – *n.* ankle, calf

bitok – *n.* parasitic worm, ascaris

bitsin – *n.* monosodium glutamate, Chinese *bi chin*

bitukon – *n.* person infected with parasitic worm, or ascariasis

bituon – *n.* star

biyahe – *n.* trip, travel, journey; *v.* to travel, Spanish *viaje*

biyernes – *n.* Friday, Spanish *viernes*

biyúos – *n.* sprout, bud

bóla – *n.* ball, Spanish *bola*

bolo – *n.* small cleaver

Bombay – *n.* Indian national or descent

boses – *n.* voices, Spanish *voces*

botante – *n.* voter, Spanish *votante*

botika – *n.* drugstore, pharmacy, Spanish *botica*

bráso – *n.* arm

buák – *v.* to break open, split in half

buaw – *adj.* fake, bogus

bubon – *n.* well, spring, baby fontanel

bubot – *n.* buttocks, rectum

buka – *v.* to open

bukád – *n.* flower, blossom; *v.* to bloom

búkad – v. to dig out
bukás – v. to open, to unfold
bukatkat – n. firefly
bukaw – n. owl
bukawil – n. shell fish, marine snail, whelk
bukbok – n. powder
bukid – n. mountain
bukidbukid – adj. hilly, mountainous
bukidnon – n. mountain dweller
buking – v. to discover a secret, to reveal
buklad – v. to unfold, to unfurl
búko – n. node in tree or bamboo
bukó – v. to rebuff, to confront, to rebuke
bukod – v. to run after, to chase
bukog – n. bone, skeleton, fishbone; v. to get fishbone stuck in the throat
bukol – n. lump, tumor, swelling
buksing – n. boxing, English *boxing*
buksingero – n. boxer, English *boxer*
buktot – n. hunchback
bukugon – adj. bony, spiny
bukulbukol – adj. lumpy, several skin bumps
bukya – n. large jellyfish
budiga – n. warehouse, Spanish *bodega*
budlay – n. exasperation; v. to exasperate, to get mad
budlayon – adj. impatient, impetuous

budlot – n. bulging eyes, knucklehead; adj. bulging, protruding
budyong – n. conch shell
buga – v. to breathe out, to exhale
bugas – n. milled rice, husked rice
búgat – n. weight
bugbog – v. to maul, to manhandle
bugkot – v. to be possessed by spirits, to disappear
bugkuton – adj. sneaky
bughat – n. ailment relapse; v. to relapse
bugíot – v. to pack full, to cram, to crowd; adj. crammed, overcrowded
búgos – n. whole, totality
bugoy – n. street child
bugsay – n. paddle, oar; v. to paddle
bugsok – n. deer
bugto – n. brother, sister, sibling
bugtong – n. only child
buhát – v. to rise, to stand up
búhat – v. to work; n. origin, source, provenance
buhawi – n. water spout, tornado
buhi – adj. alive, free; v. to set free
buhó – n. hole in the ground, pit, digging
búho – v. to dig a hole
buhok – n. hair
buhol – n. knot; v. to make a knot
buhos – n. flush, pour; v. to flush, to pour; adj. torrential
buhukon – adj. hairy

13

buhulbuhol – *adj.* knotty, gnarly, messy, mixed-up

bulad – *n.* dried fish; *v.* to dry under the sun

bulag – *v.* to separate, to divorce, to split

bulagaw – *n.* ruby color, deep red

bulalakaw – *n.* meteorites streaking in the sky

bulalo – *n.* large cowry

bulan – *n.* moon, month

bulanon – *n.* full moon, moonlit

búlang – *n.* cockfighting match in an arena; *v.* to collide

búlangan – *n.* cockpit, cockfighting arena

bulaw – *n.* yellow color, blond, brown pig

bulawan – *n.* gold

bulawanon – *adj.* golden, precious

bulbol – *n.* pubic hair, fuzz

bulbulon – *adj.* fuzzy

bulkan – *n.* volcano, Spanish *volcan*

bulkas, hilkas – *v.* to take off from hanging like clothes, to unhook

bulhog – *n.* blue-eyed person, blue color, eye cataract

bulig – *n.* help, cluster of banana fruit; *v.* to help

bulinaw – *n.* small anchovy

búliw – *v.* to let go, to release grip, to resign

bulnot – *v.* to pull

bulong – *n.* treatment, medication; *v.* to treat medically

bulok – *adj.* dull, unintelligent, slow learner

bulós – *n.* spear, retaliation; *v.* to retaliate, to spear

búlos – *v.* to slip foot into a hole

bulsa – *n.* pocket, Spanish *bolsa*

bulyas – *v.* to rinse

bumba – *n.* pump, bomb, Spanish *bomba*; *v.* to pump water or gasoline, to bomb

bumbero – *n.* fire fighter, Spanish *bombero*

bumbilya – *n.* electric light bulb, Spanish *bombilla*

bumbo – *n.* drum, Spanish *bombo*

bunal – *v.* to hit with the fist, to box

bunay – *n.* egg; *v.* to lay eggs

bundo – *n.* anthill

bundol – *v.* to poke with a pole, to thrust, to jab

bunga – *n.* fruit; *v.* to bear fruit

bungad – *n.* scorpion

bungalos – *n.* ingrate; *adj.* ungrateful

bungansiso – *n.* whale

bungat – *v.* to open the eyes

bungaw – *adj.* silly, stupid, idiot

bungbong – *n.* wall

bungkag – *v.* to dismantle, to destroy

bungkaras – *v.* to wake up suddenly, to startle

bungkog – *n.* back of chest

bunggo – *v.* to hit, to collide, to crash, to smash

bungí – *n.* harelip, cleft lip

bungisngis – *n.* chatter; *v.* to chatter

bungog – *n.* stun, shock; *v.* to stun, to shock

bungól – *n.* deafness, deaf person
bungot – *n.* beard
bungsaran – *n.* opening like window or door
bungto – *n.* town, municipality
bungtuhanon – *n.* town residents
bunguton – *adj.* fully bearded
buni – *n.* fungal skin infection
bunó – *v.* to stab
bunok – *n.* torrential rain, downpour; *v.* to rain heavily
búnog – *n.* bruise, contusion; *v.* to bruise
bunót – *n.* coconut husk; *v.* to husk coconut
búnot – *v.* to pull up
buntog – *n.* epilepsy, seizure
buntugon – *adj.* epileptic
buntol – *adj.* obese, stout, bouncy
bunúan – *n.* bamboo fish pen
bunyag – *n.* baptism, christening, revelation; *v.* to baptize, to give a name, to reveal
bunyog – *v.* to follow, to join a funeral procession
búog – *n.* ear infection pus
buóng – *n.* broken pieces like glass or ceramic
búong – *v.* to break apart
buót – *n.* consciousness, conscience, will; *v.* to decide
búot – *adj.* suffocating, stifling
buótan – *adj.* obedient, honest, truthful, conscientious
bura – *n.* bubble, sea foam, lather
burabod – *n.* spring, fountain
burahag – *n.* red color

buranday – *n.* variety of small clam
buras – *n.* genitals
buraw – *n.* mackerel
buray – *n.* crusted drool
burda – *n.* embroidery; *v.* to embroider, Spanish *border*
buri – *n.* fan palm, talipot *Corypha umbraculifera* used to make and embroider mats or hats
burikat – *n.* prostitute
burikbutik – *n.* bumpy, coarse skin
buring – *n.* thick dirt on skin
buringon – *adj.* dirty, unwashed clothes
buringot *adj.* disheveled, shabby, dirty
burit – *v.* to puncture, to burst
burlo – *n.* cricket
burod – *n.* pregnancy; *adj.* pregnant; *v.* to get pregnant
burong – *n.* fog
burra – *v.* to erase, Spanish *borra*
burrador – *n.* eraser, Spanish *borrador*
burublag, bublag – *v.* to disintegrate, to come apart, to scatter
burublig, bublig – *v.* to cooperate, to work together
buruhaton – *n.* job, assignment, work to do
burungon – *adj.* foggy
burungos – *n.* pubic hair
busá – *v.* to scold
buság – *adj.* white; *v.* to whiten
busbos – *v.* to cut, to operate
buskay – *n.* brightly colored cowrie
busisi – *v.* to investigate

buslong – *v.* to stare
busni – *v.* to excise an abscess, to squeeze out
busog – *adj.* full as in eating
busyo – *n.* temper tantrums, fuss; *v.* to have tantrums, to fuss
butá – *n.* blindness, blind person; *adj.* blind
búta – *v.* to blind
butagtok – *n.* backbone
butang – *n.* thing; *v.* to put down
butas – *n.* boots, Spanish *botas*
butangbútang – *v.* to falsely accuse
butkon – *n.* arm
buti – *n.* psoriasis
butig, binutig – *n.* sweet banana variety with tiny, hard fruit boiled to become edible
butihon – *adj.* afflicted with psoriasis or similar skin disease
butilya – *n.* bottle, Spanish *botella*
butiti – *n.* puffer fish
butlaw – *n.* fatigue, tiredness
butnga – *n.* middle, center; *prep.* between, in the middle of
butó – *n.* explosion; *v.* to explode
búto – *n.* female genitalia
butod – *n.* stale, putrid
butok – *n.* bundle, faggot; *v.* to tie as a bundle, to bind, to bundle
bútol – *n.* bump, protrusion, swelling
butól – *n.* throat, larynx
butóng – *n.* mature coconut
bútong – *v.* to pull

butonis – *n.* button, Spanish *boton*
butubutó – *n.* fireworks
butulbutol – *adj.* bumpy, coarse
búwa – *n.* coconut embryo, coconut seed
buwá – *v.* to lie, to deny; *n.* lie, falsehood, denial, mendacity
buwáon – *n.* liar; *adj.* untruthful, mendacious
buwas – *n.* tomorrow
buwasbuwas *v.* to procrastinate
buwaya – *n.* crocodile
buwisit – *n.* bad luck, misfortune; *adj.* unlucky
buyag – *n.* curse, bad luck; *interj.* expression of concern
búyay – *n.* protuberant belly
buyayaw – *n.* curse, profanity, obscene expletive; *v.* to curse
búyayon – *adj.* rotund, stout, fat belly
buynas – *adj.* lucky, Spanish *buenas*
búyo – *n.* betel nut, gum
buyóg – *n.* bee
búyog – *v.* to follow, to accompany
búyong – *n.* scrotum
buyóng – *v.* to groom, to abduct, to kidnap
buyungon – *n.* enlargement of scrotum from hydrocele or inguinal hernia
byulin – *n.* violin, Spanish *violin*

K:k

ka – *pron.* you; *adv.* very, so
kaabtik – *n.* expertise, being skillful
kaadlawan – *n.* birthday, anniversary, days; *adv.* daily
kaadlawon – *n.* daytime
kaagahon – *n.* daybreak, early morning
kaagi – *n.* way, method, struggle, adverb
kaapuhan – *n.* descendants, grandchildren
kaapuyan – *n.* ancestors, grandparents
kaaraman, kaadman – *n.* knowledge, know-how, skill
kaarawdan – *n.* shameful act, embarrassment
kaawa – *n.* envy; *v.* to envy
kaaway – *n.* enemy
kaawod – *n.* shame
kababuyan – *n.* piggery, pigs
kabak – *n.* fried sesame balls
kabakhawan – *n.* mangrove
kabag – *n.* abdominal colic, stomach ache, flatulence; *v.* to have abdominal pain
kabagwakan – *n.* wild forest, badlands
kabahin – *n.* shareholder, dividend
kabaltukan – *n.* intelligence, smartness
kabaraka – *adj.* worried, worrisome
kabarasan – *n.* sandbar, sandy beach
kabarkada – *n.* gang member
kabat – *v.* to grab another's space, to invade

kabatasanan – *n.* customs, tradition
kabatsihan – *n.* bumpy road
kabayo – *n.* horse; *v.* to horseback ride, Spanish *caballo*
kabidúan – *n.* deep sorrow
kabít – *n.* mistress
kábit – *v.* to cling, to hang on
kablas – *adj.* poor, impoverished, needy, modest
kablasanon – *n.* poverty, poor person
kablit – *v.* to flick, to pull the trigger
kabó – *n.* pail, water scoop, Spanish *cubo*
kabog – *n.* large bat
kabos – *adj.* impoverished, deprived
kabubwason – *n.* future, posterity
kabudkiran – *n.* mountain range, mountains
kabudlay – *n.* exasperation, displeasure, hatred
kabugtuan – *n.* brothers, sisters
kabukugan, kabukgan - *n.* bones, skeleton
kabulanan – *n.* menstruation, monthly occurrence, *adv.* monthly
kabulig – *n.* helper, servant, assistant
kabunyog – *n.* follower, chaperone, partner
kaburúton – *n.* will, disposition, consciousness, mood
kabusugan – *n.* gluttony
kakablasan – *n.* poverty
kakahuyan - *n.* woodland, forest

17

kakaiba – *adj.* different, unusual
kakampi – *n.* group member, *adj.* complicit
kakáno – *pron.* when
kakanog – *n.* large moth
kakaw – *n.* cacao, cocoa, Mexican *cacahuatl*
kakawayan – *n.* bamboo grove
kakilala – *n.* acquaintance
kakulangan – *n.* deficit, lacking, need, deficiency
kakulba – *n.* anxiety, palpitation
kakulop – *n.* yesterday
kakurian – *n.* hardship, poverty, misfortune
kakurulpon – *n.* dusk, late afternoon
kada – *adj.* each, every, Spanish *cada*
kadaan – *n.* old times
kadabutang – *n.* everything
kadagatan – *n.* open seas
kadagmitan – *adv.* hurriedly, immediately
kadal – *v.* to shiver, to tremble from fear or cold
kadamó – *n.* party, gathering
kadámo – *n.* multiplier; *adj.* plentiful, many
kadamuan, kadáman – *n.* majority, multitude, abundance
kadang – *n.* pair of poles, each with footrest, used to walk above the ground, bamboo stilts; *v.* to walk above the ground using stilts
kadayaw – *n.* full moon
kadayunan – *n.* forever, eternity
kadi – *v.* to come

kadimalas – *adj.* unlucky, unfortunate
kadimalasan – *n.* misfortune, mishap
kadina – *n.* chain, Spanish *cadena*
kadto – *v.* to go
kadugo – *n.* blood relations
kadugtong – *n.* segment, continuation, sequence, connection; *conj.* in continuaton of
kadungan – *adj.* simultaneous, coincidental; *adv.* simultaneously, coincidentally
kadurog – *n.* bedfellow
kagábi – *n.* last night
kagabihon – *n.* midnight
kagamhanan – *n.* power, authority
kagamitan – *n.* equipment, utility, usefulness
káganak – *n.* parent
kagang – *n.* single-clawed, small mud crab
kagaramo – *adj.* overwhelmed, hands full
kagát – *n.* bite, claw of a crab or critter, pincers; *v.* to bite
kagaw – *n.* germ, diease-bearing organism, microbe
kagkag – *n.* rake
kagíd – *n.* thick, dirt on the skin, dirty stain
kagiron – *adj.* dirty as skin
kagís – *n.* scratch; *v.* to scratch
kagiyanan – *n.* addiction
kagod – *v.* to grate coconut
kagrupo – *n.* group member, Spanish *grupo*
kagugubaan, kagugúban - *n.* deep forest, hinterlands
kaguol – *n.* sentiment, fatigue

kagupong – *n.* state of confusion, *adj.* confused, flummoxed

kaguran – *n.* coconut grater

kagurangan – *n.* deep forest, hinterlands

kagustuhan – *n.* liking, favorite, taste, preference

kagutom, katgutom – *n.* famine, hunger, starvation

kagwang – *n.* flying lemur

kaha – *n.* case, box, Spanish *caja*

kahababawan, kahababwan – *n.* shallow water

kahadian – *n.* kingdom, realm

kahadlok – *n.* fear, trepidation, fright

kahalaruman, kahaladman – *n.* depth

kahaluagan – *n.* widest part; *adj.* wide-open

kahalutan – *n.* greed, selfishness

kahanangan – *n.* muddy brackish water, marshland, swamp

kahangturan – *n.* eventuality, destiny, forever

kahayag – *n.* brightness, enlightenment

kahibabawan, kahibabwan – *n.* shallow part of the sea

kahibaro – *n.* knowledge, intelligence

kahidlaw – *n.* nostalgia

kahig – *n.* rake; *v.* to make pile

kahilaruman, kahiladman – *n.* depth, deepest part of water, bottom

kahimayaan – *n.* glory

kahímo – *n.* pattern, technique

kahimó – *n.* face

kahimutangan, kahimtang – *n.* plight, situation, peace of mind

kahingadtuan – *n.* consequence, result, eventuality

kahingatungdan – *n.* recognition, importance, acknowledgement

kahiusa – *n.* exclamation, interjection

kahoy – *n.* wood

kahubugan – *n.* drunkenness, inebriation

kahubya – *adj.* lazy

kahubyaan – *n.* laziness

kahulop – *n.* doubt, indecision, hesitancy

kahulugan – *n.* meaning, significance, translation

kahumayan – *n.* rice field

kahumok – *n.* softness, suppleness

kahurakan – *n.* fullness, abundance, plenitude

kahuynon – *n.* tree fairies

kaiban – *n.* subtrahend, minuend

kailaruman, kailadman – *n.* bottom, lowest place

kaingin – *n.* slash-and-burn farming

kaiskwela – *n.* schoolmate

kairiniton, kainiton – *n.* hatred, anger, animosity

kairo – *adj.* pitiful

kairo man! – *interj.* expression of sympathy

kaladkad – *v.* to boil

kaladngan, kalarangan – *n.* willpower

kalag – *n.* soul, ghost, spirit

kalagasan, kalagsan – *n.* old folk, elderly

19

kalahingan – *n.* maturity
kalalawdan – *n.* vast ocean
kalamay – *n.* sugar block
kalamira – *adj.* clumsy, scatterbrain, careless
kalamutan – *n.* greed, selfishness
kalan – *n.* stove
kalangitan – *n.* skies, heavens
kalapi – *n.* rattan fruit
kalarakan – *n.* open space, universe
kalaradngan – *n.* creation, nature, destiny
kalas – *n.* startle, surprise; *v.* to startle
kalatsutsi – *n.* kalachuchi flower
kalaw – *n.* Samar hornbill *Penelopides samarensis; interj.* expression of good intention
kalawasan – *n.* health, human body, state of health
kalawat – *n.* small basket-like bamboo contraption to support the circumsized penis for healing
kalawuran, kalawdan – *n.* vast ocean
kalayo – *n.* fire, flame
kaldero – *n.* kettle, Spanish *caldera*
kalduhan – *n.* bowl, Spanish *caldo*
kaliawan – *n.* entertainment, recreation
kalibutan – *n.* world, earth, awareness, consciousness
kalidad – *n.* quality, class, Spanish *calidad*
kaliding – n. wheel; *v.* to roll as a wheel

kaligiran – *n.* sides, surroundings, environment
kalimaan, kalíman – *num.* fifty
kalindaryo – *n.* calendar, Spanish *calendario*
kalingawan – *n.* pastime, hobby, diversion
kalinturon – *n.* high fever, malaria, Spanish *calentura*
kalinurungan – *n.* malfeasance, corruption, perfidy, foolishness
kalipayan – *n.* happiness
kalisang, kalisangan – *n.* anxiety
kalit – *adj.* sudden, quick; *adv.* suddenly, quickly
kaliwat – *n.* lookalike
kalkag – *v.* to spread grain or soil using a rake; *n.* rake
kalma – *adj.* calm, Spanish *calma*
kalo – *n.* hat
kalot – *v.* to scratch
kalsada, karsada – *n.* street, road
kalugaringon – *n.* oneself, ownership
kalukuhan – *n.* foolishness
kalugo – *n.* wart
kaluluthan – *n.* joints
kalumpihig – *n.* small crab with single pincers
kalundiis – *n.* dimple
kaluoy – *n.* pity, sympathy, mercy; *v.* to pity, to empathize
kalupad, kalpad – *n.* flight; *v.* to fly
kalye – *n.* street, Spanish *calle*
kaípa – *n.* envy; *v.* to get envious
kama – *n.* bed, Spanish *cama*
kamaaram – *adj.* knowing, knowledgeable

kamádan – *n.* dryland
kamaihaan – *n.* old times, ancient; *adj.* old-fashioned
kamalungay – *n.* leaves of *Moringa oleifera* tree
kamanampan, kamananapan – *n.* animal kingdom, animals
kamanduhan – *n.* authority, command, Spanish *mando*
kamang – *v.* to crawl
kamanukan – *n.* poultry chickens
kamatayan – *n.* death
kamatis – *n.* tomato
kamatuóran – *n.* truth
kamaúo – *n.* fist
kami – *pron.* we (first person plural, excluding listener)
kamingaw – *n.* silence, nostalgia
kamingawan – *n.* silence, serenity
kamisita – *n.* shirt, Spanish *camisa*
kamo – *pron.* you (plural)
kamot – *n.* hand; *v.* to eat with bare hands
kamoti – *n.* sweet potato, Nahuatl (Mexican) *camote*
kampana – *n.* large bell
kampanilya – *n.* small bell
kampay – *v.* to beckon, to summon with the hand
kampi – *n.* group, party, connivance; *v.* to connive, to join, to take side
kampo – *n.* camp, Spanish *campo*
kamras – *n.* scratch, cat scratch; *v.* to scratch with fingernail or claw
kamulay – *n.* playmate

kamurayaw, kamurayawan – *n.* peace, orderliness
kamutangan – *n.* situation
kan – *prep.* to, of, by
kanaway – *n.* east wind
kanay – *pron.* whose, whom; *conj.* whose, whom
kandado – *n., a.* lock, padlock – Spanish candado, pagkandado
kandila – *n.* candle, Spanish *candela*
kanding – *n.* goat
kangalason, kangaralson – *n.* hatred
kangaran – *n.* adjective, namesake
kangaranngraran – *adj.* in name only, nominal
kanhi – *v.* to come here
kanina – *adv.* earlier
kaningag – *n.* cinnamon
kanser – *n.* cancer, English
kanta – *n.* song, Spanish *canto;* *v.* to sing
kantor – *n.* singer
kanugon – *adj.* useless, futile, wasteful; *v.* to waste
kanunay – *adj.* persistent, earnest, persevering; *adv.* always, earnestly, persistently
kánon – *n.* cooked rice
kanyon – *n.* cannon, Spanish *cañon*
káon – *v.* to eat
kapa – *n.* smegma, cape, Spanish *capa*
kapagal – *n.* fatigue, tiredness
kapalaran – *n.* fate, destiny
kaparyintihan – *n.* relatives, Spanish *pariente*
kapatagan – *n.* flatlands, plains

kapatas – *n.* boss, foreman, Spanish *capataz*

kapaugan – *n.* absurdity, stupidity

kapawaan, kapáwan – *n.* brightness, clarity, enlightenment

kapaya – *n.* papaya

kapkap – *n.* frisk; *v.* to body search for concealed weapon

kape – *n.* coffee, brown color, Spanish *café*

kapirawan – *n.* sleepiness, drowsiness

kapituàn – *num.* seventy

kaplag – *v.* to break apart, to scamper

kapot – *v.* to hold

kapoy – *n.* tiredness, fatigue, short of breath

kapri - *n.* fanciful giant

kapulungan – *n.* saying, vocabulary, dictionary

kapurúan – *n.* archipelago

kapyot – *v.* to cling, to hang on

karabaw – *n.* water buffalo

karadol – *n.* low-pitched dragging sound

karag – *n.* waste; *v.* to waste

karaha – *n.* frying pan, wok

karaksutan – *n.* ugliness

karal-karal – *n.* gurgling sound; *adj.* gurgling like an engine

karambula – *v.* to jumble

karamsaw – *n.* mayhem, confused fight, scuffle; *v.* to scuffle

karangkang – *adj.* rash, impetuous

karasá *n.* taste

karasikas – *n.* scratchy noise; *v.* to produce scatchy noise

karatong – *n.* hollow tube drum made from bamboo; *v.* to sound like one

karáunan – *n.* dining room

karáunon, karanon – *n.* food, meal, bread, cookie

karautan, karátan – *n.* danger, temptation, misfortune

karawat – *v.* to receive, to accept

karaykay – *n.* string of colorful paper trimmings hung over streets

karayhakan – *n.* ecstasy, exuberance

kargador – *n.* porter, Spanish *cargador*

kargamento – *n.* cargo, Spanish *cargamento*

karigo, parigo – *v.* to take a bath or shower

karígon – *n.* firmness, sturdiness

karigudigo – *n.* happenings, commotion

karigusan *n.* bathroom, shower

karikhi – *v.* to scrape roots from tuber

karikuhan – *n.* wealth, fortune

karinggal – *n.* worry, apprehension

karinggalon – *adj.* worrisome, anxious, apprehensive

karit – *n.* skill, expertise, greatness; *v.* to anxious about something or someone

karitilya – *n.* small cart, Spanish *carretilla*, wheelborrow

kariton – *n.* cart, Spanish *carreta*

karnabal – *n.* carnival, Spanish *carnaval*

karni – *n.* meat, beef, Spanish *carne de vaca*

karniro – *n.* sheep, Spanish *carnero*

karpintero – *n.* carpenter, Spanish *carpintero*

karro – *n.* decorated cart used for religious procession, Spanish *carro*

karsonsilyo – *n.* boxer shorts, Spanish *carsoncillo*

karubasa – *n.* squash, gourd, Spanish *calabaza*

karuhaan – *num.* twenty

karukaliding – *v.* to cartwheel; *adv.* roll over

karukatutang – *n.* rancid odor

karukayakan – *n.* talk, conversation, discussion

karuwahi – *n.* carriage, Spanish *carruaje,* cart

karuyag – *v.* to like, to want, to admire

karuyagon – *adj.* likable

kasabid – *n.* doing for the sake of doing

kasabwat – *n.* accomplice, connivance; *adj.* complicit

kasagaran – *adv.* often times

kasagingan – *n.* banana patch or plantation

kasagsagan – *n.* peak; *adj.* extreme, ultimate

kasakit – *n.* sickness, sacrifice, anguish

kasakitan – *n.* state of poor health, disease and poverty

kasal – *n.* wedding; *v.* to wed, to marry, Spanish *casar*

kasanggabi – *n.* night before last night

kasangkayan – *n.* friends, comrades

kasangkot – *n.* complicity

kasangkulop – *n.* the day before yesterday

kasanhi – *n.* past, yesteryears

kasayuran – *n.* information, verification

kasiguraduhan – *n.* security

kasili – *n.* eel

kasilyas *n.* toilet

kasina – *adj.* hatred, animosity; *v.* to be angry, to get mad

kasing – *n.* pivot, turning point of a top, core

kasingkasing – *n.* heart

kasirangan – *n.* east, sunrise

kasisidman – *n.* darkness

kasiyaman – *num.* ninety

kaso – *n.* case, instance, Spanish *caso*

kastigo – *n.* punishment; *v.* to punish, to castigate, Spanish *castigar*

Kastila, Katsila – *n.* Spaniard, Spanish language

kastulindas – *n.* traditional water splashing during feast of St. John the Baptist

kasubo – *n.* sadness

kasumatan – *n.* story telling, history

kasumpay – *n.* conjunction, segment, connection

kasunod – *adj.* next

kasurat – *n.* alphabet, penmanship

kasuratan – *n.* scripture

katadungan – *n.* reason, right, duty, righteousness; *adv.* straight ahead

kataghuman – *n.* coldness, frigidity

kataisan – *n.* point, tip of peninsula

kataliwan – *conj.* then

kataliwas – *adv.* later, afterwards

kataliwasan, katalwasan – *n.* liberty, freedom, ending, end of bondage

katamsihan – *n.* birds

katanuman, katanman – *n.* garden, vegetable patch

katapangan – *n.* ignorance

katapusan – *n.* end, ending, end-point, finality

kataruman, katarman – *n.* sharp tip, point

katatawa – *n.* laughing, laughter

kataw – *n.* mermaid, siren, fish with human form

katawanan – *adj.* funny, hilarious

katawuhan, katawhan – *n.* crowd, people, multitude, mankind

katbari – *n.* harvest time for rice

katig – *n.* bamboo or timber rig outfitted to prevent canoe from tipping, outrigger

katiguban – *n.* gathering, meeting, organization

katikangan – *n.* beginning, onset, start, provenance, time of creation

katilimban, katilingban – *n.* multitude, populace

katitirok – *n.* gathering, meeting, reunion

kato – *n.* insanity, craziness

katol – *n.* skin irritation, itchiness, skin infection

katoliko – *adj.* catholic, Spanish *catolico*

katorse – *num.* fourteen, Spanish *catorce*

katri – *n.* bed

katugkop – *n.* attachment

katugma – *adj.* fitting, corresponding; *n.* corresponding parts

katuhayan – *n.* orderliness

katuígan – *n.* decade

katuluàn – *num.* thirty

katumanan – *n.* fullfillment

katunaan – *n.* land owner, land holdings or ownership

katungá – *adj.* half

katungdanan – *n.* obligation, duty

katungod – *n.* counterpart, preposition

katunog – *n.* consonant

katunuran, katundan - *n.* west, sunset

katurog – *v.* to sleep

katurugan – *n.* bedroom

katutnga – *n.* midnight

katutungaydan – *n.* essence, reality, truth; *adj.* basic, essential, real

katuyawan – *n.* foolishness

kaugatan – *n.* blood vessels, arteries and veins

kaunman – *num.* sixty

kaunuran, kaundan – *n.* muscles and tendons

kaupatàn – *num.* forty

kaupayan – *n.* common good, wellness, progress, prosperity

kaupod – *n.* companion, chaperone

kaurupdan – *n.* relatives, clan

kaúsa – *n.* mate, fellow

kauswagan – *n.* progress, prosperity

kautod – *n.* cut-end

kauyag – *n.* playmate
kawaluàn – *num.* eighty
kawang – *adj.* futile, useless
kawara – *n.* new moon
kawat – *v.* to steal
kawatan – *n.* thief
kawayan - *n.* bamboo
kawil – *n.* line, hook and sinker; *v.* to fish with line, hook and sinker
kawit – *n.* bamboo tube container with hooked handle
kay – *conj.* because
kaya – *n.* capability; *adj.* able, capable; *v.* to be able
kayamas – *n.* inedible, tiny mud crab
káyano – *adv.* why
kayhingan – *interj.* expression of attestation
kerida – *n.* mistress, Spanish *querida*
keso – *n.* cheese, Spanish *queso*
kibord – *n.* computer keyboard, American *keyboard*
kikidlat – *n.* lightning
kikiro – *n.* small pompano-like fish
kikik – *n.* raven, vulture, large crow
kidni – *v.* to hit head with knuckle
kido – *n.* dance, sexual intercourse; *v.* to dance, to thrust as in coitus
kidya – *n.* Philippine lime, calamansi; *v.* to squeeze and add calamansi to a dish
kigol – *n.* coccyx
kiha – *v.* to file lawsuit, to sue

kilala – *v.* to recognize, to know, to introduce
kilalado – *adj.* famous, popular
kilaw – *v.* to pickle
kilkig – *n.* wood file madefrom sting ray skin
kilikid – *v.* to lie on one side, to turn to one side
kilikili – *n.* armpit
kilid – *n.* side
kilíng – *adj.* listing to one side as a boat or ship
kilingkiling – *v.* to list from side to side as a boat
kilya – *n.* keel, Spanish *quilla*
kimas – *n.* recklessness, carelessness; *v.* to be reckless
kimbig – *v.* to quake, to shake
kimbot *v.* to swing the hips, to sashay
kimpit – *n.* clothes pin, clamp, clip, tongs
kinaadman – *n.* skill, experience, knowledge, expertise, insight
kinabatasanan – *n.* customs, tradition, morals
kinablas – *adj.* poor, modest, humble
kinabuhi – *n.* life
kinabuwasan – *adv.* following day, afterwards, day after tomorrow
kinadaan – *adj.* old-fashioned, past
kinahanglan – *n.* necessities, needs; *v.* must, should
kinaiya – *n.* character, nature, manner
kinalibutanon – *adj.* mundane, worldly, earthly
kinasabang – *n.* chattering, shenanigan; *v.* to chatter

25

kinasal – *n.* newlywed couple, bride and groom

kinasingkasing – *adv.* heartfelt, heartily, sincerely, wholeheartedly

kinastila, kinatsila – *n.* Spanish language; *adj.* pertaining Spanish

kinawilan – *n.* fish

kinilaw – *n.* pickled fish with coconut milk

kinis – *n.* crab

kinse – *num.* fifteen, Spanish *quince*

kipot – *adj.* tightly closed

kiray – *n.* eyebrow

kirig – *v.* to convulse

kirigta – *n.* meeting, reunion

kirikisi – *v.* to roll the beater handle between the hands, to stir, to shuffle

kiripot – *adj.* puckered

kiris – *v.* to rinse rice

kirítan – *n.* theater, movie house

kiríton – *n.* show, movies

kiró – *v.* to wink an eye as in flirting; *n.* wink

kirot – *adj.* irritating pain

kirugtol – *v.* to crouch

kisam – *v.* to chew, to nibble

kisiyo – *n.* cheese from carabao milk,

kiskis – *n.* full shaven head; *v. to* shave the head

kita – *pron.* we (first person plural, including listener)

kíta – *n.* income, funds, proceeds, salary; *v.* to meet

kitá – *v.* to see, to witness, to look

kitakita – *n.* observation, intuition; *v.* to observe, to watch

kitkit – *v.* to nibble

kiwa – *n.* movement; *v.* to move

kiyod – *v.* to thrust hips forward, to twerk

klasmeyt – *n.* classmate, English *classmate*

ko – *pron.* I

kolira – *n.* cholera el tor, Spanish *colera*

kompyuter – *n.* computer, American *computer*

kongresista – *n.* congressman, Spanish *congresista*

konseho – *n.* council, Spanish *concejo*

kontrol – *n.* remote control, English *control*

kostumre – *n.* custom, Spanish *costumbre*

kotse – *n.* car, automobile, Spanish *coche*

krus – *n.* cross, Spanish *cruz*

krusipiho – *n.* crucifix, Spanish *crucifijo*

kúan – *interj., verb, adj.* all-purpose word to substitute any word; inflected like any noun, verb, adjective

kubal – *n.* callus

kubalon – *adj.* thick bumpy like the sole

kubit – *v.* to tap, to touch with the finger to get attention

kubita – *n.* toilet, Spanish *cubeta*

kubra – *v.* to withdraw money

kudal – *n.* fence

kudkod – *v.* to scrape

kudos – *n.* sign of the cross; *v.* to do sign of the cross

kugita, pugita – *n.* octopus

kugon – *n.* tall, coarse grass used for thatching, Cogon grass, *Imperata cylindrical sp.*

kugos – *v.* to carry in the arms

kuha – *n.* component, taken from; *v.* to take, to remove

kuhakuha – *adj.* removable, adjustable

kuhida – *n.* income; *v.* to gather, to grasp, Spanish *cogida*

kuhit – *v.* to scoop cooked rice

kulalapnit – *n.* fruit bat

kulambutan – *n.* cuttlefish

kulang – *n.* lack, deficit; *v.* to lose, to lack, to take away, to reduce

kulangkulang – *n.* mentally retarded

kulaw – *v.* to look, to stare, to inspect

kulba – *n.* palpitation, anxiety, worry; *v.* to palpitate, to throb, to worry

kuló – *n.* nail, fingernail, or toenail

kulob – *n.* prone position: *v.* to assume prone position, to lie on the belly, to prostrate

kulop – *n.* afternoon

kultson – *n.* mattress, Spanish *colchón*

kumbensido – *adj.* convinced, Spanish *convencido*

kumo – *n.* fist; *v.* tomake a fist; *adj.* fistful

kumpra – *n.* commodities; *v.* to buy

kumulgar – *v.* to take communion, Spanish *comulgar*

kumunidad – *n.* community, Spanish *comunidad*

kumunyon – *n.* communion

kumusta – *v.* to greet how one is doing, Spanish *como esta*

kun – *conj.* if

kuna – *adj.* taken, made of; *v.* to get, to take

kundi – *conj.* but

kunggo, sunggo – *n.* nosebleed; *v.* to bleed from the nose

kuno – *adv.* accordingly

kunot – *adj.* crumpled; *v.* to crumple

kunsuylo – *n.* sweetheart, Spanish *consuelo;* *v.* to court, to woo

kunta, unta – *adv.* wishfully, hopefully

kuntador – *n.* electric meter, Spanish *contador*

kuntra – *prep.* against, Spanish *contra*

kupkop – *v.* to cuddle, to embrace

kupos – *v.* to shrink; *adj.* shrunken

kupras – *n.* dessicated coconut

kupya – *n.* copy; *v.* to copy, Spanish *copia*

kurason – *n.* heart, Spanish *corazon*

kuratsa – *n.* courtship dance that imitates movement of a rooster and a hen.

kurbata – *n.* necktie, Spanish *corbata*

kuri – *n.* difficulty; *v.* to try hard

kuripot – *adj.* stingy, miserly

kurisom – *n.* furrow between eyebrows in anger, scowl; *v.* to scowl, to furrow between eyebrows, to sulk

kuro – *v.* to shrink

kurog – *n.* tremors, chills; *adj.* shaky, trembling

kurong – *adj.* curly; *v.* curly hair coiffure

kuros – *adj.* sagging skin, wrinkles

kurot – *v.* to pinch

kurti – *n.* looks, appearance

kurukod – *n.* sweet rice in coconut milk rolled in banana leaf and boiled

kurukuso – *v.* to wash clothes by hand

kurumos – *adj.* crumpled, wrinkled; *v.* to crumple, to wrinkle

kuryente – *n.* electricity, electric current, Spanish *corriente*

kusat – *v.* to smash; *adj.* smashed; *n.* mishmash

kusatkusat – *adj.* jumbled, mishmashed

kusina – *n.* kitchen, Spanish *cocina*

kusinero, kusinera – *n.* cook, Spanish *cocinero, cocinera*

kusing – *n.* penny, centavo

kuskos – *n.* scrub; *v.* to scrub

kusóg – *n.* strength; *v.* to force

kustomer – *n.* customer, English *customer*

kusugan, kusgan – *adj.* strong, muscular, forceful

kuta – *n.* stone wall

kutak – *n.* cackle; *v.* to cackle as a hen

kutil – *n.* concoction of coconut wine, chocolate and raw egg, believed to cure measles and chicken pox

kuting – *n.* cat

kutkot – *v.* to nibble

kuto – *n.* louse, lice

kutob – *n.* hunch, pulse, heartbeat

kutol – *v.* to pinch

kutsara – *n.* spoon, Spanish *cuchara*

kutsilyo – *n.* knife, Spanish *cuchillo*

kutuon – *n.* lice-infested hair; *adj.* lice-infested

kuyahaw – *n.* loud cry, scream, yell; *v.* to cry loudly, to scream, to yell

kuying – *n.* cat

kuykoy – *n.* hoarse coughing, asthmatic attack, croup, pertussis; *v.* to cough vigorously

kwarenta – *num.* forty, Spanish *cuarenta*

kwarta – *n.* money, coin, Spanish *cuarta*

kwarto – *n.* room, Spanish *cuarto*

kwatro – *num.* four, Spanish *cuatro*

kwintas – *n.* necklace

kwitis – *n.* fireworks

D:d

daan – *adj.* old

daba – *n.* clay pot

dakmol – *n.* thickness

dako – *adj.* big, large

dakop – *v.* to catch, to arrest, to kidnap

dakupdakupay – *v.* to play tag

dadá – *n.* aunt

dadakuro – *adj.* very large
dagaang – *n.* dry and hot air, scorching heat
dagat – *n.* sea
dagit – *v.* to catch like a bird using its beak or claws
dagkot – *v.* to light a fire, to ignite
dagdag – *n.* addition; *v.* to add
dagmit – *adv.* quickly
dagol – *v.* to knock head with knuckles
dagom – *n.* needle
dágom – *v.* to become cloudy; *adj.* overcast
dagsa – *v.* to drift ashore
dagway – *n.* face, profile
dahon – *n.* leaf
dalagan – *v.* to run
dalaganan – *n.* refuge, protector, shelter
dalaganay, dadlaganay – *n.* run race, sprint
dalan – *n.* path, way, trail, road
dalí – *v.* to hurry
dalían – *adv.* hurriedly, quickly, immediately
dalikyat – *adj.* fleeting, sudden, immediate
dalisay – *n.* nipa palm wine
dalos – *v.* to cut grass
dalugdog – *n.* thunder
dalumdom – *n.* cloudiness, overcast
dalunot – *n.* slime, slip
dalusdos – *v.* to slide
dalusdusan – *n.* slide
damo – *adj.* many, plenty
damudamo – *n.* multiplication; *v.* to multiply
dampog – *n.* cloud
damyo – *n.* plank
danas – *v.* to drag

danaw – *n.* lake, lagoon
danay – *adj.* sometimes
dangas – *n.* receding forehead, bald
dangat – *v.* to arrive
dangatan – *n.* consequence, result, arrival
dangaw – *n.* finger breadth, measurement using distance between thumb and index finger
dangop – *v.* to seek help, to take refuge
dangupan, dangpanan – *n.* refuge, sanctuary, shelter
danyos – *n.* damages, Spanish *daño*
daóg – *n.* winnings, prize, victory, triumph; *v.* to win
daol – *n.* pith, core
dapa – *v.* to prostrate, to lie down on the belly
dapadapo – *n.* resin used for smoking rituals
dará – *n.* carried item; *v.* to bring, take, to carry, to manage; *conj.* because
dára – *v.* to be influenced
daradara – *adj.* always carried
darág – *n.* yellow color, jaundice
daraga – *n.* unmarried woman, lady
daragita – *n.* damsel, maiden
darahog – *n.* physical abuse, maltreatment; *v.* to maltreat, to cast a spell by evil spirits
darahunon – *n.* saying, proverb, word of wisdom
darangpan – *n.* refuge, protection, sanctuary
daraon – *v.* to get closer

darudalugdog – *n.* thunderstorm

dasig – *n.* pride; *v.* to boast

dasigay – *v.* to show off, to compete

dasok – *adj.* compact, packed; *v,* to compact, to pack tightly

data – *n.* goodness, plesantness

daugan – *n.* winner, victorious

daugdaog – *v.* to bully, to annoy, to belittle

daw – *adv.* just, really

dayag – *adj.* revealing, exposed, obvious

dayaw – *v.* to praise

dayig – *v.* to worship

dayo – *v.* to visit; *adj.* foreign

dayon – *adv.* straight ahead; *v.* to continue, to pass; *n.* eternity, beyond

dayuday – *adv.* forever

dayuhan – *n.* visitor, foreigner

dekada – *n.* decade, Spanish *decada*

dekorasyon – *n.* decoration, Spanish *decoracion*

demanda – *n.* demand; *v.* to file a complaint in court, Spanish *demanda*

demokrasya – *n.* democracy, Spanish *democracia*

demonyo - *n.* demon, evil spirit, Spanish *demonio*

dentista – *n.* dentist, Spanish *dentist*

departamento – *n.* department, bureau, Spanish *departmento*

depensa – *n.* defense, Spanish *defense*

deposito – *n.* deposit (money), depot (fuel), Spanish *deposito*

desisyon – *n.* decision, English *decision*

destap – *n.* desktop computer, American *desktop*

dida – *adv.* there (specific)

didi – *adv.* here

didto – *adv.* there (nonspecific)

dígon – *n.* hardness, sturdiness, conviction; *v.* to reason out

diin – *pron., adv., conj.* where

dikit, dukot – *n.* glue; *adj.* sticky, adherent

dikitdikit, dukutdukot – *adv.* close-knit

díla – *n.* tongue

dilá, diláp – *v.* to lick

dimalas – *n.* misfortune

dinhi – *adv.* here

diretso – *adv.* straight ahead, Spanish *derecho*

diri – *n.* no; *v.* to prohibit, to negate

dirig, durog – *n.* person to sleep with; *v.* to sleep with someone

diripala, dipala – *interj.* expression of negative anticipation or surprise

dirudilain, durudilain – *n.* variety, miscellaneous, kaleidoscope

diskurso – *n.* speech; *v.* to speak in public, Spanish *discurso*

disenyo – *n.* design, Spanish *diseño*

disgrasya – *n.* accident, English *disgrace*

distansya – *n.* distance, Spanish *distancia*

Disyembre – *n.* December, Spanish diciembre

diwara – *n.* denial; *v.* to deny

diwata – *n.* superstition, enchanted being

diwindi – *n.* dwarf

Diyos – *n.* God, Spanish *Dios*

doktor – *n.* doctor, English *doctor*

Domingo – *n.* Sunday, Spanish *domingo*

don – *n.* Mr., honorofic for a rich man, Spanish *don*

donya – *n.* Mrs., honorific for a rich woman, Spanish *doña*

dos – *num.* two, Spanish *dos*

dose – *num.* twelve, Spanish *doce*

dosena – *n.* dozen, Spanish *docena*

druga – *n.* drugs, narcotics, Spanish *droga*

duás – *adj.* pale, sick; *n.* pallor

dúaw – *v.* to visit, to attend

dubdob – *v.* to smoke like cigar or cigarette

duble – *adj.* double, Spanish *doble*

dukdok – *v.* to poke with a stick

dukit – *n.* stain; *v.* to stain

duklat, suklat – *v.* to poke an eye

dukot – *v.* to attach, to paste, to catch fire

dukuti, dukti – *v.* imperative to attach, to light fire

duda – *n.* doubt; *v.* to doubt, Spanish *duda*

dugang – *v.* to add

dugangan, durugangan – *adj.* lacking, deficient

dughan - *n.* chest

dugmok – *v.* to mash like potato or taro

dugnit – *n.* clothes, garment, clothing

dugo – *n.* blood

dugos – *n.* honey

dugtong – *v.* to connect, to continue in sequence

dugyok – *n.* flood, deluge

duhá – *num.* two

duhaduha – *v.* to hesitate, to have second thoughts, to equivocate

duhol – *v.* to give, to reach over

dulas – *v.* to slip

dulaw – *n.* yellow color, turmeric plant

duling – *n.* cross-eyed person, squinting; *v.* to squint

dulom – *n.* new moon, darkness

dúlong – *n.* prow of boat; *v.* to deliver, to send

dulóng – *v.* to wrestle, to fight

dulot – *v.* to pierce

dulse – *n.* candy, Spanish *dulce*

dumara – *n.* management; *v.* to manage

dumdum – *v.* to recall, to remember, to memorize

dumog – *n.* rotten as wood

dumot – *n.* animosity, hatred, revenge, grievance

dumutanon, dumtanon – *adj.* vengeful, aggrieved, hateful

dungan – *v.* to coincide, to synchronize; *adv.* simultaneously

dungaw – *v.* to view, to look out

dungawan – *n.* window, lookout, viewpoint

dungganan, dungugan – *adj.* honorable, famous

dungog – *n.* honor, hearing; *v.* to hear, to honor

dunot – *adj.* overripe, rotten as fruit

duón – *v.* to press

dúong – *v.* to arrive, to approach a pier like a boat

dupa – *n.* one arm-length breadth, measurement, about one fathom

dupay – *v.* to freeze from fear, unable to move, *n.* inability to move, transient immobility

dupol – *adj.* blunt

dupot – *n.* interest, intention

durante – *conj.* during, Spanish *durante*

duro – *adv.* very, intensely

dúrog – *n.* orange color; *v.* to pound into powder

duróg – *v.* to sleep with someone

duron – *n.* locust

duroy – *n.* aggravation

durugtong – *adj.* interconnected

durungan – *adj.* simultaneous

dusó – *v.* to push

dúsog – *v.* to move a little, to budge

dusuduso – *adv.* moveable

duungan, duruungan – *n.* landing place, wharf

duyan – *n.* hammock; *v.* to swing a hammock

duyog – *n.* sympathy; *v.* to join, to accompany, to empathize

dyep – *n.* jeep, American *jeep*

dyes – *num.* ten, Spanish *diez*

dyesinoybe – *num.* nineteen, Spanish *diecinueve*

dyesiotso – *num.* eighteen, Spanish *dieciocho*

dyesisais – *num.* sixteen, Spanish *dieciseis*

dyesisyete – *num.* seventeen, Spanish *diecisiete*

G:g

gaba – *n.* curse, karma; *v.* to curse

gábi – *n.* night, nighttime

gabot – *v.* to pull out as tooth, to uproot

gagad – *v.* to enjoin, to entrust

gahin – *n.* share, gain, profit

gahom – *n.* power, might

gamaw – *n.* wild duck

gamay – *adj.* thin, small

gamhanan – *adj.* powerful

gamit – *n.* usage, tool, equipment; *v.* to use, to equip

gamot – *n.* roots; *v.* to grow roots

gana – *n.* appetite

ganansya – *n.* gain, profit, Spanish *ganancia*

ganggang – *n.* edge, precipice

ganghis – *n.* cicada, cricket

gangsa – *n.* goose, Spanish *ganso*

gantsilyo – *n.* crochet; *v.* to crochet, Spanish *gancho*

gaod – *v.* to tie to something

gapas – *n.* cotton

gapos – *v.* to tie down, to immobilize

garagara – *n.* audacity, insolence, impudence

garagaraan – *adj.* rash, audacious, insolent

garamiton – *n.* tools, equipments

garapon – *n.* glass jar, container

garawasan, garawsan – *n.* exit

garbo – *n.* elegance, gracefulness, Spanish *garbo*

garbuso – *adj.* flamboyant, elegant, graceful, Spanish *garboso*

garhob – *n.* deep baritone voice

garing – *v.* to grind grain in stone mill

garingan – *n.* stone mill

gasgas – *n.* scratch; *v.* to scratch like a smooth surface

gasolina – *n.* gas, gasoline, Spanish *gasolina*

gasto – *v.* to spend, Spanish *gastar*

gastos – *n.* expenditure, expenses

gatas – *n.* milk

gatós – *num.* hundred

gawas – *n.* outside, exterior; *v.* to go outside; *prep.* out of, except

gaway – *n.* taro

gawgaw – *n.* starch

gihap, gihapon – *adv.* also

gihay – *n.* midrib of coconut or nipa palm leaf

gikan – *v.* to begin, to start a journey; *conj.* due to, because

giling – *n.* stone grinder; *v.* to grind

gilingan – *n.* rice mill

ginbúhatan – *adj.* done, realized, source, origin, provenance

ginhadían – *n.* kingdom, realm

ginhawa – *n.* breath, rest; *v.* to breathe in, to rest

ginikanan - *n.* ancestors, grandparents

gininhawaan – *n.* expired air, breath air

ginsabutan, sinabutan – *n.* agreement

gintikangan – *n.* cause, origin

gintiupay – *adj.* abused, harrassed

Ginúo – *n.* Lord

giok – *v.* to thresh harvested rice

gipit – *n.* financial difficulty

gira – *n.* war, Spanish *Guerra*

girikgitik, gitikgitik – *v.* to tickle

girikgitikon, gitikgitikon – *adj.* ticklish

giringgiting – *n.* zigzag pattern

girok – *n.* ticklish or tingling sensation

gisa – *v.* to sauté

gísi, gúsi – *v.* to tear

gisí, gusí – *adj.* torn

gisígisí, gusígusí - *adj.* tattered, ragged

gitara – *n.* guitar, Spanish *guitarra*

gitgit – *n.* sparrow

giyan – *n.* addict, addiction: *v.* to become addicted

graba – *n.* gravel, Spanish *grava*

grabe – *adj.* serious, grave, Spanish *grave*

grado – *n.* grade, Spanish *grado*

grano – *n.* grain, Spanish *grano*

grasa – *n.* grease, Spanish *grasa*

gripo – *n.* faucet, Spanish *grifo*

guba – *v.* to destroy; *n.* forest

gubaguba – *adj.* broken into several pieces
gubot – *n.* war, chaos
gubyerno – *n.* government, Spanish *gobierno*
gud – *adv.* always, surely, certainly
gudla – *adv.* only, solely
gugma – *n.* love, affection
guhó – *n.* hole; *v.* to create a hole
gulaman – *n.* agar, gelatin
gulíat – *v.* to shout, to yell
gulong – *n.* wheel
gulpi – *v.* to beat up, to hit; *adj.* critical, serious; *adv.* mercilessly, Spanish *golpe*
guma – *n.* rubber, Spanish *goma,* tire
gumamela – *n.* red china rose *Hibiscus rosa-sinensis*
gumo – *v.* to mold with the hand
gumok – *n.* entangled thread; *v.* to entangle as in thread
gunting – *n.* scissors; *v.* to cut with scissors
guol – *n.* tiredness, exhaustion
gupong – *n.* confusion; *v.* to confuse
gurot – *n.* slice of meat; *v.* to slice meat
gusak – *adj.* chipped
gusakgusak, gurakgusak – *adj.* rough, coarse, chipped edges
gusok – *n.* ribs
gusto – *v.* to like, to want, Spanish *gusto*
guti – *adj.* small in size or quantity
gutiay – *adj.* small, little, few
gutóm – *adj.* hungry; *v.* to make hungry, to famish

gútom – *n.* hunger, famine
gwano – *n.* bird dung, fertilizer, Spanish *guano*
gwapo – *adj.* handsome, Spanish *guapo*
gwardabano – *n.* soursap fruit

H:h

ha, sa – *prep.* to
haara – *v.* to get used to, to accustom
hababaw, hibabaw – *adj.* shallow
habagat – *n.* southwest monsoon, choppy seas, west wind
hablos – *v.* to adopt
hakog – *adj.* greedy, selfish
hakot – *v.* to carry, to bring
hadi – *n.* king
hadlok – *n.* fear, fright, trepidation; *v.* to scare, to frighten
hadlukon – *adj.* fearful, afraid
hadto, sadto – *adv.* before, prior to; *pron.* that in time
haganas – *n.* rushing water
hagkot – *n.* coldness, frigid weather
hagdan – *n.* stairs, staircase
hagikhik – *n.* laugh with snorting sound, chortle; *v.* to chortle
hagilap – *n.* chance encounter; *v.* to encounter, to meet by chance
hagong – *n.* snoring; *v.* to snore
hagos – *adj.* past; *v.* to pass in time
hagupit – *n.* sandpaper

hagurong – *n.* reverberating sound, tinnitus, ringing in the ear

háin – *adv.* where, used in question

halaba, hilaba – *adj.* long

halad – *n.* offering; *v.* to offer

halaghag – *adj.* sparse, thinly spread

halapad, hilapad – *adj.* wide

halarom, hilarom – *adj.* deep

halas – *n.* snake

haligot, hiligot – *adj.* narrow

halipot, hilipot – *adj.* short

haló – *n.* monitor lizard, gecko

hálo – *v.* to mix, to stir

halot – *adj.* selfish, greedy

halúag – *adj.* wide, loose, roomy; *v.* to loosen

haluhago – *adj.* loose

hambog – *adj.* boastful, show-off

hamon – *n.* ham, Spanish *jamon*

hamot – *n.* scent, fragrance, smell; *v.* to smell

hampang – *v.* to join in conversation

hamtik, hantik – *n.* large ants, fire ants

hamumuong – *n.* hornet

han, san – *prep.* for

hanang – *n.* brackish, muddy water

hanaw – *v.* to fade away, to disappear, to die

hangad – *v.* to look up

hangag – *n.* tortoise, small land turtle

hangaran – *n.* pronoun; *adj.* titular, only in name, nominal; *prep.* in the name of

hangaron – *n.* wish, ambition

hangga – *n.* chicken pox

hangin – *n.* wind, air hangit – *v.* to be mad, to get angry

hangkop – *n.* embrace, cuddling; *v.* to embrace, to cuddle

hangol – *adj.* greedy, selfish

hangos – *n.* breath, deep beath

hangtod – *conj.* until

hangyo – *v.* to request, to ask

hantak – *n.* beans

hantakan – *n.* round smooth surface piece of rock used in coin-toss gambling

hanting – *n.* hunting knife, English *hunting*; *v.* to hunt

hapa – *v.* to prostrate, lie down on the belly, to lie in prone position

hapdos – *n.* stinging pain

hapilan – *n.* garbage dump site

hapit – *v.* to drop by

haplas – *v.* to caress; *n.* caresses

hapo – *n.* shortness of breath; *v.* to have breathing difficulty

Hapon – *n.* Japanese

haráging – *v.* to reverberate like bell, to echo

harampang – *v.* to gather around the table; *n.* gathering, meeting

harana – *n.* to woo a lady through music

haráng – *n.* pepper, spice

harangdon – *adj.* honorable, honorific for majesty, highness

haráni, hiráni – *adj.* near, nearby

haraní, hiraní– *v.* to come closer, to approach

harap – *n.* night blindness, blurred vision

harapaw – *adj.* superficial

harapihap – *v.* to caress, to fondle

harapit – *adv.* almost, nearly

haras –*v.* to slash, to cut tall grass

haraw – *v.* to steal food

harayo, hirayo – *adv.* far away, distant

harigi – *n.* post, wooden vertical support of a house

harok – *n.* kiss; *v.* to kiss

harón – *v.* to alight like birds or insects

harop – *n.* palm scoop, handful; *v.* to scoop with the palm

háros – *adv.* almost

harós – *v.* to dislodge, to slip

harumamay – *n.* exaggeration; *adv.* incredibly, unbelievably; *interj.* expression of exaggeration or hyperbole

harupay – *n.* fern that closes when touched

harupoy – *n.* breeze

hasahasa – *n.* mackerel

hasang – *n.* fish gills

hasta – *prep. and conj.* until, Spanish *hasta*

hat – *adj.* honorific for the deceased person

hataas, hitaas – *adj.* tall

hatag – *n.* gift, grant, present; *v.* to give, to grant

hatak – *v.* to pull

hataw – *v.* to surface, to reveal

hatok – *n.* coconut milk; *v.* to mix with coconut milk

hawa – *v.* to spread disease, to infect another person with communicable disease

háwak – *n.* waistline, *v.* to hold around the waist

hawan – *v.* to clear up vegetation, to clean up mess

háwas – *v.* to dismount, to disembark

hawol – *n.* exhaustion, tiredness, fatigue

hayag – *n.* light, brightness, enlightenment; *v.* to enlighten

hayahay – *v.* to relax, to take easy, to refresh; *adv.* easily

hayhat – *adj.* arrogant, snubbish

hayukat! – *interj.* expression of contempt

hi, si – *arti.* the, used in proper names of person

hiagi – *n.* occupation, source of income

hiara – *v.* to be accustomed, to get used to; *adj.* habitual

hibang – *v.* to be injured, to damage

hibangkaagan – *n.* preoccupation, concentration, attention

hibaro – *n.* learning, knowledge; *v.* to learn, to know

hibol – *n.* lump-in-throat feeling, thirsty

hikay – *v.* to dig, to find, to discover, to research

hikog – *v.* to hang as in suicide

higante – *n.* giant, Spanish *gigante*

higayon – *n.* occasion, opportunity

higda – *v.* to lie down

higdáan - *n.* bed

higop – *v.* to sip, to suck

higot – *n.* string, twine, rope; *v.* to tie with a string

higugmáon – *n.* loved one, beloved, sweetheart

hila – *v.* to drag

hilarom – *adj.* deep

hilaw – *adj.* not fully cooked, unripe as fruit

hilawig, halawig – *adj.* long (life)

hilig – *n.* liking, proclivity, tendency, propensity

hiling – *n.* to peep

hilkas – *v.* to take down hung clothes

hílo – *n.* dizziness, fainting; *v.* to faint, to feel dizzy

hiló – *n.* poison; *v.* to poison

hilom – *v.* to keep quiet, to shut up

hilot – *n.* masseur, massage

hilúan – *n.* poison dispenser

hiludibila – *n.* thread, small twine, string, Spanish *hilo de vela*

hilwas – *v.* to utter, to speak

himaga – *n.* libido, coitus, orgasm; *v.* to have orgasm

himangraw – *n.* conversation, discussion; *v.* to talk, to converse, to discuss

himamágon – *adj.* horny, libidinous, sexually excited

himatay – *v.* to faint, to pass out

himaya – *adj.* glorious

himo – *v.* to make, to create, to build

himos, hipos – *v.* to keep, to hide

himsaw – *v.* to wash feet

himtang – *n.* situation, condition

himuhimo – *n.* invented falsehood, fictitious allegation; *v.* to trump up

himurayaw – *n.* rest, peace and order

hin, sin – *prep.* with

hini, ini – *pron.* this, these

hinablusan – *n.* foster child, adopted child

hinanakit – *n.* grievance

hinatukan – *n.* coconut milk dish

hinay – *v.* to slow down, to be careful

hinayhinay – *adv.* slowly, carefully

hingadtuan – *n.* destiny, eventuality

hingal – *v.* to put out of breath

hingalo – *v.* to be in agony, to struggle

hingaran – *v.* to enumerate, to name

hingas – *v.* to chortle, to laugh with a snorting sound

hingbis – *n.* fish scale

hinggok – *v.* to breathe in, to snort

hingit – *v.* to grimace

hingpit – *adj.* earnest

hingyap – *n.* wish, desire; *v.* to wish, to desire

hini, sini – *pron.* this, these

hinigugma – *n.* sweetheart, soul mate; *adj.* beloved

hinikay – *n.* research

hinimo – *n.* product; *adj.* made, done

hinin, sinin – *pron.* these

híno – *pron.* who

hinog – *adj.* ripe

hinukay – *n.* diggings, dirt

hinumduman – *n.*
remembrance, memento
hinungdan – *n.* significance,
meaning, cause, reason
hipag – *n.* sister-in-law
hipon – *n.* sauce of salted
ground shrimp ; *v.* to cook
with this sauce
hira – *pron.* they
hirámos – *v.* to wash face
hiranat – *n.* fever
hiribhirib – *adj.* scary, frightful
hiris – *n.* lemon
hírit – *adv.* fast
hiróg – *n.* rubbing ointment,
topical medication, pumice
rock used to scrub or scour
hírog – *v.* to rub, to scrub
hírot – *adj.* careful, cautious
hirót – *v.* to be careful, to
beware, to be cautious
hiruhimangraw – *n.*
conversation, discussion,
meeting
hisgot – *n.* discussion; *v.* to
discuss
hit, hiton – *prep.* of
hita – *n.* inner thigh, hips
hitabo, hinabo – *n.* happening,
occurence; *v.* to happen, to
occur
hito – *n.* catfish
hiton, siton – *pron.* that, those
hitsura – *n.* shape, looks, facet
Spanish *hechura*
hiunong – *prep.* about,
pertaining to; *v.* to cause
hiwa – *v.* to slice; *n.* slice
hiwí – *adj.* lopsided
hiwihiwi – *adv.* haphazardly in
disarray
hiya, siya - *pron.* he, she, it
hiyak – *v.* to suck the belly in

hiyay! – *inter.* expression of
fear or trepidation
hiyom – *n.* smile; *v.* to smile,
to sigh
hiyos – *v.* to deflate like tire
hubad – *v.* to untie, to
untangle
hubag – *n.* swelling, abscess
hubang – *n.* ditch, canal; *v.* to
dig a ditch
hubas – *n.* low tide; *v.* to dry
up or scorch food being boiled
or cooked
hubo – *adj.* butt naked, nude
hubog – *n.* drunken person;
adj. drunk, wasted
hubsak – *adj.* lazy
hubya – *adj.* lazy
hukab, hikab – *n.* asthma
hukad – *v.* to scoop cooked
rice, to empty out especially
food
hukal – *adj.* loose
hukay – *v.* to excavate, to dig
hukip – *n.* bribe; *v.* to bribe
hukom – *n.* judge, justice; *v.* to
judge
hudlom – *n.* shade
hudno - *n.* oven, Spanish
horno
hudnuhan – *n.* bakery
hudo – *interj.* expression of
contempt
hugador – *n.* gambler, Spanish
jugador
hugas – *v.* to wash
hugáw – *n.* dirt, garbage; *v.* to
get dirty
húgaw – *n.* dirt, soil, stain; *v.*
to make dirty, to stain
hugdon – *v.* to land as an
airplane

hugót – v. to pull out, to tighten

húgot, húot – adj. tight

hulabtog – n. green pepper

hulagway – n. rest, refresh, relaxation; v. to rest

hulampag – v. to fall flat

hulang – adj. fruitless, barren, infertile

hulashulas – n. miliaria, sweat rashes

hulat – v. to wait

hulatan – n. waiting station

hulbot – v. to pull out, to draw out

hulins – n. marbles; v. to play with marbles

huló – n. uncircumcised penis; v. to draw back foreskin over the glans

hulóg – v. to fall, to drop, to fail in an examination or test, to translate

húlog – v. to pay by installment, to translate

hulogan – n. installment, place to drop; v. to pay by instalment

hulop – v. to be indecisive, to have second thoughts, to hesitate, to waver, to equivocate

húlos – adj. wholehearted, sincere

hulós – v. to wet, to moisten

hulso – v. to take off

hulupanon, hulpanon – adj. indecisive, hesitant, equivocating

Hulyo – n. July, Spanish julio

human – v. to finish; adj. finished, done

humatol – n. swell, long wave, surf

humay – n. unhusked rice, palay

humba – n. dish of slow cooked fatty pork premarinated with soy sauce and vinegar

humla – n. understanding, kindness, pleasant

humog – adj. wet, moist; v. to wet, to moisten

humok – n. softness; v. to soften

hunahuna – n. mind, thinking, imagination; v. to think, to imagine

hunaw – v. to wash hands

hundaray – v. to lie down, to rest

hungaw - v. to leak air or gas

hungit – v. to spoon feed

hungot – n. coconut or bamboo spoon or scoop

huni – n. sound

hunong – v. to stop, to stall

hunsoy – n. tobacco pipe

Hunyo – n. June, Spanish junio

huot – adj. tight; v. to tighten

hupong – n. edema, swelling; v. to become edematous

hurak – n. abundance, fullness, plenitude

huram – v. to borrow

huraw – n. dry season

huring – n. whisper; v. to whisper

hurma – v. to form, to mold

hurmaan – n. mold

hurnal – n. a person who works in the waterfront loading and unloading ships or boats, stevedore

hurom – v. to soak

hurón – *n.* remote village, rural areas, hinterlands; *adj.* rural, rustic

húron – *v.* to sleep over

hurós – *v.* to slip, to slide, to dislodge

hurubhurob, huribhurib – *n.* rumor mongering, gossip; *v.* to spread rumor

hurushuros – *adj.* adjustable

hurót – *n.* all, everything

hurunanon – *adj.* rural, rustic, lacking sophistication

hurunanon – *n.* rural area inhabitants; *adj.* pertaining to rural areas

husga – *v.* to judge, Spanish *juzga*

husgit – *v.* to mention, to tell

husog – *adv.* forcibly, forcefully

husto – *adj.* enough

huthot – *n.* sucker, parasite; *v.* to snort

hútok – *adj.* concentrated, thick like syrup

huwad – *v.* to pour

huwang – *adj.* loose, wide open

huwaw – *v.* to expose private parts

huwebes – *n.* Thursday, Spanish *jueves*

huwes – *n.* judge, Spanish *juez*

huweteng – *n.* illegal numbers game, Chinese *jue teng*

huyam – *n.* yawn; *v.* to yawn

huyang – *v.* to lie down on the back, to be in supine position

huyayag – *adj.* supine, clear, obvious

huygo – *n.* gambling; *v.* to gamble, Spanish *juego*

huyop – *v.* to blow; *n.* wind gust, breeze

huyuhoy – *n.* breeze

I:i

ibá – *adj.* different, unlike; *v.* to differ

íba – *n.* succulent, sour plum-like fruit, kamias

ibáibá – *adj.* miscellaneous

iban – *v.* to reduce, to subtract

ibas – *v.* to thin out from constant use, to wear the sole down like shoes

ibos – *n.* salted sweet rice wrapped in coconut leaf

ikagusa – *adv.* rarely, once

ikaw – *pron.* you

ikid – *n.* to tiptoe

ikinatawo – *n.* genitalia, sex

ikmat – *v.* to watch, to beware, to be cautious

ikog – *n.* tail

Iks-re – *n.* X-ray machine; *v.* to undergo an X-ray

iksamen – *n.* examination, exam , test; *v.* to take a test, to be examined, Spanish *examen*

iksport – *n.* export, English *export*

idad – *n.* age, Spanish *edad*

ídro – *n.* airplane, Spanish *aeroplano*

igbaw – *n.* upper level of a house; *prep.* above, over

igbusay – *adj.* almost, swiped

igindidiri – *adj.* prohibited, forbidden

igkasi – *adj.* fellow

igkasitawo – *n.* fellowmen

igo – v. to hit a target; adj. exact, fit, precise

iguigo – n. estimate, approximation

igos – n. fig tree

igot – n. black berry

igsyapa – n. first cousin

iha – n. duration

ihalas – adj. wild, savage

ihap – n. number; v. to count

ihaw – v. to slaughter like pig

ihawan, irihawan – n. slaughterhouse, abattoir

ihi – n. urine; v. to urinate

ilarom – prep. below, under

ilawod – adv. seabound, towards the sea

iliw – v. to miss

ilob – n. endurance; v. to endure

ilop – v. to elope, English elope

imbis – adv. instead, in place of

imbistigar – v. to investigate, Spanish investigar

imbitar – v. to invite, Spanish invitar

imbitasyon – n. invitation, Spnaish invitacion

imim – n. lips

imo, im – pron. you, yours (singular)

imod – v. to consume everything, to leave nothing

imot – n. greed, stinginess

impleyado – n. employee, Spanish empleado

inaanak – n. godchild

inangkop – n. adopted child

inarikawot – adv. hardly, inadequately, insufficiently

inay – n. mother

indigan – n. intrigue

Inero – n. January, Spanish enero

inganyar – v. to trick, to deceive, Spanish engañar

ingka – n. unsteady gait, wobble; v. to walk wobbly

inggat – n. glitter, sparkle, shine

ini – pron. this (singular)

inin – pron. these (plural)

init – v. to get upset, to be irritated

inop – n. dream, ambition; v. to dream

insulto – n. insult; v. to insult, Spanish insultar

intablado – n. stage, Spanish tablado

intawon – interj. expression of sympathy

intonsis – conj. therefore, then, Spanish entonces

intoy – n. little boy

intríga – n. intrigue, embroil; v. to intrigue, Spanish intrigar

intrigá – v. to offer, to present, to introduce

intrimis – n. trick, joke; v. to trick, to make fun of

Intsik, Intsika – n. Chinese person

intyinde – v. to understand, to attend to, Spanish entender

inukab – n. pit, excavation, diggings

inulang – n. thread, yarn

inulunan, inúlnan – n. placenta

inungod – adv. really, truly, seriously

ipa – n. jealousy, envy, craving; v. to crave

ipis – *v.* to pour slowly
ipit – *v.* to squeeze, to clip
ira – *pron.* their, theirs, them
iraid – *n.* delicacy of mashed tuber with coconut and sugar; *v.* to make such delicacy
iraira – *interj.* expression of wishful thought or second-guessing
irapa – *n.* illness, sickness; *adj.* ill, sick
iras – *n.* restlessness
iraya – *adv.* inland
irihis – *adj.* irreverent, impious
iring – *n.* kitten
iró, idó – *n.* puppy
írok – *n.* armpit
irong – *n.* nose
iroy – *n.* mother
iskina – *n.* corner, Spanish *esquina*
iskolar – *n.* scholar, English *scholar*
iskor – *n.* score, English *score*
iskrin – *n.* screen, English *screen*
iskwelahan – *n.* school, Spanish *escuela*
isda – *n.* fish
isla – *n.* island, Spanish *isla*
isnak – *n.* snack; *v.* to snack, English *snack*
ísog – *n.* bravery, courage
isóg – *v.* to scold, to reprimand
ispada – *n.* sword, Spanish *espada*
ispiker – *n.* speaker, English *speaker*
ispiho – *n.* mirror, Spanish *espejo*
istatuwa – *n.* statue, Spanish *estatua*

istorya – *n.* story, Spanish *historia*
istrikto – *adj.* strict, Spanish *estricto,* mean
istudyante – *n.* student, Spanish *estudiante*
isturbo – *v.* to disturb, to bother, Spanish *turbar*
iton, it – *pron.* that, those (sometimes used as a linking verb)
itay – *n.* father
itik – *n.* duck
itip – *n.* scorched bottom of cooked rice
itlog – *n.* testicle
itom – *adj.* black; *v.* to blacken
itsa – *v.* to throw, to pitch, to toss
iwas – *v.* to drive away, to avoid, to leave
íya – *pron.* his, her, hers, its
iyá – *interj.* take this
íyaíya – *v.* to claim for oneself; *adj.* selfish
iyagiti – *interj.* expression of contempt or disgust
iyo – *pron.* you, yours (plural)
iyot – *n.* sexual intercourse, coitus; *v.* to have sexual intercourse

L:l

la – *adv.* only
laag – *v.* to wander
lábas – *adj.* fresh (fish)
laba – *v.* to wash, to launder, Spanish *lavar*
labakara – *n.* face towel
labad – *n.* trouble, blurry sight

labada – *n.* laundry, Spanish *lavada*

labandera – *n.* washerwoman, Spanish *lavandera*

labar – *v.* to wash body, Spanish *lavar*

labasiro – *n.* fisherman

labaw – *adj.* beyond; *prep.* above, over

labáy – *v.* to pass by, to drop by

lábay – *v.* to throw, to hurl

labi – *adv.* especially

labilabi – *v.* to pamper; *adj.* stubborn, recalcitrant

labog – *v.* to throw away, to waste

lábot – *conj.* except, despite, aside from

labót – *v.* to touch, to steal, to intervene, to get involved

laburos – *n.* blustering wind and rain

labyog – *v.* to swing

lakat – *v.* to walk, to travel

lakatlakat – *n.* stroll, aimless walking

lakha – *n.* brown rice

lako – *n.* throat secretions, mucus

lakob – *n.* bamboo tube container

lakog – *v.* to choke

laksi – *v.* to play, to trick someone

laktaw – *v.* to skip a sequence or order

lakwatsa – *n.* unproductive use of free time; *v.* to spend time with friends, to galivant

ladawan – *n.* image, picture, photograph

lága – *n.* light; *v.* to light, to switch on, to boil meat

lagas – *n.* old person

lagaslagasoy – *adj.* behaving like an old person

lagay – *n.* mud, clay

lagtak – *v.* to hit the head with an object

lagtok – *v.* to soak rice

lahi – *n.* race

lahid – *v.* to wipe

lahing – *adj.* mature coconut, unripe fruit

lahos – *v.* to pass beyond target, to overshoot

láin – *n.* other, another; *adj.* different

laín – *v.* to be different

láing – *n.* taro leaves cooked with coconut milk

lamay – *n.* wake, funeral

lambong – *n.* shadow; *v.* to shadow

lamiri – *n.* dirt, soil

lamisa – *n.* table, Spanish *mesa*

lamot – *adj.* greedy, selfish

lámoy – *v.* to devour, to swallow

lampara – *n.* lamp, Spanish *lampara*

lampaso – *n.* floor scrub of coconut husk; *v.* to scrub the floor

lamrag – *n.* light, brightness; *v.* to brighten

lana – *n.* oil

lanat – *v.* to chase, to follow, to catch up

lanay – *v.* to flow, to drip

langka – *n.* aromatic, spiky fruit

landingan – *n.* airport, English *landing*

langaglangag – *n.* pharynx, throat

langan – *n.* wait; *v.* to delay

langanlangan – *v.* to waste time, to gallivant, to delay

langaw – *n.* fly; *v.* to infest with flies

langit – *n.* sky, heaven

langitnon – *adj.* holy, heavenly

lango – *n.* stupidity

langoy – *v.* to swim

langsa – *n.* putrid odor like rotten fish

langulango – *adj.* stupid

langyaw – *n.* foreigner, stranger; *adj.* foreign; *v.* to travel to foreign lands

lanoy – *n.* mellow sound

lantaka – *n.* cannon, bamboo cannon

lantawan – *n.* tower, lookout

lantsa – *n.* launch, boat, barge, Spanish *lancha*

lanyug – *n.* very tall coconut trees; *adj.* tall and slender

láom – *n.* hope; *v.* to hope

lapad – *n.* width

laparag – *v.* to fall on the ground

lapinig – *n.* wasp

lapirit – *v.* to squeeze out air, to make this kind of sound

lapis – *n.* pencil, Spanish *lapiz*

lapok – *n.* mud, clay

lapos – *v.* to go through; *conj.* beyond, through

lapsaw – *adj.* dilute

laptap – *n.* laptop computer, American *laptop*

lapos – *v.* to go or pass beyond a certain point

lapuslapos – *adv.* through and through

lará – *n.* virulence, sting; *adj.* virulent, poisonous

lára – *v.* to weave

larang – *v.* to decide, to plan, to create

laray – *n.* display; *v.* to display, to outline

larayulohan – *n.* headline as in news

larga – *v.* to embark

larog – *n.* sediment

lasagas – *v.* to walk barefoot; *adj. adv.* barefoot

lasaw – *n.* puddle, pool of stagnant water

laso – *v.* to boil

lastiko – *n.* rubber band, Spanish *elastico*

lasuna – *n.* garlic

lasurbo – *n.* splatter, splash; *v.* to splash

laswak – *v.* to overflow

lata – *n.* tin can, Spanish *lata*

latak – *v.* to bleach, to lose a game with big margin

latag – *v.* to spread, to display

latagaw – *n.* wanderer, vagabond

látang – *n.* interval, gap

latay – *v.* to walk on narrow plank or bamboo bridge

latayan – *n.* bamboo foot bridge, narrow plank

latik – *v.* to flick with a finger; *n.* coconut syrup

latigo *n.* whip; *v.* to whip, Spanish *latigo*

lato – *n.* sea weed

latob – *v.* to whip; *n.* whip

latos – *n.* long range distance, projectile; *v.* to travel at speed and distance

lauya – *n.* boiled meat dish

lawaan – *n.* lumber tree used to make furnitures and boats, Philippine mahogany

lawak – *n.* lake

lawalawa – *n.* cobweb

lawas – *n.* body, torso

lawáy – *v.* to salivate

láway – *n.* saliva, obscenity, profanity

lawayan – n. small, slimy flat fish

lawlaw – *n.* fermented anchovy

lawod – *n.* ocean

láya – *n.* fishing net

layá – *v.* to wilt, to wither

layag – *n.* sail; *v.* to sail

layaw – *adj.* wild, not domesticated

layas – *v.* to flee, to leave, to run away

layog – *v.* to dive, to jump

layon – *adv.* please

Letenyo – *n.* Leyte native or resident; *adj.* pertaining to or about Leyte Island, Spanish *Leyteño*

liaw – *v.* to entertain

libak – *v.* to gossip

libag – *n.* skin dirt

libat – *n.* cross-eyed person, squint; *v.* to squint

libay – *n.* doe, female deer

libo – *num.* million

libong – *n.* yard, surrounding

libot – *v.* to run around a circle, to surround, to rotate

libutlibot – *n.* rotation, revolution

libro – *n.* book, Spanish *libro*

likaw – *v.* to deny

likay – *v.* to avoid, to prevent

liko – *v.* to turn on a corner

likod – *prep.* behind

lider – *n.* leader, Spanish *lider*

lidgid – *n.* sweet, coconut milk taro delicacy

lidong – *n.* circle, round

ligas – *v.* to dislodge

ligbos – *n.* umbrella-like mushroom

ligid – *n.* side

ligidligid – *adv.* sideways

ligidligiron – *n.* surroundings

ligis – *v.* to run over, to injure in a vehicular accident

ligoyligoy – *v.* to gallivant

ligwat – *n.* lever; *v.* to pry

lihi – *n.* pregnant cravings; *v.* to crave during pregnancy

lilinti – *n.* sky lightning

lilipak – *n.* ground lightning

lima – *num.* five

limás – *n.* scoop for bailing

límas – *v.* to bail a boat

limba – *n.* red color

limbaglimbag – *v.* to roll side to side

limbahon, limbawon – *n.* pink color

limbasog – *n.* resolve, initiative, effort, stoicism

limbong – *v.* to cheat

limbungan – *n.* cheater, swindler, shill

limon – *n.* lemon

limos – *n.* alms, pittance; *v.* to beg, Spanish *limosna*

limot – *v.* to forget

limpyo – *n.* cleanliness

limukon – *n.* wild dove

limugmog – *n.* gargle; *v.* to gargle

limutanon, limtanon – *adj.* forgetful

linaga – *n.* boiled meat with vegetables

lindog – *n.* shade

Lineyte-Samarnon – *n.* other name for Waray language; *adj.* pertaining to Leyte and Samar

linga – *adj.* mentally retarded, confused

lingaw – *v.* to pass time, to entertain

lingganay – *n.* bell

lingganayan – *n.* bell tower, belfry

lingi – *v.* to look back

lingit – *n.* pair, counterpart

lingkod – *v.* to sit down

lingkuran – *n.* seat, chair, bench

lingkuranay – *n.* dwarf coconut tree, coconut sapling

lingo – *n.* betrayal; *v.* to betray

linog – *n.* earthquake

linubid – *adj.* intertwined, twisted

linupak – *n.* delicacy of smashed cooked potato, banana or taro sweetened with sugar and grated coconut

linurong – *n.* betrayal, malfeasance, perfidy

linya – *n.* line, Spanish *linea; v.* to fall in line, to mark with a line

liog – *n.* neck

lipat – *n.* confused, perplexed; *v.* to cheat, to confuse

lipatlipat – *v.* to obfuscate, to hide

lipay – *n.* happiness, joy

lipóng – *adj.* crazy, demented, confused

lípong – *v.* to get dizzy, confused

liro – *n.* calm recess of a stream, pool, pond

lisang – *adj.* anxious, careless, disorderly

lisík – *n.* testicle

liso – *n.* seed

lison – *n.* sphere

listo – *adj.* alert, ready, prompt, Spanish *listo*

lisuliso – *n.* tiny bumpy lesion

lítag – *n.* trap; *v.* to trap

litra – *n.* letter, Spanish *letra*

litson – *n.* roasted pig; *v.* to roast whole pig by rotisserie

liwán – *v.* to change clothes

líwan – *v.* to exchange, to substitute

liwanliwan – *adj.* constantly changing

liwas – *n.* past, past event

liwat – *v.* to repeat, to revise; *adv.* again

liwatliwat – *adj.* changeable, fickle, capricious

lola – *n.* grandmother

lolo – *n.* grandfather

lubád – *v.* to fade, to discolor

lúbad – *adj.* faded, discolored

lubas – *adj.* half-naked

lubay – *n.* flexibility, suppleness

lubi – *n.* coconut

lubid – *n.* twine, string; *v.* to twist strings

lublob – *n.* carved step on tree trunks

lubo – *n.* balloon; *v.* to inflate

lubog – *n.* murkiness, turbidity

lubong – *v.* to bury

lubos – *n.* whole, total
lubungan – *n.* grave, graveyard
lubnganan – *n.* cemetery
lukad – *n.* dessicated coconut meat; *v.* to separate coconut meat from shell
lukat – *v.* to redeem, to retrieve
lukay – *n.* leaf of coconut
lukba – *v.* to pry, to detach
lukmay – *v.* to bewilder, to spellbind, to empathize
lukon – *n.* prawn, large shrimp
lukop – *v.* to complete, to occupy completely
lukot – *v.* to fold like clothes, to lie down as a dog, to roll mat
lukso – *n.* jump, leap; *v.* to jump
ludgod – *n.* stone scrub for skin; *v.* to scrub skin
lugar – *n.* place, Spanish *lugar*; *v.* to place, to stop
lugáring – *conj.* but, only that
lugaríng – *v.* to be alone
lugas – *v.* to dislodge, to dislocate
lugaw – *n.* porridge; *v.* to cook porridge
lugit – *n.* dessicated coconut meat, copra; *v.* to process copra
lugod – *adv.* instead, else, differently
lugos – *v.* to force someone, to intimidate, to rape
lugsong – *v.* to come down, to descend
lugtok – *n.* toddler
luha – *n.* teardrop, tears
luhaw, lunghaw – *n.* green color
luhó – *n.* hole

lúho – *n.* luxury
luhod – *v.* to kneel, to genuflect
lumalabay – *n.* passerby; *adj.* temporary, transient, fleeting
lumatod – *n.* toddler
lumay – *n.* love potion; *v.* to poison
lumos – *v.* to drown
lumot – *n.* moss
lumpya – *n.* spring roll
lumuton – *adj.* mossy
lunay – *v.* to sit on the floor or the ground, to lie down
lunes – *n.* Monday, Spanish *lunes*
lungá – *n.* sesame seeds
lunggan – *n.* swimmer's ear; trapped water in the ear; *v.* to trap water in ear
lungib – *n.* cave, cavern
lungón – *n.* coffin
lúngon – *v.* to cohabit, to live together before marriage
lungot – *n.* mischief
lunlon – *adv.* aggravating; annoyingly
lunod – *v.* to sink, to drown
lunop – *n.* deluge, flood
luntog – *n.* boredom
luob – *v.* to squat on
luon – *n.* dessicating coconut meat by smoking; *v.* to smoke
luoy – *v.* to pity
lupad – *v.* to fly
lupak – *n.* blister
luparan – *n.* airport
lupaypay – *adj.* frail, weak
lupig – *adj.* lost as in a game or fight, inferior to
lupiglupig – *adj.* abused; *v.* to be bullied

lupiglupigon – *n.* bullied person
lura – *n.* spit; *v.* to spit
lurab, larab – *v.* to burst in flames, to flare up
lurong – *adj.* mentally deranged, crazy, lunatic, bipolar; *v.* to become mentally deranged luronglurong – *n.* foolish, crazy person, psychotic patient
lurop – *v.* to dive, to submerge
lusad – *v.* to come down
lúsay – *n.* baby burp and spit; *v. to* spit; *adv.* solely
luslos – *n.* inguinal hernia; *v.* to slide down
lusob – *v.* to invade, to attack
lusong – *n.* wooden mortar for pounding rice with wooden pole
lusot – *v.* to slip through, to avoid, to give excuses
lutaw – *n.* to float
luthang – *n.* bamboo cannon
lúto - *v.* to cook, *n.* cooked rice
lutó – *v.* to mourn
lutop – *adj.* transparent, tight fitting
lutúan – *n.* kitchen, cooking pot
lutúon – *n.* uncooked meal
luwad *n.* feeling of fullness, satiety
luwag – *n.* ladle
luwas – *v.* to say, to speak, to utter
lúya – *n.* ginger
luya – *n.* weakness
luyat – *adj.* soft and wilted, overriped

luyo – *prep.* behind; *n.* place behind a certain point

M:m

maabo – *adj.* ashen, gray, grayish
maabtik – *adj.* hyperactive, industrious
maabugho – *adj.* jealous, nagging, overbearing
maadlaw – *adj.* sunny
maalikaya – *n.* affable, pleasant
maalin – *adj.* introvert
maalindanga – *adj.* scorching hot weather
maalinsuob – *adj.* hot and humid, suffocating hot
maamhok – *adj.* smelling like spoiled rice, moldy
maan – *v.* to regret, to make amends
maanghit – *adj.* smelly like armpit
maangso – *adj.* smelly like urine
maangtod – *adj.* smelling like burnt or scorched
maanyag – *adj.* bright, brilliant
maaraksidente – *adj.* accident-prone
maaram – *adj.* knowledgeable, educated, skillful
maaram – *adj.* skillful, smart, knowledgeable
maaringasa – *adj.* noisy, boisterous
maaruga – *adj.* hospitable
maasin – *adj.* salty
maaslom – *adj.* sour, acidic
maaso – *adj.* smoky

maasul – *adj.* blue, bluish
maataman – *adj.* caring, loving
maatamanon – *adj.* hospitable
maayos – *adj.* orderly, neat, tidy
mabaho – *adj.* smelly, stinky
mabaliknon – *adj.* resilient, mailob
mabalod – *adj.* choppy, rough sea
mabangis – *adj.* brave, courageous, intrepid
mabanhod – *adj.* numb
mabaskog – *adj.* stiff, hard
mabaysay – *adj.* beautiful, pretty
mabirde – *adj.* green, greenish
mabudlay – *adj.* expasperating, impatient
mabúgat – *adj.* heavy
mabulaw – *adj.* brown, brownish
mabuligon – *adj.* helpful
mabusag – *adj.* white
mabusisi – *adj.* meticulous, investigative
mabutlaw – *adj.* tired, fatigued
makaarawod – *adj.* shameful, embarassing
makakurulba – *adj.* causing to palpitate, scary, worrisome
makagarahom – *n.* powerful, Almighty, omnipotent
makahalawhaw – *n.* faintness, acrophobia, fear of heights; *adj.* faint, dizzying height
makaharadlok – *adj.* scary, frightful, horrendous
makahihilo – *adj.* poisonous, toxic
makahiridlaw – *adj.* sentimental, nostalgic

makahuhulop, makahurulop – *adj.* causing hesitancy, doubt, indecision, uncertainty
makairinit – *adj.* annoying, irritating
makalilimos, makililimos – *n.* beggar, Spanish *limosnero*
makalilipay – *adj.* causing happiness
makalilisang – *adj.* dreadful, stressful
makaluluoy – *adj.* pitiful, pathetic
makangangalas, makangaralas – *adj.* irritating, anger provoking, loathesome
makangingirhat – *adj.* gross, grotesque
makangurudyot – *adj.* lovable like a child, charming
makaon – *adj.* greedy in eating, voracious
makapoy – *adj.* winded, short of breath
makarimadima – *adj.* horrible, horrendous
makaruruyag – *adj.* pleasant, admirable, lovable, exciting
makarit – *adj.* great, skilled, expert
makasasala, makasarala – *n.* sinner; *adj.* sinful
makatol – *adj.* itchy, scratchy
makauulang – *adj.* obstructive, obstinate
makauurit – *adj.* annoying, irritating
makawiwili – *adj.* exciting, amusing, interesting, entertaining
maki – *adv.* liking, tendency; used as prefix of adjective or verb

makiaangayon – *adj.* friendly, extrovert, hospitable, accommodating

makiawayon – *adj.* quarrelsome, belligerent, cantankerous

makiíyaíya – *adj.* selfish, greedy, egotistical

makina – *n.* machine, engine, Spanish *maquina*

makisangkay, makisasangkayon – *adj.* friendly

makiwá – *adj.* hyperactive, wobbly, shaky

makugi – *adj.* industrious

makupa – *n.* pink, heart-shaped fruit

makuri – *adj.* hard, difficult

makusóg – *adj.* strong

makuti – *adj.* meticulous

madagaang – *adj.* dry and hot, scorching

madagmit – *adj.* fast, quick

madágom – *adj.* cloudy, overcast

madakmol – *adj.* thick

madali – *v.* to hurry; *adv.* hurriedly

madalumdom – *adj.* cloudy, overcast

madalunot – *adj.* slippery, slimy

madaog – *adj.* lucky, always winning

madarahog – *adj.* cruel, bully

madaya – *adj.* deceitful

madi, mari – *n.* honorific for mother of a godchild

madígon, marígon – *adj.* sturdy, hard, firm, durable

madlos – *n.* wind gusts, raging storm; *adj.* gusty, stormy

madre – *n.* mother, nun, honorific for Roman Catholic nun, Spanish *madre*

madrina – *n.* godmother, Spanish *madrina*

madukot – *adj.* sticky

madulas – *adj.* slippery, greasy

madulaw – *adj.* yellowish

madulot – *adj.* sharp, penetrating

madumot – *adj.* hateful, unforgiving, cynical, vengeful

maduruto – *adj.* industrious, workaholic

magáan – *adj.* light, not heavy

magasá – *adj.* thin, emaciated

magasáwa – *n.* married couple, husband and wife; *v.* to get married

magasto – *adj.* wasteful, spendthrift

magkadirudilain – *n., kan.* assortment, miscellaneous, assorted

magin – *pron.* whoever, whomever, whatever

magirhang – *adj.* itchy

magirok – *adj.* ticklish

magkadirudilain – *n.* variety, collection of different things, kaleidoscope

maglalará – *n.* mat weaver

magmarango – *n.* guardian, baby sitter

magparahot – *n.* mat embroiderer

magtiayon – *n.* couple, husband and wife

magtirindog – *n.* founder, builder

magturutdo, manunutdo – *n.* teacher, instructor

magtutúon, magturúon– *n.* student, pupil

maguol – *adj.* tired, exshauted, fatigued

magurang – *n.* older sibling; *adj.* older

magutom – *adj.* hungry

mahagkot – *adj.* cold

mahal – *adj.* dear, expensive, costly; *v.* to love, to cost expensive

mahamis – *adj.* clean, tidy, smooth

mahamot – *adj.* fragrant

mahangin – *adj.* windy

mahapdos – *adj.* stinging painful

maharang – *adj.* spicy

maharaw – *adj.* sneaky to find food

mahatagon – *adj.* generous

mahawol – *adj.* tired, exhausted

mahayag – *adj.* bright

mahibulong, mahiblong – *adj.* desirous, unrequited, unquenchable as thirst

mahidlaw – *adj.* nostalgic

mahilig – *adj.* fond, inclined, attracted

mahilwason – *adj.* frank, tactless

mahimyang – *adj.* peaceful, orderly

mahinay – *adj.* slow

mahinhin – *adj.* graceful, modest

mahinungdanon – *adj.* important, significant

mahirot – *adj.* careful, cautious

mahitungod – *prep.* about, in accordance with; *conj.* because, according to

mahiyumhiyom – *adj.* always smiling, affectionate, pleasant, graceful

mahudlom – *adj.* shaded, overcast

mahugaw – *adj.* dirty

mahulos – *adj.* wet, moist

mahumla – *adj.* empathetic, pleasant, understanding

mahumok – *adj.* soft, supple

mahuyo – *adj.* calm, quiet as a person

maiha – *adj.* protracted, prolonged

mailob – *adj.* enduring, brave, tenacious, insensitive, resilient

maimot – *adj.* stingy, greedy, selfish

mainggat – *adj.* shiny, glittering

mairas – *adj.* restless

maís – *n.* corn

maísog – *adj.* brave, fearless, intrepid

maistra – *n.* female teracher, Spanish *maestra*

maistro – *n.* male teacher, Spanish *maestro*

maitom – *adj.* dark, black

malabad – *adj.* troublesome, mischievous, blurry as in vision

malabinagong – *n.* coral rock

malabyaw – *adj.* snobbish

malagay – *adj.* muddy

malaksi – *adj.* quick, agile

malamiri – *adj.* dirty, soiled

malamrag – *adj.* bright

malangkag – *kan.* boring

malángig – *kan.* fishy

malangsa – *adj.* putrid, foul-smelling

malanhod – *adj.* lukewarm

malapok – *adj.* muddy

malasugi – *n.* blue marlin

malatos – *adj.* far-flung, shooting far

maláway – *adj.* obscene, profane, salacious, salivating

malaybalay, balaybalay – *n.* shack, playhouse

malibak – *adj.* gossipy, backbiter, rumormonger

malimbasog – *adj.* resolved, impassive, stoic

malidong – *adj.* round, circular

maligno – *n.* evil spirit

malimbong – *adj.* cheat, deceitful, fraudulent

malimpyo – *adj.* tidy, clean, Spanish *limpio*

malinaw – *adj.* clear, calm, well understood

malingo – *adj.* deceiving, deceitful, traitorous

malipay, malipayon – *adj.* happy

malipong – *adj.* confusing, dizzy

malison – *adj.* spherical

malubay – *adj.* flexible, limber, supple

malubog – *adj.* turbid, dirty

malulúyon – *adj.* merciful, benevolent

malumot – *adj.* mossy, slippery

malungot – *adj.* annoying, mischievous, troublesome, belligerent

maluntog – *adj.* bored

maluwad – *adj.* distasteful

maluyá – *adj.* unsteady, restless

malúya – *adj.* weak

máma – *n.* mother

mamá – *v.* to chew betel nut; *n.* spit of chewed beetle nut

mamamasa, mambarasa – *n.* readers

mamara – *adj.* dry

mamaralit – *n.* custumers

mamaratbat – *n.* prayer leader

mamingaw – *adj.* quiet, silent

mana – *n.* honorific for an older woman, mistress

manamok – *adj.* mosquito infested

mananabang – *n.* saviour

mananahi, manarahi – *n.* dressmaker, tailor

mananakop – *n.* invader

mananambal, manarambal – *n.* physician, doctor of medicine

mananangot, manaranggot – *n.* tuba gatherer, coconut wine maker

mananap – *n.* animal, critters

mananggiti – *n.* coconut climber

manaragat – *n.* fisherman, seaman, sailor

manaragna – *n.* prophet

mandato – *n.* command, mandate, Spanish *mandato*

mandaw – *interj.* expression of approval

mando – *n.* command, order, rule; *v.* to order, to command, Spanish *mandar*

mangarangara – *han.* severely itchy

mangangadi, mangaradi – *n.* prayer group

mangarol – *adj.* blunt, rough

mangga – *n.* mango

manggad – *adv.* perchance, perhaps

manggagabot – *n.* dentist

manggod – *adv.* surely, certainly, definitely

manghod – *n.* younger sibling; *adj.* younger

mangidlis – *adj.* high-pitched, annoying

mangilad – *adj.* ugly, gross, vulgar, profane

mangingisda, mangirisda – *n.* fisherman

mangiras – *adj.* noisy, boisterous

mangirhat – *adj.* gross, vulgar, grotesque

mangirísda - *n.* fisherman

mangno – *n.* watchman, guard, guardian; *v.* to watch, to guard

mangulinguli – *adj.* annoying, irritating as sound

manguruwat – *n.* swindler, con artist, shill, fraud

mangutngot – *adj.* achy, gnawingly painful

mani – *n.* peanut

manipis – *adj.* thin, flimsy

maniringba – *n.* churchgoers

maniubra – *n.* maneuver, operation, Spanish *maniobra;* to maneuver

manlibasog – *n.* determination, resolution; *adj.* resolute, determined

mano - *n.* honorific for older man, mister

manok – *n.* chicken

manta – *adv.* only, solely, finally

mantika – *n.* fat, lard, butter, Spanish *manteca*

mantikahon, matikáon – *adj.* oily

mantikilya – *n.* butter, Spanish *mantequilla*

mantinir – *v.* to maintain, Spanish *mantener*

manunubos – *n.* redeemer

manunudlis – *n.* surgeon

manunulay – *adj.* evil, treacherous, temptress

mao – *adj.* correct, confirmed; *adv.* agreeably

maong – *n.* durable, twilled cotton pants, jean

mapágad – *adj.* salty

mapaít – *adj.* bitter

mapalad – *adj.* lucky, fortunate

mapános – *adj.* rancid, stale

mapaso – *adj.* hot, warm

mapilit – *adj.* sticky

mapinaubusanon, mapinaubsanon – *adj.* humble, lowly, understanding

mapintas – *adj.* sour and tart

mapula – *adj.* red, reddish

mapunga – *adj.* short of breath

mapuot – *adj.* smoky

maraksot – *adj.* ugly, unsightly

maragumo, maragumok – *adj.* crunchy, crispy

marampag – *adj.* luxuriant

marangya – *adj.* ostentatious

maraot – *adj.* bad, wrong

marasa – *adj.* tasty, delicious

maraton – *n.* marathon, English *marathon*

mareklamohon – *adv.* always complaining, demanding

maribhong – *adj.* lively, vibrant, luxuriant, colorful

marígon, madígon – *adj.* sturdy, hard, strong, firm

marigoso, amariguso – *n.* bitter squash, Spanish *amargoso*

marihayaw – *n.* goose bumps

marisyo – *adj.* lively, noisy, fun

marol – *adj.* tiny, white flower

Marso – *n.* March, Spanish *marzo*

Martes – *n.* Tuesday, Spanish *martes*

martilyo – *n.* hammer, Spanish *martillo*

martsa – *n.* march, military parade; *v.* to march, to join a parade, Spanish *marcha*

marupok – *adj.* brittle

maruruyagon – *adj.* pleasure seeking, wanting

mas – *adj. adv.* more, Spanish *mas*

masabal – *adj.* annoying, obstinate, stubborn

masakit – *adj.* sick, painful

masakiton – *adj.* sickly, moribund

masag – *n.* blue slender crab

masamok – *adj.* (thing) messy, confusing, (person) disturbing, troublesome, troublemaker, belligerent

masapara – *adj.* gritty, rough, sandy, coarse

masaplod – *adj.* astringent, tart

masapnot – *adj.* draggy, dull, coarse

masawi – *adj.* annoying as something causing discomfort

masayon – *adj.* easy

masilaw – *adj.* blinding brightness, glaring as sun

masilhag – *adj.* transparent

masinggit – *n.* teaser

masirak – *adj.* sunny, hot

masirom – *adj.* dark

masubad – *n.* imitator, copycat

masukasuka – *adj.* nauseous

masukot – *adj.* frequent, often

masugot – *adj.* obedient, obsequious

masulog – *adj.* torrential, strong as current or flow

masulúbon – *adj.* sad, sorrowful

masumo – *adj.* boring, monotonous

masungit – *adj.* mean, cruel, strict

masungot – *adj.* suffocating odor, offensive

masunod – *adj.* imitating, unoriginal

masuok – *adj.* overcrowded, compact, tight

masuson – *adj.* overcritical, self-righteous

masustansya – *adj.* nutritious, substantial, Spanish *sustancia*

maswirte – *adj.* lucky, comedic, fond of making jokes

masyado – *adv.* very

masyaw – *n.* play of numbers, illegal gambling

matá – *n.* eye; *v.* to wake up

matábang – *adj.* unsalted, unsavory

matadong – *adj.* righteous, straight

matag – *adj.* every, each

matagak – *a.* will fall

matagamtam – *v.* to taste, to savor

matagudtod – *adj.* gritty to taste

matahom – *adj.* pleasant, pretty, exquisite

matámis – *adj.* sweet

matamay, magtamay – *adj.* spiteful

matambok – *adj.* fat

matansero – *n.* butcher, Spanish *matanzero*

matapubre – *adj.* spiteful of poor people

matapon – *adj.* contagious

mataputapo – *adj.* dusty
matari – *adj.* starchy
matarom – *adj.* sharp
matatag – *adj.* durable, tough, enduring, stoic
matawa – *adj.* ticklish, easily laughing
matíga – *adj.* hard to touch, tough, stiff
matigás – *adj.* brave, tough, intrepid
matignos – *adj.* hard to chew
matinahuron – *adj.* respectful
matínaw – *adj.* crystal clear (water)
matinguhaon – *n.* inventive, creative, resourceful
matinumanon – *adj.* faithful, trustworthy, obedient, obsequious
matinuohon – *adj.* faithful
matiwugtiwog – *adj.* unstable, wobbly, shaky
matris – *n.* womb, uterus, Spanish *matriz*
matugnaw, mabugnaw – *adj.* cool, refreshing
matulin – *adj.* fast, speedy
matuok – *adj.* crybaby
matuoron – *adj.* gullible
matuskig – *adj.* stiff
mauhaw – *adj.* thirsty
maúlol – *adj.* painful
maungod – *adj.* daring, intrepid
maunat – *adj.* elastic, resilient
maupay – *adj.* good
maurán – *adj.* rainy
maus – *n.* computer mouse, America *mouse*
mautot – *adj.* flatulent
mauyam – *adj.* bored

mauyatom – *adj.* resourceful, meticulous, industrious
may – *v.* to have, to own
maya – *n.* ricefield finch
mayakan – *adj.* talkative, garrulous, loquacious
mayakimbot – *adj.* garrulous, loquacious
mayada – *n.* owner, ownership, *adj.* rich, wealthy,
mayaguta – *adj.* mushy
mayamang – *adj.* bed wetter
mayamuit – *adj.* sloppy, wet and dirty
Mayo – *n.* May, Spanish *mayo*
mayor, mayora – *n.* mayor, English *mayor*
mayuyo – *v.* to cherish
mestiso – *n.* half-breed, Spanish *mestizo*
mga – *adj.* preceding plural noun; *adv.* approximately, about
miki – *n.* flour noodle
mikrubyo – *n.* disease-producing microscopic organism, Spanish *microbio*
mil – *num.* thousand, Spanish *mil*
milagruso – *adj.* miraculous, Spanish *milagroso*
minatay – *n.* corpse, funeral
minayuyo – *adj.* precious, cherished
mingaw – *n.* silence
ministiblis – *adj.* limited, austere, marginal
minsahe – *n.* message, Spanish *mensaje*
minuto – *n.* minute, Spanish *minute*
mirisi – *adv.* consequentially

miryenda – *n.* snack, Spanish *merienda; v.* to eat light food between meals

misa – *n.* holy mass, Spanish *misa*

misay – *n.* cat

mismo – *adj.* same, self, very; Spanish *mismo*

Miyerkules – *n.* Wednesday, Spanish *miercoles*

mudmod – *v.* to stumble and hit the face

múdot – *v.* to pout in sulky mood, to sulk

muhog – *n.* mucus, nasal secretions, snot

mulay – *v.* to play

mulayan – *n.* toy, plaything

mulinohan – *n.* rice mill, Spanish *molino*

mulmol – *v.* to suck, to slobber, to lick

mulupyo – *n.* populace, constituents

mulye – *n.* wharf, pier, loading platform, Spanish *muelle*

mumbon – *n.* sandbar

mumo – *n.* tiny food particles, cooked rice grain

munggos – *n.* small, green bean, mung bean *Vigna radiate sp*

murantang – *v.* to make fun of

muron – *n.* delicacy of boiled ground sweet rice and coconut milk with chocolate flavor rolled in banana leaf

muronilyo – *n.* chocolate beater, Spanish *molinillo*

murto – *n.* ghost, Portuguese *morto muerto*

murulayan – *n.* playground

murusot – *n.* sulky mood, pout; *v.* to sulk, to pout

muskitero – *n.* mosquito net, Spanish *mosquitero*

mustasa – *n.* mustard, Spanish *mostaza*

mutato – *n.* toddler

mutó – *n.* brown jellyfish

mutukoy – *adj.* insignificant

mutya – *n.* pearl

myentras – *conj.* while, Spanish *mientras*

N:n

na – *adv.* already

naabuyon – *adj.* agreeable

náawa – *adj.* jealous, envious

naayon – *adj.* comfortable, liking, enjoying

nabangad – *adj.* backward incline of a boat

nabigar – *v.* to travel, to navigate, Spanish *navegar*

nabungól – *adj.* deafened

nabúta – *adj.* blinded

nakaladkad – *adj.* boiling hot

nakon – *pron.* me, mine

nakiling – *adj.* listing to one side as a boat

nadako – *adj.* growing, enlarging, increasing in size

nadamo – *adj.* plentiful, increasing in quantity

nadiri – *v.* to dislike, to refuse

nadugang – *adj.* aggravating; *adv.* increasingly

nadunot – *adj.* overriped, rotten

naduroy – *adj.* aggravating, worsening

naga – *n.* narra tree, *Ptecarpus palido*
naglabay – *n.* past times, memories
nagkagaramo – *adj.* busy
nagpaparagpag – *adj.* unkempt, disheveled
nagutiay – *adj.* diminishing in size or quantity
nahangos – *adj.* winded, heavy breathing, short of breath; *v.* to be out of breath, to breath heavily
nahiaraan – *n.* customs, tradition
nahihimaga – *n.* orgasm
nahingadtuan – *n.* consequences, eventuality
nahingaturog – *adj.* sleepy, dowsy
nahitatabo – *n.* happenings, events
nahiunong – *conj.* due to, as a result of
nahurak – *adj.* abundant, plentiful
nahuyo – *adj.* calm, keeping quiet
naípa – *adj.* envious, jealous
nalaya – *adj.* wilted, withered
nalubad – *adj.* faded, discolored
namimingaw – *adj.* nostalgic, sentimental
naminos – *adj.* mitigating, diminished
namok – *n.* mosquito
namon – *pron.* our, ours (excluding listener)
nana – *n.* pus; *v.* to suppurate
nanang – *n.* aunt
nanaon – *adj.* infected wound, suppurative

nanay – *n.* mother
nangangandoy – *adj.* melancholic, nostalgic
napaka – *adv.* pretending, prefix to adjective
napiyait – *v.* to make high-pitched piercing sound, to shrill
napúlô – *num.* ten
narkotiko – *n.* narcotics, English *narcotics*
narimadima – *adj.* terrified, horrified
narra – *n.* hard red wood *Pterocarpus indicus species*
nars – *n.* nurse, English *nurse*
nasiga – *adj.* shining, lighted
nasod – *n.* nation, country
natádan – *adj.* found, discovered
natawhan, natawuhan – *n.* birthplace
natawo – *n.* birth; *v.* to be born
nati – *n.* young water buffalo (carabao)
natipa – *adj.* disagreeable; *v.* to disagree
naton – *pron.* our, ours (including listener)
natuwad – *adj.* forward incline of a boat
nauba – *adj.* feeling unworthy or snubbed
nauso – *n.* fad, trend
nauyon – *adj.* aggreable, conforming
nawa – *v.* to be alone
nawong – *n.* face
negatibo – *n.* negative, Spanish *negative*
negosyante – *n.* businessman, merchant, dealer, Spanish *negociante*

negosyo – *n.* business; *v.* to conduct business, Spanish *negocio*

nigo – *n.* round and flat basket of woven rattan strips used to winnow rice

nipa – *n.* nipa palm leaves

nirbyos – *n.* anxiety, nervousness

nirbyuso – *adj.* nervous, agitated, anxious

niyan – *adv.* later; *conj.* then

nobenta – *num.* ninety, Spanish *noventa*

Nobyembre – *n.* November, Spanish *noviembre*

noybe – *num.* nine, Spanish *nueve*

numero – *n.* number, Spanish *numero*

núos – *n.* squid

nyus – *n.* news, English *news*

nyuspepor – *n.* newspaper, English *newspaper*

NG:ng

nga – *arti.* the

ngada – *adv.* there; *prep.* until

ngadi – *adv.* here

ngadto – *adv.* there; *prep.* to , towards; *v.* to go there

ngahaw – *interj.* expression of affirmation

ngalas – *n.* anger, wrath; *v.* to be angry, to upset

ngan – *conj.* and

ngánga – *n.* dried nasal mucus

ngangá – *v.* to open one's mouth

nganhi – *prep.* to come back here

ngani – *interj.* expression of denial

ngaralson – *adj.* hateful, irritable, angry

ngaran – *n.* name, noun

ngarangara – *n.* itch, severe itchiness

ngarat – *n.* nightmare; *v.* to have nightmare

ngarukaliding – *adj.* wheel-like, reeling

ngatanan – *n.* all, everything, everyone

ngawingawi – *n.* jaws, snout

ngáyan – *adv.* so, by the way

ngidlis – *n.* high-pitched, scratching sound

ngihab – *n.* missing tooth, toothless

ngílad – *n.* vulgarity

ngípon – *n.* tooth

ngirhat – *adj.* gross, grotesque, gruesome

ngirisi – *n.* grinning

ngirit – *n.* grin, grimace

ngisí – *n.* grin; *v.* to grin, to smile

ngitngit – *n.* violin

ngudyot – *v.* to tease

ngúla – *n.* mute, dumb

ngurahab – *n.* loud, shameless cry; *v.* to cry out loudly

ngurudo – *n.* growl; *v.* to growl

ngurutob – *n.* mumble, mumbling; *v.* to mumble

nguso – *n.* snout

ngutngot – *n.* gnawing pain, ache

nguya – *v.* to chew

nguyit – *n.* speech impairment

nguyngoy – *n.* loud sobbing; *v.* to sob loudly

O:o

o – *conj.* or
obispo – *n.* bishop, Spanish *obispo*
obra – *n.* work, toil, Spanish *obra*
obriro – *n.* worker, laborer, Spanish *obrero*
okong – *interj.* expression of doubt or indifference
Oktubre – *n.* October, Spanish *octubre*
oday – *n.* little girl
odayka – *interj.* expression of disappointment
odog – *interj.* expression of empathy
ohales – *n.* button-hole, Spanish *ojal)*
oho – *interj.* to emphasize attention especially to directions
onse – *num.* eleven, Spanish *once*
oo – *n.* yes
opisina – *n.* office, Spanish *oficina*
opisyal – *n.* government official, Spanish *oficial*
oras – *n.* hour, Spanish *hora*
orasan – *n.* timepiece, clock, watch
orasyon – *n.* incantation, prayer, Spanish *oracion*
ordinaryo – *adj.* ordinary, Spanish *ordinario*
ospital – *n.* hospital, English *hospital*
otoy – *n.* little boy

otsenta – *num.* eighty, Spanish *ochenta*
otso – *num.* eight, Spanish *ocho*

P:p

pa – *prep.* to, towards; *adv.* yet
páa – *n.* thigh
paabat – *n.* clairvoyance, extrasensory perception; *v.* to perceive supernaturally
paabot – *n.* welcome, anticipation; *v.* to welcome, to anticipate
paak – *v.* to bite
paado – *n.* wedding dance; *v.* to make a couple
paagahan – *n.* oil lamp
paagi, pinaagi – *n.* method, process
paanak – *v.* to deliver baby, to impregnate, to be pregnant out of wedlock
paás – *adj.* hoarse
pabalabag – *adv.* crosswise, across
pabilo – *n.* wick, Spanish *pabilo*
pabo – *n.* turkey, Spanish *pavo*
pabor – *n.* favor, Spanish *favor*
paburito – *adj.* favorite, Spanish *favorite*
pabuto – *n.* explosives
pakabuhi – *n.* occupation, business, source of income
pakdol – *n.* hoofs; *v.* to stumble

59

pakiana – v. to ask, to question, to inquire; n. question, query

pakiangay – v. to accommodate, to be hospitable

pakighilawas – n. sexual intercourse, coitus

pakipot – adj. unyielding, hard to get

pakla – n. frog

pakli – v. to turn a page

pakó – n. wing, edible fern

pakot – v. to pin

pakpak, palakpak – v. to clap hands, to applaud

paksiw – n. fish or meat dish cooked in salt and vinegar; v. to cook this dish

pakwan – n. watermelon

padára – adj. swayed, influenced, conned

padará – n. parcel, package; v. to send package

padayon – v. to proceed, to continue

pádi – n. priest

padí, parí– n. honorific for father of a godchild

padis – n. pair, partner

padog – v. to walk while ignoring surroundings

padre – n. father, honorific for Roman Catholic priest, Spanish *padre*

padrino – n. godfather, Spanish *padrino*

pag – conj. prefix denoting condition, upon, when, if; adv. prefix used to inflect verb infinitive

págad – n. salinity, salt

pagampo – n. prayer, worship; v. to pray, to worship

pagantos – n. suffering, sacrifices

pagaw – adj. hoarse

pagbalos – n. to return a favor, to repay

pagbasol – n. repentance, regret; v. to repent

pagbuot – n. will, decision

pagka, ka – adv. very, truly

pagkalimot, pangalimot – v. to forget

pagkalupad, pagkalpad – v. flying

pagkáon - n. food, meal

pagkasigurado – v. to be sure, to be certain

pagkatawo – n. personality, incarnation

pagkatitirok - n. gathering, meeting

pagkaurosa – n. reunion, unity

paggasto – v. to spend

paghalad – n. offering, sacrifice; v. to offer, to sacrifice

paghigugma - n. love affair, romance

paghinay – n. being careful; adv. slowly

paghingaturog – n. sleepiness, drowsiness

pagi – n. stingray

pagikan – n. send-off party; v. to send off

paglaom – n. hope

paglarang – n. creation, making, willpower; v. to create, to decide

pagmata – v. to awaken

pagong – n. small sea turtle

pagpabaya – v. to neglect

pagpaubos – *v.* to be humble, to lower in status
pagsalinurog – *n.* celebration
pagsiguro, paniguro – *v.* to to work hard, to exert extra effort, to secure
paguma – *v.* to farm, to plow the field
pagwara – *v.* to forgive
paha – *n.* belt
pahabila – *n.* barracuda
pahak – *n.* hairless part of scalp
pahalipay – *n.* gift, reward
pahamot – *n.* perfume
pahayag – *n.* declaration, statement; *v.* to declare, to announce, to enlighten
pahayagan – *n.* newspaper, bulletin, magazine
pahibaro – *n.* announcement, notice; *v.* to announce, to inform
pahid – *v.* to wipe
pahimangno – *n.* advisory, caution, beware; *v.* to warn, to advise
pahimutang – *n.* assurance; *v.* to calm down, to settle down
pahimuwa – *v.* to allege falsehood on someone
pahiran – *n.* rag, doormat, wipe
pahitungod – *n.* preposition
pahiusa – *v.* to wonder
pahot – *v.* to embroider mat
pahoy – *n.* scarecrow
pahuway – *n.* rest, relaxation; *v.* to rest, to relax
pahuwayan – *n.* rest area, resting place

paìd – *n.* compassion, sympathy; *v.* to pity, to understand, to empathize
paít – *n.* bitter taste, bitterness
palá – *interj.* expression of positive anticipation or surprise
pála – *n.* shovel, propeller, Spanish *pala*
palabilabi – *v.* to pamper, to praise
palakínon – *n.* masculine female, tomboy, lesbian, butch, dyke
palakpak – *v.* to clap hands
palakpakan – *n.* applause
pálad – *n.* palm
palád – *n.* flat fish, flounder, fluke, halibut
palanas – *n.* flagstone, waterfall, cascade
palangga – *n.* beloved; *v.* to pamper, to spoil
palanggana – *n.* wash bowl, Spanish *palangana*
palasyo – *n.* palace, Spainsh *palacio*
palawan – *n.* large edible tuber that take years to grow
palawod – *kaa.* towards the sea, downstream
palaypay – *v.* to hang on clothes line to dry; *n.* vine-like parasitic plant with wide leaves
palid – *v.* to be blown away
palikoliko – *n.* zigzag course; *v.* to zigzag
palit – *v.* to buy, to trade
palito – *n.* match stick
palpag – *n.* mallet
paluparan – *n.* airport

palwa – *n.* palm leaf, Spanish *palma*
pamaagi – *n.* management
pamahaw – *n.* breakfast
pamalod – *n.* graceful dancing style
pamahungpahong – *n.* flare, style of talking and walking, sashay, swagger
pamalandong – *n.* introspection, self-assessment, recollection; *v.* to own one's mistakes, to pray for forgiveness
pamarigo – *n.* beach party, picnic at a beach or in the water
pamasko – *n.* Christmas gift
pamaspas – *n.* brush; *v.* to brush off
pamatbat – *v.* to lead a prayer
pamati – *v.* to listen, to pay attention
pambot – *n.* motorized outrigger, American *pump boat*
pamilya – *n.* family, Spanish *familia*
pamughat – *n.* herbs used for relapse
pamulong – *n.* sentence
pamunyag, panbunyag – *n.* baptism, christening
pamusa – *v.* to wash feet
pamyenta – *n.* pepper, Spanish *pimientos*
pan – *prep.* for
paná – *n.* arrow, bow and arrow, spearfishing, harpon
pána – *v.* to shoot with bow and arrow
panáaran – *n.* sacred place, shrine

panakna – *n.* prophesy, forecast; *v.* to foretell, to forecast, to prophesy
panakot – *n.* cooking ingredients, spices
panagang, panagangan – *n.* shield, protection, defense; *v.* to protect, to defend, to shield
panahon – *n.* time, weather
panalagsa – *adj.* rare, uncommon; *adv.* seldom, rarely
panamilit – *n.* farewell, goodbye; *v.* to bid farewell
panamkon – *n.* conception
pananglit – *v.* to set example
pananglitan – *n.* example; *conj.* if, whether
panaon – *n.* artichoke-like fruit full of edible seeds
panapton – *n.* clothes, clothing, garment
panas – *v.* to flatten, to thin out as in slippers or shoes; *adj.* flattened, worn down like shoes
pandemya – *n.* pandemic
pangadi – *v.* to pray
pangahulugan – *n.* vocabulary, translations, significance
pangalimot – *v.* to forget
pangamaya, pangamuyo, – *n.* plea, prayer, supplication; *v.* to pray, to plead
pangandoy – *n.* melancholia, nostalgia
pangasal, pankasal – *n.* wedding
pangastos – *n.* expendenture, budget
pangatadungan – *n.* justification, reason; *v.* to justify, to reason

pangatubang – *n.* animistic ritual of ancestral offering of slaughtered pig
pangawil – *v.* to fish with line, hook and sinker
panggal – *n.* basket-like crab trap; *v.* to catch crab
panggasto – *n.* expenses, expenditure
pangiklop – *n.* supper
panginabuhi – *n.* livelihood, occupation
panginano – *n.* care, concern
panginlabot – *n.* intervention, involvement; *v.* to intervene
pangipa – *n.* craving, *v.* to crave
pangisda – *v.* to catch fish
pangkag – *adj.* stale as bread
pangpang – *n.* riverbank
pangtion – *n.* general term for clam
pangumpirma, pankumpirma – *n.* confirmation
pangumpisal, pankumpisal – *n.* confession
pangumunyon, pankumunyon – *n.* communion
panhimalad – *n.* palm reading, palmistry
panhimsaw – *v.* to clean feet, to wash feet
panhiramus – *v.* to wash face
panhulugan – *n.* dropping place
panhunahuna – *n.* thinking, imagination
panhunaw – *v.* to wash hands
panigurado – *n.* assurance
paniguro – *n.* hard word, tireless effort
pánihap – *n.* number

pangihápan, panngihapan – *n.* counter, calculator
panihapon – *n.* supper
panikas – *n.* theft, robbery, corruption
panigaman, panigamnan – *n.* guide, punctuation marks
panimalay – *n.* family, household
paningkamot – *n.* hard work, effort
paníngudto, paníudto – *n.* lunch
pánit – *n.* skin, peel; *v.* to peel
panluto – *n.* cooking, catering
panrasa – *n.* appetite
pansit – *n.* sautéed noodles with vegetables and meat
pantalan – *n.* wharf
pantat – *n.* catfish
pantog – *n.* urinary bladder
pantyon – *n.* tomb, cemetery, Spanish *panteon*
panugaok – *n.* cock crowing, daybreak, dawn, early morning
panulay – *n.* devil
panumdom – *v.* to recall, to remember
panurundon – *n.* custom, tradition, heritage, example
pánus – *n.* stale, moldy, rancid odor
panutduan – *n.* doctrine, teachings, dogma
panyo – *n.* veil, head scarf, shawl, Spanish *paño*
panyolito – *n.* handkerchief, Spanish *pañuelo*
paon – *n.* bait; *v.* to bait
papa – *n.* father
papag – *n.* wide bamboo bench, recliner
papas – *v.* to happen, to fade

papil – *n.* paper, Spanish *papel*

papilit – *n.* paste; *v.* to paste

pará – *n.* eraser; *v.* to erase; *adj.* faded like memory, forgotten

pára – *v.* to stop, Spanish *parar; prep.* for, by

paraarot, parapangarot – *n.* barber, hair stylist

parakatpakat – *n.* slipshod haircut

paragbusbos – *n.* surgeon

paragsamwak – *n.* broadcaster, newscaster, TV anchorman

paragsukot – *n.* debt collector

paraguma, parauma - *n.* farmer

parahubog – *n.* alcoholic, drunkard

paraihaw, paragihaw, parapangihaw – *n.* butcher

parapanganak – *n.* midwife

parasingba – *n.* parasingba

paraw – *n.* sailboat

parayaw – *n.* pride, show-off; *v.* to show off, to boast

parehistro – *v.* to register, Spanish *registro*

pariho – *adj.* similar, like, Spanish *pareja*

parik – *v.* to break into smithereens or tiny fragments

parokya – *n.* parish, Spanish *parroquia*

parol – *n.* lantern, Spanish *farol*

parong – *v.* to put off the light, to switch off

parot – *n.* skin or rind of fruit; *v.* to peel

parti – *n.* part, Spanish *parte*

partira – *n.* midwife, Spanish *partera*

parukat – *n.* barnacle

parula – *n.* lighthouse, Spanish *faro*

parumba, paprumba – *n.* race, speed competition

parutpot – *n.* edible, small, slimy fish

paryinte – *n.* relative, Spanish *pariente*

pasá – *n.* bruise, contusion

pása – *v.* to pass the ball, Spanish *pase*

pasabot – *n.* information, revelation, meaning; *v.* to inform, to reveal

pasahi – *n.* fare, Spanish *pasaje; v.* to pay fare

pasamano – *n.* counter

pasamwak – *n.* news broadcast, announcement; *v.* to announce, to broadcast

pásan – *v.* to carry over the shoulder

pasangyaw – *n.* to show off, to display ostentatiously

pasar – *v.* to pass an exam or grade, Spanish *pasar*

pasayan – *n.* shrimp

pasaylo – *n.* forgiveness; *v.* to forgive

pasí – *n.* pig suckling

pasibayá – *n.* neglect, negligence; *v.* to neglect

pasikat - *v.* to show off; *adj.* arrogant, show-off, frivolous

pasipara – *v.* to go against advice, to violate

pasirit – *v.* to squirt

pasko – *n.* Christmas; *v.* to give gift

pasma – *n.* faintness from hunger, hypoglycemia; *v.* to faint from hunger

pasó – *n.* scorching heat

páso – *v.* to burn, to scorch

paspas - *adj.* fast, English *fast*; *adv.* swiftly

paspas – *v.* to move fast; to brush aside

pastilan – *adv.* please

pasuba – *kaa.* upstream

pasubra – *n.* extra, excess, exaggeration, Spanish *sobra*

pasundayag – *n.* lively celebration, program of singing and dancing

pasyada – *v.* to stroll, to walk leisurely; *n.* stroll, promenade, Spanish *paseo*

pasyinsya – *n.* patience, Spanish *paciencia*

pasyinte – *n.* patient, Spanish *paciente*

patakas – *v.* to take advantage of; *adj.* opportunistic

patag – *n.* flatland, plains; *v.* to level, to flatten like terrain

patagbo – *n.* commemoration, death anniversary; *v.* to commemorate a dead person

patani – *n.* black beans

pataráwan – *adj.* funny, laughable

patas – *adj.* even

patáy – *n.* corpse, dead person

pátay – *v.* to kill, to murder

pati – *conj.* including

pating – *n.* shark

patintiro – *n.* hopscotch; *v.* to play hopscotch

patis – *n.* fish sauce

pato – *n.* duck, Spanish *pato*

patod – *n.* cousin

patok – *n.* ax, pickaxe

patong – *v.* to lay on top of another, to stack

patungpatong – *n.* pile; *v.* to pile on top of another

patron – *n.* town fiesta, religious festival, yearly thanksgiving feast in honor of a saint

patron, patrona – *n.* patron saint

patula – *n.* zuckini-like fibrous gourd

patunga – *v.* to appease, to placate, to satisfy

patunog – *n.* vowel

patúo – *adv.* towards the right

paugpaog – *adj.* stupid, idiot

paumaya – *v.* to sacrifice, to give up one's priority to another

paunhan – *v.* to advance

paura – *v.* to pamper, to spoil

pausa – *v.* to surprise, to wonder, to be in awe

pawa – *n.* light

pawala – *adv.* towards the teft

pawikan – *n.* sea turtle

páwod – *n.* nipa shingle

payag – *n.* hut, shack

payong – *n.* umbrella; *v.* to use umbrella

paypay – *n.* fan, page

Pebrero – *n.* February, Spanish *febrero*

piang – *v.* to fracture as bone, to dislocate as bone joint, to cripple

piáy – *n.* disabled person, cripple, handicap

pidlit – *v.* to press, to squeeze

pígi – *n.* hips, buttocks

pigil – *v.* to restrain, to control

pigos – *n.* runt, smallest animal of a litter

pigsot – *v.* to squirt

piho – *adj.* sure, certain

piit – *v.* to squeeze

pika – *v.* to pick a fight, Spanish *pica*

pikat – *v.* to flirt; *adj.* to flirtatious, spoiled

piklat – *n.* scar

piknit – *v.* to pinch the ears

piko – *n.* pickaxe, Spanish *pico*

pikon – *adj.* sensitive, thin-skinned, easily insulted

pikot – *adj.* slit eyed

pikoy – *n.* parrot

piksi – *v.* to tear

piktaw – *v.* to hop, to skip, to hopscotch

pihing – *kan.* lopsided, unbalanced

pilak – *v.* to throw, to hurl

pilas – *n.* scratch, abrasion; *v.* to get abrasions or scratches

pili – *v.* to select, to elect; *n.* hazelnut

pilidong – *n.* misshapen, irregular circle, deformity, asymmetry; *adj.* uneven, lopsided, asymmetric

pilingpiling – *v.* to shake the head sideways as a sign of disagreement; *n.* negative head gesture

pilipig – *n.* mortar-pounded toasted rice

pilit – *n.* glutinous rice; *v.* to stick, to glue

pilo – *n.* a fold, crease; *v.* to fold as clothes

pilyo – *adj.* naughty, mischievous

pinaanakan, pinaangkan – *n.* pregnancy out of wedlock, to impregnate out of marriage

pinaka – *adv.* most

pinalangga - *n.* sweetheart, beloved

pinalaypay – *n.* clothes hung to dry on clothes line

pinaubusanon, pinaubsanon – *n.* humility

pinaulnan – *n.* placenta

pinaurog – *adj.* favorite, favored

pingak – *adj.* flat nosed

piniliay – *n.* election

pinit – *n.* morsel, piece of bread, segment, fraction; *v.* to break off a piece

pinitpinit – *v.* to break into many pieces

pinsar – *v.* to think, Spanish *pensar*

pintakasi – *n.* communal work

pintor – *n.* painter, Spanish *pintor*

pintura – *n.* paint

pinubre – *adj.* menial, poorly

pipi – *n.* vagina

pipino – *n.* cucumber

pirá – *n.* value, cost, price; *v.* to value, to set the price

pirapira – *adj.* insignificant, small in quantity

piraw – *adj.* sleepy; *v.* to sleep late

pirde – *v.* to lose, Spanish *perder, perdido*

pirdible *n.* safety pin, Spanish *imperdible*

pirikot – *adj.* puckered, crumpled, distorted

piristihon – *n.* disgusting, abominable person

pirit – *v.* to force

pirma – *n.* signature; *v.* to sign, Spanish *firmar*

pirme – *adj.* firm, steadfast, Spanish *firme*

piro – *conj.* but, Spanish *pero*

pirok – *n.* eyelash; *v.* to blink

piruwisyo – *n.* damage, harm, trouble, Spanish *perjuicio*

pisá – *v.* to flatten, to press

pisara – *n.* blackboard, Spanish *pizarra*

pisaw – *n.* dagger, sharp and pointed kitchen knife

pisi – *n.* rope, twine

pisít – *n.* neutered animal; eunuch

písit – *v.* to neuter, to castrate

pisnga – *v.* to blow the nose

piso – *n.* peso, American *peso*

pisó – *n.* chick

pisók – *v.* to blink

pisokpisok – *adj.* blinking, twinkling; *v.* to twinkle

pisót – *n.* sprout, bud; *adj.* uncircumcised

pispis – *adj.* stingy, miser, austere

pisti – *n.* plague, pandemic, Spanish *peste*

pitad – *n.* step; *v.* to take steps

pitig – *v.* to walk in quick short steps

pitik – *v.* to leap like a frog, to flick with a finger

pitikay – *n.* game of flicking bundled rubber bands

pitikbirik – *adj.* flirtatious

pitlok – *v.* to strangulate

pitó – *num.* seven

pitrolyo – *n.* petroleum, kerosene, Spanish *petroleo*

pitsa – *n.* date, appointment, Spanish *fecha*

pitsay – *n.* chinese cabbage, bokchoy

piyait – *n.* high, piercing sound, shrill; *v.* to shrill, to giggle

piyano – *n.* piano, English *piano;* *v.* to play piano

piyóng – *n.* cockle clam

píyong – *v.* to close eyes

piyós – *adj.* uncircumcised

plaka – *n.* vinyl or metal plate, music disc, license plate, Spanish *placa*

plais – *n.* pliers, American *pliers*

plantsa – *v.* to iron clothes, Spanish *plancha*

plataporma – *n.* political agenda, Spanish *plataforma*

platito – *n.* saucer, Spanish *platillo*

plato – *n.* dinner plate, Spanish *plato*

pliti – *n.* rent, rental; *v.* to rent

portahan – *n.* doorway, Portuguese *porta*

positibo – *n.* positive, Spanish *positivo*

posteso – *n.* denture, Englsh *dental prosthesis*

presidente – *n.* president, Spanish *president*

prinda – *v.* to pawn

printe – *n.* front, Spanish *frente*

priso – *n.* prisoner, Spanish *preso; v.* to put in jail

prisuhan – *n.* prison, jail

prisya – *n.* scallion, green onion, shallot

prito – *v.* to fry, Spanish *frita*

progresibo – *adj.* progressive, prosperous, Spanish *progresivo*

prutas – *n.* fruits, Spanish *frutas*

puag – *v.* to box, to hit

publiko – *n.* public, Spanish *publico*
pubre – *adj.* poor, impoverished, Spanish *pobre*
pukaw – *v.* to awaken
pukis – *v.* to come last, to be last
pukot – *n.* fishing net
pukpok – *n.* mallet, hammer; *v.* to strike with hammer or mallet
puday – *n.* female pudendum, vagina
pudhay – *n.* big toe
pudngan – *v.* to forbid, to prevent
pudo – *n.* youngest child
pudol – *v.* to bump
pudong – *n.* turban, crown, cloth worn around the head; *v.* to crown
púga – *n.* escapee, flight; *v.* to escape, Spanish *fugar*
pugá – *v.* to squeeze by hand, to extract as in coconut milk
pugo – *n.* bald head, shaven head; *v.* to shave the head
pugong – *v.* to forbid, to prohibit, to prevent
pugos – *v.* to force, to intimidate
pugot – *v.* to sever, to amputate, to behead
pugtot – *n.* buttocks, butt, gluts, ass
puhunan – *n.* capital (business); *v.* to capitalize, to provide capital
pula – *adj.* red; *v.* to redden
puliki – *v.* to short of hands, to become helpless
pulilid – *v.* to roll over
puling – *n.* foreign body on the eye

pulis – *n.* policeman, Spanish *policia*
pulod – *v.* to fell a tree
pulong – *n.* word
pulos – *n.* worth, usage, value; *v.* to utilize
pulungpulong – *n.* discussion, conversation
pulso – *n.* pulse, Spanish *pulso*
punas – *v.* to wipe
punaw – *n.* hardshell clam
pundo – *n.* anchor, fund; *v.* to anchor, to fund
pundok – *n.* pile, aggregate; *v.* to pile, to aggregate, to gather as a crowd
punga – *n.* out of breath; *v.* to be short of beath
púnggod – *n.* pimple, zit
pungko – *v.* to squat
pungkol – *n.* amputee
pungo – *n.* nipa palm fruit
pungos –*n.* coiled hair coifed to the back of the head
pungot – *v.* to harbor hatred, animosity
pungtanon – *adj.* vengeful, hateful, irritable, petulant
pungtod – *n.* graveyard
puníkas – *n.* daybreak
puniti – *n.* fisticuffs, squabble; *v.* to fight with fists
punó – *adj.* full; *v.* to fill
púno – *n.* tree trunk, leader of a group or organization
punsúan – *n.* stingray
punúan – *n.* leader, head of organization
punyal – *n.* dagger, Spanish *puñal*
purak – *v.* to break like day, to break like waves
purát – *n.* cicada

purbida – *interj.* expression of disappointment

purdoy – *n.* failed business, bankruptcy; *v.* to bankrupt

purga – *v.* to purge, Spanish *purga*

purgatoryo – *n.* purgatory, Spanish *purgatorio*

purluminos – *adv.* at least, Spanish *por lo menos*

púro – *adj.* pure, Spanish *puro*

puró – *n.* island

purok – *n.* cockfight, zone, district; *v.* to collide

purog – *n.* red clay colorant, ferruginous soil

puros – *pron.* everything, everyone

purot – *v.* to pick up, to lift up, to choose a partner at a dance

purtona – *n.* fortune, Spanish *fortuna*

pursuso – *adj.* biological child

puruko – *v.* to stay in one place, to keep still

purulungan – *n.* vocabulary, dictionary, agenda

purupsilay, pupsilay – *n.* gunfight, gunbattle; *v.* to fight with guns

purupulilid – *adv.* continuously rolling over, cartwheeling

pusak – *n.* to hit with the fist

pusas – *n.* handcuffs, Spanish *esposa;* *v.* to handcuff, to manacle

pusdak – *v.* to drop forcefully

pusil – *n.* handgun, pistol, rifle, Spanish *fusil*

púso – *n.* banana blossom, buds of banana fruit

pusó – *n.* steamed rice in heart-shaped woven palm leaf

pusod – *n.* navel, umbilicus

puson – *n.* pubes

pusong – *n.* fool, simpleton; *adj.* silly

puspuro – *n.* match, Spanish *fosporo*

pusta – *v.* to bet, to gamble

pustahan – *n.* bet, betting, wager

pusti – *n.* post, pole, Spanish *poste*

pustrira – *n.* blame, hindsight, Spanish *postrero*

pustura – *n.* posture, attitude, Spanish *postura;* *v.* to display an attitude

puthaw – *n.* iron, steel

pútik – *n.* ass, vagina, buttocks, rear

putík – *n.* coitus; *v.* to have sexual intercourse

putingad - *adj.*casually indifirrent, nonchalant

putli – *n.* pure

puto – *n.* steamed rice cake

putok – *n.* heartbeat; *v.* to throb, to pulsate

putong – *adj.* short-tempered, impetuous

putos – *n.* paper wrapper; *v.* to wrap

putpot – *v.* to honk as a car

putyukan – *n.* beehive

puwaki – *n.* shortage, shortfall, lack, uneven

puya – *n.* toddler, little child

puyas – *v.* to consume, to finish

puyde – *a.* can, could, Spanish *puede*

puyit – *n.* vagina

puyo – v. to reside
puyúan, púyan – n. residence, address

R:r

raksot – n. unsightly person or thing, ugliness
radyo – n. radio, American radio
ragaak – n. squeaking sound; adj. squeaky
ranggat – n. glitter, sparkle; v. to glitter, to sparkle
rangrang – v. to flare up like healing wound
rangya – n. luxury
rantas – v. to unravel
rantok – v. to bump the head
rapádapa – n. sole of foot
rasa – n. taste, appetite
rason – n. reason, motive, Spanish razon
rayandayan – n. ornaments, decorations
rayaraya – n. mesentery
rayhak – n. enjoyment, exuberant celebration
rayna – n. queen, Spanish reyna
raysang – n. nail; v. to nail
rayuma – n. rheumatism, Spanish reuma
reklamador – n. complainer, claimant, Spanish reclamador
reklamo – n. protest, complaint; v. to complain, to protest, Spanish reclamo
rekwerdo – n. remembrance, souvenir, keepsake, Spanish recuerdo

relo – n. watch, clock, Spanish reloj
resibo – n. receipt
rigla – n. menstruation, Spanish regla
rikado – n. bayleaf, laurel leaf
riko – adj. rich, Spanish rico
rimadima – v. to terrify, to terrorize
rimalaso – n. misfortune, disaster
rimas – n. breadfruit
rimedyo – n. remedy, help, recourse; v. to remedy, to avoid
rimurki, rimulki – v. to tug as boat, Spanish remolquer
ringgal – n. worry, apprehension, anxiety; v. to be apprenhensive
ripike n. pealing of bells; v. to peal, Spanish repique
ripolyo – n. cabbage, Spanish repollo
risidente – n. resident. Spanish residente
risyo – n. lively celebration
rosa – n. rose flower, Spanish rosa;
adj. pink
rosaryo, rosaryohan – n. rosary, Spanish rosario
ruba – v. to destroy, to break apart
ruhaduha, duhaduha – n. wavering, indecision; v. to waver, to falter
rulyo – n. roll; v. to roll
rumba – n. race as sports; v. to compete as speed
rumok, rugmok – n. bread crumbs; v. to break into crumbs; v. to crumble, to crush

rumpag – *v.* to collapse, to break apart like a structure or building
rúnog – *v.* to fall as a structure, to collapse
ruwang – *n.* sala, large room, hall

S:s

sáad – *n.* promise; *v.* to promise, to swear
sáag – *v.* to delay, to snag
sába – *n.* variety of cooking banana
sabá – *v.* to silence, to shut up
sábak – *n.* pus, pustule
sabák – *v.* to carry
sabado – *n.* Saturday, Spanish *sabado*
sabaw – *n.* soup
sabid – *adj.* habitual
sablay – *v.* to hang
sabod – *v.* to swipe, to hit someone by accident
sabon – *n.* soap; *v.* to lather with soap, Spanish *jabon*
sabót – *n.* knowledge, awareness; *v.* to know, to be aware
sábot – *v.* to agree
sabrang – *v.* to scatter, to break into smithereens
saburak, sabrak – *v.* to spread by throwing into the air
saka – *v.* to climb, to go up
sakang – *adj.* bow-legged
sakáy – *v.* to ride
sákay – *n.* passenger
sakayán – *n.* boat, vehicle

sakayón – *n.* travel, journey
sakaysakay – *n.* pleasure trip by boat
sakit – *n.* illness, sickness, pain
saklang – *v.* to climb
saklay – *v.* to carry upon the shoulder
sakma – *v.* to tap, to gently slap
sako – *n.* sack, bag, Spanish *saco*
sakob – *v.* to enter; *prep.* inside, interior
sakop – *n.* boundary; *v.* to integrate, to include
sakot – *v.* to mix
saksi – *n.* witness; *v.* to witness
sakutsakot – *n.* assortment
sada – *n.* door panel, window panel
sadang – *adv.* enough, sufficiently; *v.* to suffice
sadok – *n.* wide-brimmed hat of nipa palm leaves
sagang – *n.* shield, defense; *v.* to shield, to defend
sagapot *v.* to get entangled walking
sagabal – *n.* hindrance; *adj.* obstinate
sagbang – *v.* to interrupt a convensation
sagdon – *n.* advice; *v.* to advise, to counsel
saghid – *v.* to sag to ground
saging – *n.* general term for banana
sagipo – *adj.* busy, helpless, handful
sagka – *n.* dryland, upland
sagmak – *v.* to tap, to slap
sagrado – *adj.* sacred, Spanish *sagrado*

sagubay, sagbay – v. to put arm around another person's shoulder

sagudida – n. top

sagudsod – v. to step deep an hard forward

saha – n. banana sprout

sahid – n. sharing; v. to share, to distribute

saho – *interj.* expression of indifference or defiance

sahog – n. sweet rice with coconut milk delicacy; v. to cook this delicacy

sahusaho – v. to defy, to hesitate

sahumeryo – n. incense, resin, Spanish *sahumerio*

sais, sayis – *num.* six, Spanish *seis*

sála – n. large room, guest room

salá – n. sin, mistake; v. to make mistake

salabay – n. stinging jellyfish

salaki – v. to trip, to stumble

salag – n. bird's nest

salagubang – n. beetle

salagunting – n. two-fist game of scissors, stone and paper

salamat – n. thanks, gratitude; v. to give thanks

salaming – n. glass, mirror

salapi – n. money

salapían – *adj.* rich, wealthy

salbahi – n. savage, Spanish *salvaje; adj.* wild, immoral

salbahi – *adj.* wild, savage, Spanish *salvaje*

salikway – v. to reject, to abandon, to disown

salin – n. left-over; v. to leave something unfinished

salínurog – v. to celebrate, to commemorate

salipod – v. to obscure from light or view

salipungog – n. silly, foolish

salit - *conj.* then, thence

saliwan – n. reliever, proxy, substitute; v. to change, to substitute

salmon – n. salmon, Spanish *salmon*

saló – v. to catch

sálog – n. river

salóg – n. floor

salsal – v. to masturbate

salwak – n. overflow; v. to overflow

sama – *adj.* similar

samad – n. wound; v. to inflect wound on someone, to injure

Samarenyo – n. Samar Island native or resident; *adj.* pertaining ot or about Samar, Spanish *Samareño*

sambi – n. intimate friend; v. to make friend

sambalagi – n. tamarind

samok, saramok – n. disturbance, mess, fight, turmoil, mayhem

samót – n. aggravation

sampaga – n. violet color

sampagita – n. fragrant, tiny lobed, white flower *Jasminum sambac*

sampurado – n. sweet chocolate rice porridge

samtang – *conj.* while

samurang – *adj.* careless, disorderly

samwak – v. to broadcast

sandig – v. to lean on, to rest on

sandigan – n. support, bureau

sandiya – n. sunflower seed

sandok – n. ladle

sanga – n. branch; v. to branch

sangbuwas, sarusangbuwas – n. day after tomorrow

sangbay – n. nickname, moniker

sangkúan – n. hindrance, obstruction

sanghid – n. permission, v. to ask permission

sanghiran – n. advisor, reference, academy

sangit – v. to hit a snag, to tangle, to get stuck

sangkay – n. friend; v. to make friends

sangko – v. to block, to obstruct, to snag

sangkop – n. part, equipment

sangkot – v. to implicate, to be involved in a crime

sangkuan – n. blockage, hindrance

sanglad – v. to run aground as a boat

sanglag – n. fried rice; v. to fry rice

sanglit, salit – conj. therefore, then, so

sangpit – v. to call, to beckon

sangpot – v. to finish, to win, to succeed

sangyaw – v. to announce

sanhi – n. past, cause

sáno – adv. when

santik – n. sling-shot

santol – n. large tree with golf-size, sour fruit and sweet, slimy seed

santop – n. lesson, learning, memory; v. to learn, to understand, to memorize

santos – n. wooden image of saints, Spanish santo

saop – n. land tenant

saot – n. talisman, amulet

sapa – n. brook, creek, lake

sapak – n. nice

sapatos – n. shoes, Spanish zapatos

sapaw – n. excess, extra; v. to overflow, to exceed

saphid – adj. incomplete, almost full, swept

sapiki – v. to trip one intentionally by the legs

sapin – n. shoes, sole support

saping – v. to swipe, to start a fight

sapit – adj. next

sapitsapit – adj. close-knit

saplot – n. clothing

sapod – v. to save

sapsap – n. small, slimy flat fish

sapyo – n. plane; v. to plane, to shave off wood

sára – v. to strain, to filter

sará – n. strainer, sieve, filter; v. to close, Spanish cerra

sarakot – adj. mixed

saradang – adj. equally shared

sarahuon – adj. stubborn, indifferent, recalcitrant,

sarakan – v. to mix grains, to adulterate

saramok – n. chaos, war; v. to create chaos

sarang – v. to scatter, to spread

sarapati – n. dove, pigeon

sarawayon – n. disorderly, disrespectful, knucklehead

sarawayon – *adj.* knuckle headed, stubborn

sarayawon – *n.* folk dance

sardinas – *n.* sardine, Spanish *sardine*

sari – *n.* wrestling contest; *v.* to wrestle

sarig – *v.* to lean on, to depend on for support

saring – *adj.* confused

saringsing – *n.* sprout, twigs; *v.* to sprout

sarit – *v.* to ask for permission

saritsarit – *n.* insistence, persistence

saro – *v.* to share

sarop – *n.* plug, patch; *v.* to plug a leak, to patch a hole

sarusarakot – *n.* assortment; *adj.* mixed, assorted, miscellaneous, cornucopia

sarusaro – *n.* party

saruwal – *n.* trousers, pants

saruyong – *n.* gutter, eaves

sasing – *n.* tiny geoduck clam

sastri – *n.* tailor, Spanish *sastre*

satamsatam – *n.* silent prayers or incantations, palindrome

sato – *n.* game of batting short stick to longer distance; *v.* to play such game

saurog – *v.* to celebrate, to commemorate

sawá – *n.* python, boa constrictor

saway – *v.* to rebuke, to advise

saya – *n.* skirt

sayaw – *n.* dance; *v.* to dance

sayod – *n.* witness, informer; *v.* to bear witness, to inform

sayon – *n.* ease; *v.* to take easy

sayop – *n.* fault, mistake, sin, flaw; *v.* to make mistakes

sayote – *n.* vegetable pear, Mexican *chayote*

saysay – *v.* to explain, to tell story, to discuss

sayurong – *n.* draining pipes at the eaves for collecting rain water, roof gutter

sekso – *n.* sex, Spanish *sexo*

senado – *n.* senate, Spanish *senado*

senador – *n.* senator, Spanish *senador*

serbisyo – *n.* service, duty; *v.* to serve, Spanish *servicio*

seroks – *n.* Xerox copier, copymachine; *v.* to copy by xerography

seroks – *n.*; *v.* to copy by xerography

siak – *v.* to chop wood

sibad – *v.* to devour like a fish, to take a bait

sibid – *n.* surf from the prow of a boat

sibuyas – *n.* onion, Spanish *cebolla*

sikad – *v.* to kick

sikangkang – *v.* to spread the legs

sikát – *adj.* famous; *v.* to become famous, to shine

sikì – *n.* feet

siklo – *n.* hiccup; to hiccup

síko – *n.* elbow

sikó – *v.* to shove with the elbow

sìkon – *adj.* compact, dense

sida – *n.* silk, Spanish *seda*

siday – *n.* poem, poetry

sidlit – *n.* sunray, daybreak; *v.* to break as dawn

sidras – *n.* lemon

sidsid – *n.* hem, hemline

sidula – *n.* identification card, residence certificate, Spanish *cédula*

siga – *n.* light; *v.* to light, to switch on

sighot, siot – *n.* garbage, cut grass, tree leaves and clippings, litter

sigi – *v.* to continue, to proceed, Spanish *seguir*

sigidas – *adj.* constant; *adv.* constantly, continuously, Spanish *seguida*

sigisigi – *adj.* continuous, always

siglo – *n.* century, Spanish *siglo*

sigun – *prep.* according to, Spanish *segun*

sigundamano – *adj.* second-hand, second class, Spanish *segunda mano*

sigurado – *adj.* certain, sure, safe, secured, Spanish *seguro*

siguro – *v.* to secure, Spanish *seguro*

silaw – *n.* sun glare, glare

silhag – *n.* transparency

silhig – *n.* broom bundled from palm leaf midribs

sili – *n.* small red pepper, penis

silindron – *n.* harmonica

silinggoy – *n.* penis

silipon – *n.* xylophone, English *xylophone*

silot – *n.* young coconut with soft gelatinous meat

sim – *n.* galvanized roofing

simana – *n.* week, Spanish *semana*

simangot – *n.* frowning; *v.* to frown

simbako – *interj.* expression of regret, to repent for sins

simento – *n.* cement, Spanish *cement;* *v.* to use cement as mortar

simhot – *v.* to smell, to sniff

sina – *n.* anger, hatred; *v.* to get angry, to get upset

sinamay – *n.* straw mat interwoven in alternating color pattern; *v.* to weave this pattern

sinangkayan – *kan.* possessed by evil spirits

sinanglag – *n.* garlic-flavored fried rice

sinat – *n.* low-grade fever

sine – *n.* movies

sinehan – *n.* moviehouse, cinema, English *cinema*

singa – *n.* sneeze; *v.* to sneeze

singabot – *v.* to take advantage; *adj.* opportunistic

singaw – *n.* oral thrush

singba – *v.* to worship

singbahan – *n.* church

singkadol – *n.* dirty feet

síngkit – *n.* slit eye

singko – *num.* five, Spanish *cinco*

singkwenta – *num.* fifty, Spanish *cincuenta*

singgit – *n.* ridicule; *v.* to tease, to annoy by making fun of someone

singhot – *n.* sweat; *v.* to sweat

singit – *n.* inguinal fold

síngit – *n.* sty

singsing – *n.* ring

sinsilyo – *n.* small coins, coin change; *v.* to change to smaller denomination especially coins sintunado – *adj.* out of tune, Spanish *sintonizar*

sinturon – *n.* belt, Spanish *cinturon*

sinyal – *n.* signal, sign, Spanish *señal*

sipa – *n.* kick ball game; *v.* to kick

sipelyo – *n.* toothbrush; *v.* to brush teeth, Spanish *cepillo de dientes*

siper – *n.* zipper, American *zipper*

siphid – *n.* broom; *v.* to sweep

sipi – *n.* banana bunch

siplat – *n.* glance; *v.* to glance

sipol – *n.* knife used to harvest rice

sípon – *n.* colds, sniffle, snot; *v.* to get colds

sipot – *v.* to attend, to show up

sirak – *n.* sunshine; *v.* to shine

sirang – *v.* to rise, to shine (sun)

sirangan, sinirangan – *n.* east

sirbato – *n.* whistle, Spanish *silbato;* *v.* to blow a whistle

sirkador – *n.* acrobat

sirko – *n.* circus, Spanish *circo*

siridngon – *adj.* lazy, showing lack of interest

siring *v.* to say, to answer; *prep.* according to

siringanon, siridnganon – *n.* saying, adage, proverb, words of wisdom

sirit – *n.* squirt

sirom – *n.* darkness

sirot – *n.* punishment, penalty; *v.* to penalize, to fine

sirung – *prep.* under, beneath; *v.* to go under; *n.* ground floor, basement

sirutso – *n.* saw; *v.* to cut with a saw

sisenta – *num.* sixty, Spanish *sesenta*

sisí – *n.* fermented oyster

sista – *n.* guitar

sitenta – *num.* seventy, Spanish *setenta*

Sityembre – *n.* September, Spanish *setiembre*

siwak – *n.* crow, vulture

siwo – *n.* chicklet, young chicken

siya, hiya – *han.* he, she, it

siyám – *num.* nine

siyudad – *n.* city, Spanish *ciudad*

sotanghon – *n.* bean noodle

suay – *v.* to try

suba – *n.* upstream, inland

subad – *v.* to imitate

subasko – *n.* strong winds

subasta – *n.* pulic auction, Spanish *subasta*; *v.* to sell in an auction

subay – *n.* follow-up; *v.* to follow, to trace

subaybay – *v.* to follow

subó – *n.* sadness; *v.* to be sad

súbo – *v.* to swallow

subra – *n.* excess, surplus, leftover, Spanish *sobra*

subri – *n.* envelope, Spanish *sobre*

suká – *v.* to vomit, to throw up

súka – *n.* vomit, vomitus

suklab – *v.* to flare up as in fire

sukli – *n.* change as in coin

suklob – *n.* attire, costume; *v.* to put on attire

sukmat – *v.* to confront, to rebuke

sukob – *v.* to simmer
sukol – *n.* measurement; *v.* to measure
sukot – *v.* to collect debt
suksok – *v.* to insert
sudlay – *n.* fine-toothed comb
sudlot – *n.* bedbug
sudoy – *v.* to peddle
suduysudoy – *n.* gallivanting; *v.* to gallivant
sudsod – *n.* V-shaped bamboo framed fishing contraption
suga – *n.* light, lamp, lantern, torch
sugabin – *v.* to do things at the same time; *n.* multitasking
sugad – *adj.* like, similar; *v.* to imitate, to follow; *conj.* as, like
sugadsugad – *adv.* likely, somewhat, somehow
sugal – *n.* gambling; *v.* to gamble
sugarol – *n.* gambler
sugba – *v.* to grill, to broil, to roast
sugbaan – *n.* grill
sugbo – *v.* to walk in mud or deep water
sugbong – *n.* shoulder
sugi – *n.* slender fish with long pointed snout
sugo – *n.* order, errand, command; *v.* to order, to send an errand, to command
sugod – *v.* to invade, to intrude
sugot – *v.* to follow orders, to comply
sugpo – *n.* tidal bore, prawn; *v.* to block
suha – *n.* grapefruit, pomelo
suhag – *n.* oldest child
suhí – *n.* breech birth presentation

suhito – *adj.* subjugated; *v.* to subjugate, Spanish *sujeto*
suhol – *n.* fee for service
suhot – *v.* to pass under
suhuton, suruhuton – *n.* underpass
sulam – *adj.* toothless
sulangan – *n.* channel
suláy – *v.* to tempt
súlay – *n.* baby spit; *v.* to spit or drool like a baby
sulbar – *v.* to resolve, to come up with solution, Spanish *resolver*
sulibangko – *conj.* by the way
suliot – *n.* pebble
suló – *n.* bamboo torch; *v.* to use a bamboo torch
súlod – *n.* room; *prep.* inside, within
sulód – *v.* to enter, to come inside
sulog – *n.* current, torrent
sulong – *v.* to advance, to go forward
súlot – *n.* garment; *v.* to put on, to wear
sulpot – *v.* to appear suddenly
sulsol – *n.* bribery; *v.* to bribe
suluran, surudlan – *n.* entrance, container
suma – *v.* to sum up
sumala – *conj.* according to, regarding
sumat – *n.* story, news, information; *v.* to inform, to tell
sumó – *n.* boredom; *v.* to get bored
sumpa – *n.* oath; *v.*, to take an oath, to swear
sumpáan – *n.* compact, covenant

sumpay – *n.* connection, continuation, conjunction; *v.* to connect, to continue;

sumpit – *n.* dart

sumpong – *n.* irritability, impetuosity

sumpungon – *kan.* irritable, impetuous, cantankerous

sumsuman – *n.* appetizer in drinking spree

sumurunod – *n.* sequel, sequence, follower, descendants

sundalo – *n.* soldier, Spanish *soldado*

sundang – *n.* cutlass

sungá – *n.* sneeze; *v.* to sneeze

sungay – *n.* horn; *v.* to fight with horns

sungka – *n.* board game of piling shells

sungkod, tungkod – *n.* cane, crutch

sunggo – *v.* to wrestle

sunglog – *v.* to tease, to instigate

sungó – *n.* firewood

sungot – *n.* strong, irritating odor

sunod – *v.* to follow, to obey; *adv.* next

súnudsúnod – *v.* to follow blindly

sunúdsunód – *adv.* one after another, sequentially, consecutively

sunóg – *v.* to burn

súnog – *n.* fire

suntok – *v.* to box; *n.* fist

suntukan – *n.* punching bag

suntukay – *n.* boxing, fist-fight

sunudsunod – *adv.* sequentially

súok – *adj.* dense, compact

suoy – *n.* vinegar; *v.* to mix or cook with vinegar

supak – *n.* violation; *v.* to violate the law; *prep.* against

supla – *v.* to interrupt

suplada – *adj.* snob, arrogant, inflated ego, Spanish *soflado*

supliti – *n.* whistle; *v.* to blow a whistle

supo – *adj.* look alike, inherited; *v.* to inherit, to look like forebear

supot – *n.* pouch, paper bag; *adj.* uncircumcised penis

supsop – *n.* sucker, sycophant; *v.* to suck

surá – *n.* viand

surát – *n.* letter, alphabet, mail; *v.* to write, to send a letter

suri – *v.* to test, to examine, to investigate

surit – *v.* to light a fire, to ignite

suriyaw, susriyaw – *v.* to shout, to warn, to yell

súro – *n.* sarcasm, condescension

surod – *n.* comb

sursi – *v.* to sew, to mend with a needle, to stitch

suruksurok – *n.* epigastrium, epigastric pain, stomachache; *v.* to have stomach pain

surudlan – *n.* container

surugúon – *n.* servant, housemaid, helper

surugsurog – *v.* to prod, to goad

surundon, surundanon – *n.* guideline, commandment, order, instruction

Susmariyosep! – *interj.* expression of sympathy and

surprise, Jesus, Mary and
Joseph!
súso – *n.* breast; *v.* to suck
susó – *n.* edible water snail
susog – *v.* to follow the way, to
imitate
susón – *v.* to criticize, to
admonish
sustansya – *n.* nutrition,
essence,
substance,nourishment
susumaton, surumaton – *n.*
story, news
sutil – *adj.* naughty
sweldo – *n.* salary, Spanish
sueldo
swirte – *n.* luck, joke, Spanish
suerte
switik – *adj.* shrewd, street
smart
syahan – *adj.* first
syapa – *n.* first cousin, *adj.* first
syimpre – *adv.* always, sure,
Spanish *siempre*
syin – *num.* one hundred,
hundred, Spanish *cien(to)*
syinsya – *n.* science, Spanish
ciencia
syite – *num.* seven, Spanish
siete
syudad – *n.* city, Spanish
ciudad
syudadnon – *n.* city dweller;
adj. pertaining to the city

T:t

taas – *n.* height
tabag – *v.* to snatch, to kidnap,
to abduct, to elope
tábang – *n.* fresh water
tabáng – *n.* help, aid, rescue;
v. to rescue, to save
tabas – *v.* to cut, to cut with
scissors as cloth
tabi – *v.* to put aside, to
excuse, to ask permission to
enter; *prep.* beside
tabigi – *n.* remnant, leftover,
extra
tabili – *n.* small lizard
tabla – *n.* wooden planks
tablita – *n.* pill, medicine
tablet, Spanish *tableta*
tabliya – *n.* small tablets of
chocolate concentrate
tábo – *n.* flea market
tabó – *v.* to happen
tabog – *v.* to drive away, to
shoo
tabok – *adj.* across; *v.* to cross
tabón – *n.* cover
tabsik, tapsik – *n.* splash; *v.* to
splash
tabuan – *n.* marketplace
tabudlo – *n.* delicacy of sweet
taro in coconut milk; *v.* to
cook this delicacy
taburos – *n.* sprinkle, mist from
the rain
takbo – *v.* to throw liquid, to
spill water
taklap – *n.* blanket
taklób – *n.* cover, lid; *v.* to
cover
taklos – *v.* to wear cutlass
around the waste
takip – *n.* seam, boundary

takna – *n.* time, moment

takob – *n.* sheath for sword or machete

tákom – *v.* to close like the mouth, to shut up

takóp – *n.* bottle cap; *v.* to cap a container

tákop – *v.* to fill in with soil, to cover a pit

takos – *n.* worth, measurement; *v.* to measure

takot – *n.* reef

taksi – *n.* taxi, taxicab, English *taxi*

taktak – *v.* to fall, to drop

takuri – *n.* kettle

takuranga – *n.* hibiscus plant, gumamela flower

tadí – *n.* sharp and pointed blade fitted to one leg of the rooster in cockfights; *v.* to prepare and outfit a rooster for cockfight

tadóng – *adj.* straight

tádong – *v.* to straighten up

tadtad – *v.* to cut into pieces

tadtaran – *n.* cutting board, chopping block

tadyaw – *n.* large clay jar used to store and purify water

tag – *adj.* each, every

taga – *adj.* indicative of location or responsibility, usually a prefix

tagak – *v.* to fall

tagad – *v.* to recognize, to identify

tagam – *v.* to prevent, to be careful, to beware, to avoid

tagamtam – *v.* to benefit, to taste

tagasumat, tagsumat – *n.* newsman, announcer

tagay - *v.* to pour wine

tagaytagay – *n.* drinking spree

tagbalay – *n.* household

tagbo – *n.* death anniversary; *v.* to commemorate death anniversary

tagdal – *adj.* needy, inept, short of help

tagdok – *n.* arm wrestling; *v.* to arm wrestle

taghom – *n.* coldness

taghoy – *n.* whistle; *v.* to whistle

tagitagi – *v.* to give by instalment

tagilid, takilid – *adj.* on the edge

tagimpusuon – *n.* violet color

tagingting – *n.* high-pitched metallic sound; *v.* to sound like a small bell

tagíya – *n.* owner; *v.* to claim, to own

tagna – *v.* to predict, to prophesy

tagnok – *n.* gnat

tágo – *v.* to hide

tagó – *adj.* hidden, concealed

tagok – *n.* milky sap, resin

tagom – *n.* indigo, deep-violet blue

tagpira – *n.* price, cost; *adv.* how much

tagpo – *v.* to meet, to engage, to collide

tagúan – *n.* hide-out, hide-away

tagubilin – *n.* inheritance, will and testament; *v.* to will, to inherit

tagudtod – *n.* gritty hard grain like rice

taguminatay – *n.* wake, funeral

tagusa, tagsa – *n.* each, everyone
tagutago – *v.* to play hide and seek, to go incognito
taguto – *n.* small, house lizard
tagya – *n.* confidence
tahap – *v.* to suspect; *n.* suspicion
tahaptahap – *n.* false accusation
tahar – *v.* to sharpen pencil; *n.* pencil sharpener
tahi – *v.* to sew
tahob – *n.* lid, cover; *v.* to cover
tahod – *n.* respect; *v.* to respect
tahong – *n.* mussel
tahop – *v.* to separate the husk from the grain, to winnow, to chaff
tái – *n.* feces, animal excrement, stool
taís – *adj.* pointed, sharp
talaba – *n.* oyster
talagsa – *adv.* seldom, rare
talahib – *n.* variety of reed, *Phragmites sp.*
talaita – *n., a.* piecemeal, little by little, trickle; *v.* to trickle
talampasan – *n.* humiliation, disrespect, disregard; *v.* to humiliate, to disrespect
talikod – *v.* to turn around
talikuran – *n.* back; *prep.* behind
talimpukayan – *n.* summit, pinnacle, peak
talimsaw – *v.* to rinse, to wash the feet
talinga – *n.* ear
talinguha, tinguha – *n.* effort, perseverance; *v.* to persevere, to endure

taliwas, talwas – *adv.* afterwards; *v.* to end, to finish, to defend
talnod – *v.* to get stuck in mud
talo – *v.* to rape, to violate
taltag – *v.* to spread
taludtod – *n.* back of chest, nape
talunay – *v.* to braid, to weave
talyan – *n.* edible root crop, tuber
talyer – *n.* workshop, factory, Spanish *taller*
tama – *adj.* correct, exact, *v.* to hit, to correct, to solve
tamak – *n.* footprint; *v.* to set foot
tamarindo – *n.* tamarind
tamay – *v.* to humiliate, to spite, to deride
tambak – *v.* to fill up a hole, to pile, to collect
tambal – *n.* medicinal roots, treatment; *v.* to treat, to cure
tambalan – *n.* healer, witch doctor
tamban – *n.* herring fish
tambis – *n.* tiny red heart-shaped fruit
tambok – *n.* fat; *v.* to become fat, to fatten an animal
tambong – *n.* attendance, presence; *v.* to attend
tambulig – *n.* help, aid, relief goods
tamilok – *n.* wood worm
taming – *n.* shield
tamís – *n.* sugar, sweetness
tamod – *v.* to bow, to look down
tamoy – *n.* monkey
tampalo – *v.* to slap the face
tamsi – *n.* bird

tamuragko – *n.* thumb, big toe
tamuyingking – *n.* little finger
tanaman – *n.* plants, vegetation
tanamanan, taramnan – *n.* garden
tánaw – *v.* to view, to look out
tanawan – *n.* view point, window
tangbo – *v.* to look out
tangkal – *n.* pig pen
tangkod – *adj.* honest, dutiful, faithful
tangkong, kangkong – *n.* water vegetable, watercress
tangkop – *v.* to patch
tangday – *v.* to cuddle with the legs
tango – *v.* to nod the head in agreement; *n.* gesture of affirmation
tanggal – *v.* to take down, to remove, to fire from position
tangigi – *n.* Spanish mackerel, kingfish
tangis – *v.* to cry, to sob
tanglad – *n.* lemon grass
tanod – *v.* to thread a needle
tanom – *n.* plant; *v.* to plant
táob – *n.* high tide
taób – *v.* to capsize a boat, to turn upside down
taod – *v.* to mount a spur as in cockfight
taog – *v.* to smash as a fruit
taon – *n.* wager, bet; *v.* to bet
taoy – *n.* rust; *v.* to get rusted
tapak – *n.* footprint; *v.* to step on
tápang – *n.* guesswork; *v.* to hit by chance
tapáng – *adj.* ignorant

taplong – *n.* face slap; *v.* to slap face
tapo – *v.* to meet, to encounter
tapód – *adj.* dependent, needy
tápod – *n.* dependence, assurance, confidence, reliance; *v.* to depend, to assure, to trust, to rely
tapól – *n.* black rice flour
tapon – *n.* contamination as in communicale disease; *v.* to infect somebody
tápong – *v.* to burn dried vegetation
tapós - *v.* to end, to finish
tápos – *n.* death anniversary
tapsik, tabsik – *n.* splash, splatter; *v.* to splash
tapuran – *adj.* dependable, trustworthy
tapusok – *n.* lobster
taputapo – *n.* dust
tara – *v.* to find, to encounter accidentally
tarahiti, tarithi– *n.* shower, drizzle; *v.* to drizzle, to shower as in rain
taranta – *v.* to get upset, to scare
tarantado – *adj.* easily upset, impetuous
tarhog – *n.* intimidation, harrassment; *v.* to intimidate, to harrass
tarig – *n.* feline excrement
tarimbubunay – *n.* dragonfly
tarong – *n.* eggplant
tartanilya – *n.* horse-drawn carriage
tarukitok – *n.* pompano fish
tarum – *n.* sharpness
tarusan – *n.* riverbend
tarutarahiti – *adj.* drizzly

tasa – *n.* cup, Spanish *taza*
tata, tatang – *n.* uncle
tatag – *n.* endurance, tenacity
tatái – *v.* to defecate
tatay – *n.* father
tauyon – *adj.* rusty
tawa – *n.* laughter; *v.* to laugh
tawad – *v.* to haggle
tawag – *n.* name, title, call; *v.* to call, to name
tawgi – *n.* bean sprout
tawidil – *n.* loose end; *v.* to hang as excess clothing, to sag
tawil – *n.* copulating dog
tawo – *n.* man, person
tayakutak – *adj.* sporadic
tayod – *n.* hill
tayok – *v.* to light a candle
tayom – *n.* sea urchin
tebe, telebisyon – *n.* TV, television, American *television*
temprano – *adv.* early, Spanish *temprano*
termino – *n.* term, period, Spanish *termino*
testigo – *n.* witness; *v.* to witness, Spanish *testigo*
ti – *adv.* approximately, about
tibi – *n.* tubeculosis
tibod – *n.* jug, big earthen jar
tibway – *adv.* consequentially, finally
tíkang – *conj.* since, starting, beginning; *prep.* from
tikáng – *v.* to start, to begin; *prep.* from
tikas – *v.* to steal, to rob
tikasan – *n.* thief, robber
tikí, tuko – *n.* large house lizard, gecko
tikig – *n.* rigor mortis
tikling – *n.* crane
tiklob – *v.* to fold like umbrella

tikod – *n.* heel
tikog – *n.* sedge grass *Frimbistylis utilis sp.* woven into mats and other accessories
tikos – *n.* sacrifice, perseverance, endurance; *v.* to sacrifice, to endure
tiksop – *v.* to submerge, to dunk as bread in soup
tiktik – *n.* rice flour
tikwang – *v.* to shove, to push forcefully
tikwugon – *adj.* unstable, unsteady, wobbly, clumsy
tikyuob – *adj.* folded like umbrella
tiga – *n.* toughness, hardness
tigaman, tigamanan – *n.* marker, guide, remembrance; *v.* to mark, to remember
tigbas – *v.* to slash, to hack with a cutlass
tigbaw – *n.* reed, any tall, slender grass
tigbutigbuay – *n.* hide and seek; *v.* to play hide and seek
tigda – *adj.* sudden; *adv.* suddenly
tigdong – *v.* to straighten up, to keep upright
tigib – *n.* chisel; *v.* to chip with a chisel
tigo – *n.* sea snake
tigó – *v.* to guess
tígob – *v.* to fold, to organize
tigok – *v.* to hang oneself, to commit suicide
tigurang – *n.* old person
tigutigo – *n.* riddle, guess
tiil – *n.* foot
tíilan – *adv.* towards the foot
tilang – *n.* large variety of oyster

tilaw – *v.* to taste
timasa – *n.* house clothes
timba – *n.* well, spring
timbang – *n.* weight; *v.* to weigh
timbangan – *n.* weighing scale
timbi – *n.* shell, shell fragment
timitimi – *v.* to nibble
timo – *v.* to feed through the mouth
timog – *n.* south wind
timon – *n.* helm, rudder, Spanish *timon*
timonil – *n.* helmsman
tìmos – *adv.* earnestly
timpag – *n.,* avalanche; *v.* to crumble from a pile, to erode
timpla – *n.* mixture, formula; *v.* to mix, to moderate, Spanish *templar*
timre – *v.* to seal, to mark, to stamp, Spanish *timbrar*
tinago – *n.* secret; *adj.* hidden
tinahod – *adj.* respected, respectable, honorable
tinái – *n.* intestines, large bowel, entrails
tinamban – *v.* to count with the fingers
tinapay – *n.* bread
tinapayan – *n.* bakery
tinapuran – *n.* close and trusted friend, confidante, servant
tinda – *n.* merchandise, consumer goods, Spanish *tienda*; *v.* to sell
tindak – *v.* to kick
tindahan – *n.* store
tindero – *n.* store clerk, seller, salesman, Spanish *tiendero*
tindog – *n.* stature, height; *v.* to stand up, to build

tinedor – *n.* fork, Mexican *tenedor*
tinga – *n.* food particles between teeth
tingag – *n.* grouper
tingali – *adv.* perhaps, probably
tinggib – *v.* to chip
tinggil – *n.* clitoris
tingog – *n.* voice, sound; *v.* to say, to make a sound
tinguha – *n.* effort, perseverance, sacrifice; *v.* to exert effort, to persevere
tinìkangan - *n.* beginning, start, onset, origin
tinikling – *n.* dance where partners hop rhythmically between bamboo pools
tinigib, tingib – *n.* shaped with a chisel
tinipigan – *n.* heirloom, savings
tinta – *n.* ink, Spanish *tinta*
tinubuan, gintubuan – *n.* birthplace, place where one was raised, outgrown things and interests
tinubyan – *n.* redemption; *adj.* redeemed
tinuha – *n.* creation, innovation
tinuínan – *n.* trustee, assignee, heir
tinula – *n.* boiled fish
tinúnan – *n.* lesson, studies
tinuod – *adj.* truthful, believable, real
tinuuray – *adv.* really, seriously
tinuyaw – *n.* bad deeds, corruption, perfidy
tipá – *adv.* towards
típa – *v.* to disagree

tipak – *v.* to chip, to crack
tipasi – *n.* unhusked rice grain
tipdas, tigdas – *n.* measles
tipay – *n.* oyster, Capiz shell
tipig – *v.* to save money, to earn
tipli – *adj.* high-pitched
tipon – *n.* collection, savings; *v.* to save, to collect
tipos – *n.* typhoid fever
tipuntipon – *n.* gathering, meeting
tirik – *v.* to stall as an engine
tirok – *v.* to gather, to collect
tisa – *n.* chalk
tiso – *v.* to stand straight
tisting – *v.* to try, to test, English *testing*
titig – *v.* to watch intently, to concentrate
tisa – *n.* chalk, Spanish *tiza*
tisoy, tisay – *n.* half-breed, mestiso, Spanish *mestizo / mestiza*
titser – *n.* teacher, English *teacher*
tiunay – *n.* splinter
tiupay – *v.* to abuse, to harrass
tiwil – *n.* geoduck clam
tiwugtiwog – *n.* wobble; *v.* to wobble
tiyan – *n.* abdomen, belly
tiyangge – *n.* seasonal market, Mexica-Spanish *tianguis*
trabahador – *n.* laborer, worker, Spanish *trabajador*
trabaho – *n.* work; *v.* to work, Spanish *trabajo*
trapo – *n.* wipes; *v.* to wipe
traydor – *n.* traitor, Spanish *traidor*
tres – *num.* three, Spanish *tres*

trese – *num.* thirteen, Spanish *trece*
tripilya – *n.* small intestine
tripulante – *n.* crewmember, Spanish *tripulante*
truso – *n.* log, Spanish *troza*
tseki – *n.* check, American *check*
tsinelas – *n.* slippers
tsismis – *n.* gossip, Spanish *chisme*
tsismoso, tsismosa – *adj.* gossipy, Spanish *chismoso/a*
tsokolate – *n.* chocolate, Mexican *xocolatl*
tsuk – *n.* chalk, English *chalk*
tuakang – *n.* large anchovy
tuba - *n.* coconut sap fermented wine
tubák – *n.* ant
tubíg – *v.* to water (the plants)
túbig – *n.* water; *v.* to water like plants
tubil – *v.* to touch, to feel ; *n.* touch, feel
tubó – *n.* sugar cane
túbo – *v.* to grow; *n.* tube, Spanish *tubo*
tubód – *n.* fountain, scorched food; *adj.* scorched, burnt
tubol – *n.* turd, constipation
tubóng – *n.* hog feed
túbong – *v.* to feed
tubós – *v.* to redeem
tubtob – *n.* ending, finish line ; *prep.* until
tubyan – *v.* to entrust, to offer, to redeem
tukar – *n.* music; *v.* to play music, Spanish *tocar*
tukas – *n., a.* to uncover, to take off hat or cover

tukayo – *n.* namesake, Spanish *tocayo*

tukdaw – *v.* to stand

tukdo – *v.* to carry on the head

tukmod – *v.* to stumble down and hit the face

túko – *n.* large house lizard

tukó – *n.* house foundation, post, stilt

tukob – *v.* to bite as in dogbite or insect bite

túkod – *v.* to brace a structure

tukód – *n.* brace, support

tukso – *n.* urge, desire, temptation; *v.* to urge, to crave, to tempt, to instigate

tuktok – *n.* summit; *v.* to peck as chicken, to knock, to tap

tugaok, tuktugaok – *v.* to crow as a rooster

tudlis – *v.* to cut, to incise with sharp blade

tudlo – *n.* finger

tudlok – *n.* pointer, determiner, article; *v.* to point

tudtod – *v.* to grind, to pulverize

túgab – *n.* belching, burp; *v.* to burp

tugbang – *n.* counterpart; *v.* to counter, to oppose

tugkad – *v.* to fathom, to reach the sea bottom

tugkop – *v.* to attach, to connect

tugma – *v.* to fit, to correspond

tugnaw, bugnaw – *n.* coolness, frigidity

tugob – *adj.* fully loaded as a boat

tugon – *n.* message, advise; *v.* to advise, to relay message

tugot – *v.* to allow, to permit; *n.* permission

tugpo – *v.* to match

tugtog – *v.* to play a musical instrument

tugway – *v.* to guide, to lead an animal

tuhatuha – *n.* false allegation, invention

tuhay – *n.* order; *v.* to put in order, to arrange, to settle; *adj.* orderly, well-arranged

tuhod – *n.* knee

tuhog – *v.* to pierce through

tuhugtuhog – *adv.* though and through

tuig – *n.* year; *v.* to decide

tuin – *v.* to designate, to assign

tula – *v.* to boil fish or meat

tulak – *v.* to embark, to depart

túlan – *n.* bone

tulay – *n.* bridge

tuldok – *n.* period

tulin - *n.* speed, heir, inheritance

tulnob – *v.* to dunk, to submerge

tuló – *num.* three

tulon – *v.* to swallow

tulos – *n.* exacerbation, psychotic episode; *v.* to exacerbate

tulpok – *v.* to poke with the finger

tultog – *v.* to pound into strands, to flatten

tultol – *adj.* reliable, right, correct, coherent

tulúuhan – *n.* belief, religion, faith, superstition, cult

tuman – *v.* to fulfill

tumba – *v.* to trip, to fall

tumboy – *n.* lesbian, butch, dyke

tuminungnong – *n.* pioneer, original inhabitants, longtime dwellers

tumor – *n.* tumor, Spanish *tumor*

tumos – *n.* coconut sapling

tumoy – *n.* end, tip

tuna – *n.* soil, land

tunaw – *v.* to melt

tunga – *v.* to divide, to half, to satisfy

tungatunga, turunga – *adv.* evenly shared

tungaw – *n.* mite, tick

tungbaw – *v.* to put on top

tungkad, sungkad – *v.* to stand on the bottom of the water with head above the surface

tungod – *n.* place, cause, location; *v.* to place; *prep.* on, upon; *conj.* because

tungol – *n.* stomach

tungtong – *v.* to stand on foot stool or platform

tungtungan – *n.* booster, platform for a person to stand on

tunob – *v.* to step on

tunok – *n.* thorn, splinter; *v.* to get stuck with thorn or splinter

tunukon – *adj.* thorny, spiny

tunod – *v.* to lower down, to set as the sun

túnog – *n.* dew drop, morning mist

tunóg – *n.* sound, tune; *v.* to make sound, to play music

tunto – *adj.* foolish, stupid, Spanish *tonto*

tunton – *v.* to hang

túo – *n.* right

túob – *n.* steam therapy, confinement; *v.* to confine

tuók – *v.* to cry

tuód – *adj.* true; *n.* buried piece of wood

túod – *v.* to believe

túon – *v.* to cook

tuón – *v.* to study, to learn

tupada – *n.* cockfighting outside an arena

tupong – *adj.* equal in length or height; *v.* to equalize, to balance

tupra – *n.* spit; *v.* to spit

tuptop – *adj.* precise, honest, faithful

turá – *n.* semen

turí – *v.* to circumcise; *adj.* circumcised

turingan – *n.* bonita fish

turnilyo – *n.* screw, clamp, Spanish *tornillo*

turo – *n.* droplet; *v.* to drip

turuturo – *n.* trickle; *v.* to trickle, to drip slowly

túrok – *n.* needle; *v.* to inject with a needle, to prick

turók – *v.* to sprout

turutot – *n.* trumpet

tuskig – *n.* stiffness, rigidity; *v.* to stiffen

tusik – *v.* to peck as a chicken

tusok, tugsok – *n.* pointed stick, peg, skewer; *v.* to stick with pointed object, to penetrate

tustos – *n.* cigar, rolled tobacco leaf; *v.* to smoke cigar

tutbras – *n.* toothbrush; *v.* to brush teeth, English *toothbrush*

tutdo – *v.* to teach

tutok – *v.* to concentrate, to stare

tutulunan, turunlan – *n.* throat
tutumanon, turumanon – *n.* requirement, obligation, responsibility
tuúnan, turúnan – *n.* lesson, homework
túunan, turúunan – *n.* clay pot, kettle, rice cooker
tuwakang – *n.* large anvhovy
tuwad – *n.* forward incline of a boat; *v.* to bend over, to invert; *adj.* upside down, inverted;
tuwadtuwad – *v.* to pitch as boat, to rock and roll as in dancing
tuyaw – *v.* to fool around, to deceive
tuyawtuyaw – *n.* fool; *adj.* crazy, foolish, insane
tuyo – *n.* purpose, soy sauce; *v.* to add soy sauce to dish
tuyok – *n.* to spin
twerka – *n.* screw, Spanish *tuerca*

U:u

úba – *v.* to feel self-pity
uban – *n.* gray hair
ubanon – *adj.* gray-haired
ubas – *n.* grapes, Spanish *uva*
ubi – *n.* purple yam
ubó – *n.* cough; *v.* to cough
ubod – *n.* sprout, budding, bamboo shoot
úbos – *adj.* consumed; *v.* to consume
ubós – *n.* low place; *v.* to be humble; *prep.* under, below; *adv.* lower
ubusúbos – *adv.* lacking, always empty, unreplenished

ukab – *n.* excavation; *v.* to dig, to excavate
ukay – *v.* to stir, to mix
úkoy – *n.* mythical mermaid
ukóy – *v.* to stop, to stay, to reside
ukúyukóy – *adv.* stop-and-go
udilas – *n.* pancreas
uding – *n.* cat
udto – *n.* noon
ug – *conj.* and
ugá – *v.* to dry, to dessicate; *adj.* dried, dessicated
ugáng – *n.* hen
ugangan – *n.* mother-in-law, father-in-law
ugat – *n.* blood vessel
ugay – *n.* enticement; *v.* to entice, to prod
ugbos – *n.* vegetable sprout
ugmad – *n.* nightmare; *v.* to frighten, to terrify
ugong – *v.* low-pitched reververating sound; *n.* tinnitus, ringing in the ear
ugop – *v.* to take side, to defend
ugsa – *adv.* once
ugsod – *v.* to postpone, to procrastinate
ugtang – *adj.* burned to ashes
ugto – *n.* godbrother, godsister
uhaw – *n.* thirst; *v.* to feel thirsty
ulalahipan – *n.* centipede
ulalay – *n.* backstroke; *v.* to swim backstroke
ulang – *n.* blockage, hindrance; *v.* to hinder, to obstruct
ulaping – *n.* button-like mushroom
ulat – *n.* scar; *v.* to scar

ulí – *n.* toilet paper

úli – *v.* to return borrowed thing, to return home

ulin – *n.* stern of boat or ship

ulitawo – *n.* unmarried man

úlo – *n.* head

uló – *n.* glans penis

ulod – *n.* worm, maggot

ulol – *n.* pain

ulot – *n.* monkey

ulpot – *v.* to appear, to arrive, to emerge

ultimo – *adj.* last, final, Spanish *ultimo*

uluhan – *adv.* towards the head

ulunan – *n.* pillow

uma – *n.* farm; *v.* to farm

umagad – *n.* daughter-in-law, son-in-law

umangkon – *n.* nephew, niece

umpag – *v.* to fall forcefully

una – *adj.* first

unahan, unhan – *adv.* ahead, forefront

unano – *n.* dwarf, Spanish *enano*

unáno, unanon, unanhon – *adv.* how, in what manner or way

unat – *v.* to stretch

unatunat – *adj.* elastic, stretchable

unay – *v.* to commit suicide

undo – *n., a.* to hold breath and push, to strain

undong – *v.* to launch, to endorse

ungara – *n.* wish, desire; *v.* to wish, to desire

ungay – *v.* to get involved, to participate, to indulge

unggit – *v.* to annoy, to irritate

unggoy – *n.* monkey

ungod – *adj.* true, real

ungot – *v.* to get stuck like splinter

unina – *adv.* later, lately

uno – *num.* one, Spanish *uno*

unod – *n.* meat, muscles

unom – *num.* six

unong – *v.* to scam

unta, kunta – *adv.* wishfully

untog – *v.* to fall on the butt, to bump

untol – *v.* to bounce like a ball

upá – *n.* rice husk

upat – *num.* four

upay – *n.* goodness, prosperity, healing; *v.* to improve, to heal, to feel better

upod – *v.* to accompany, to chaperone, to include

upudupod – *n.* constant companion

ura – *v.* to pamper

urag – *n.* libido

uragon, uuragon – *adj.* horny, libidinous, lascivious, lustful

urán – *n.* rain

urangop – *v.* to blend with surroundings, to hide as camouflage

uráura – *adj.* excessive, too much; *v.* to severely damage

uray – *adj.* genuine, real, authentic, essential

urhi – *adj.* last, delayed; *v.* to be late, to arrive last

uring – *n.* charcoal

uripon – *n.* slave

urit – *n.* anger; *v.* to get angry

uro – *v.* to defecate

urog – *n.* majority; *adv.* mostly

uruhan – *n.* toilet

urukyan – *n.* station, residence, bus stop

urupod – *n.* relative, companion

urusa – *v.* to unite, to unify

urusahon – *adj.* wonderful, miraculous, awe-inspiring, strange, amazing

urúuro – *n.* diarrhea; *v.* to have diarrhea

urúutro – *adv.* repeatedly

uruúyog – *adj.* shaky, unsteady

uruwaton – *adj.* gullible, easily scammed

usá – *num.* one

úsa – *v.* to wonder

usahan, usaan – *v.* to be alone or single; *adv.* alone, singly

usahay – *adv.* once, seldom

usig – *v.* to bark

usisa – *v.* to investigate, to examine, to test

uso – *n.* fad, trend as in fashion

úsog – *v.* to budge, to move a little

uswag – *v.* to come in, to make progress, to advance; *adv.* forward

utak – *n.* cleaver

útan – *n.* vegetable dish

utang – *n.* debt; *v.* to borrow

utanon – *n.* vegetable

utin – *n.* penis

utbo – *n.* steam, vapor or heat especially coming from the ground *adj.* steamy

utod – *v.* to cut, to sever, to separate

utóg – *n.* penile erection

útok – *n.* brain

utók – *v.* to hold breath; *n.* Valsalva maneuver

utót – *n.* fart; *v.* to fart

utro – *n.* repetition; *v.* to repeat; *pron.* another; *adj.* repeated; *adv.* again, Spanish *otro*

utudutod – *adj.* breaking, interrupted, disconnected, discontinuous

uwak – *n.* crow

uwat – *v.* to con, to trick, to swindle, *n.* gullible person

uway, luway – *v.* rattan

uyab – *n.* boyfriend, girlfriend; *v.* to woo

uyag – *v.* to play

uyagan – *n.* plaything, toy

uyam – *v.* to get bored

uyog – *v.* to shake

uyon – *v.* to confirm, to agree

uyuguyog – *adj.* bouncy, shaky

W :w

waklit – *v.* to fling, to hurl

wakwak – *n.* witch

wagayway – *n.* flag, banner; *v.* to wave a flag

wagtang – *v.* to lose, to waste

wala – *n.* left

waló – *num.* eight

wara – *v.* to lose, to disappear

warawara – *v.* to mislead, to obfuscate

Waray – *n.* an Austronesian language spoken in the Samar, Leyte and Biliran provinces of the Philippines, a person who speaks the language

waray – *n.* none, nothing

waray ngani – *interj.* expression of denial

waraynon – *n.* Waray speaker

waraywaray – *adj.* carefree, nonspecific
warikwik – *v.* to sprinkle
waring – *v.* to turn like a wheel
wasak – *v.* to break
watakwatak – *v.* to break apart, to spill water or liquid
watí – *n.* worm
waydong – *n.* advice, warning; *v.* to advise, to warn
wirik – *v.* to fling
witik – *n.* a sprinkle of water or other liquids; *v.* to sprinkle
wurok – *n.* confusion; *v.* to confuse, to flummox
wutok – *n.* mosquito larva

yapad – *adj.* flat
yatot – *n.* mouse, rat
yawa – *n.* devil
yawyaw – *n.* idle talk; *v.* to talk
yaya – *n.* child caregiver
yilo – *n.* ice, Spanish *hielo*
yinakanan, yinaknan – *n.* speech, language, dialect
yirro – *n.* iron, Spanish *hierro*
yugto – *n.* chapter
yugyog – *v.* to shake, to swing
yukòt – *num.* thousand
yunal – *n.* tattoo
yupyupan – *n.* nipple

Y:y

yabag – *adj.* out of tune, disharmony
yabe – *n.* key; *v.* to lock, Spanish *llave*
yabó - *v.* to throw water, to splash
yábo – *v.* to punch, to box
yakan – *v.* to speak, to talk, to scold
yakimbot – *v.* to babble, talk incoherently
yakyak – *n.* gossip, sprinkle ; *v.* to babble, to gossip, to sprinkle
yamang – *n.* bed wetting; *v.* to bed wet
yámid – *n.* smirk; *v.* to smirk, to sneer
yana – *adv.* now
yano – *adj.* simple, ordinary, Spanish *llano*
yanta – *n.* rim of a wheel, Spanish *llanta*

91

Legend:

n – noun
v – verb
adj – adjective
pron – pronoun
adv – adverb
prep – preposition
conj – conjunction
arti – article
interj – interjection
num – numeral

Part 2

English

to

Waray

A:a

abandon – *n., a.* baya, salikway, pagbaya, pagsalikway

abandoned village – *n.* binungtuan

abattoir – *n.* ihawan, irihawan

abdomen – *n.* tiyan, suruksurok

abdominal pain – *n.* kabag, suruksurok

abduct – *n., a.* buyóng, bihag, tabag, pagbuyóng, pagbihag, pagtabag

able – *n., a., kan.* kaya, pagkaya

abominable – *kan.* piristihon

about – *kan.* mga, ti

about – *kat.* palibot

about – *s.* bahin, hiunong, mahitungod

above – *kat.* bawbaw, igbaw, labaw

abrasion – *n., a.* pilas, kagis, pagpilas, pagkagis

abscess – *n.* hubag

absurd – *kan.* kauwat, kapaog

absurdity – *n.* kapaugan, kauwatan

abundance – *n.* hurak, kahurakan, kadamúan

abundant – *kan.* nahurak

abuse – *n., a.* darahog, tiupay, abuso – Spanish *abuso*, pagtiupay, pagdarahog, pagabuso

abused – *kan.* gintiupay, lupiglupig, gindarahugan, ginabuso

acacia – *n.* akasya

academy – *n.* sanghiran

accept – *n., a.* karawat, pagkarawat

accident – *n., a.* hibang, disgrasya - English *disgrace*, aksidente - Spanish *accidente*, paghibang, pagkadisgrasya

accident-prone – *kan.* maaraksidente

accommodate – *n., a.* aruga, pakiangay, pagpakiangay, pagaruga

accommodating – *kan.* makiangayon, maaruga

accompany – *n., a.* búyog, duyog, upod, pagbúyog, pagduyog, pagupod

according – *s., kat.* mahitungod, siring, sumala, sigun - Spanish *segun*, abitapa,

accordingly – *kaa.* kuno

accustom – *n., a.* hiara, nahiara, pagpahiara

ache – *n.* ngutngot, ulol, sakit

achy – *kan.* mangutngot, maulol, masakit

acidic – *kan.* maaslom, mapintas

acidity – *n.* aslom, pintas

acknowledge – *n., a.* pahitungod, asi, pagasi, pagpahitungod

acknowledgment – *n.* kahingatungdan, pagasi, pagpahitungod

acquaintance – *n.* kakilala

acquire – *n., a.* arog, pagarog

acrobat – *n.* sirkador

acrophobia – *n., kan.* halawhawon, makahalawhaw

across – *kat.* atúbang, tabok

actor – *n.* artista nga lalaki

actress – *n.* artista nga babayi

adage – *n.* siringanon, siridnganon, kapulungan
add – *n., a.* áyaw, dugang, dagdag, pagáyaw, pagdugang, pagdagdag
addend – *n.* kadúgang, kaáyaw
addict – *n., a.* giyan, pagkagiyan
addiction – *n.* kagiyanan
addition – *n., a.* dugang, pagdugang
address – *n.* puyuan, púyan, inuukyan, urukyan
adherent – *kan.* nadikit, nadukot, madukot
adjective – *n.* kangaran
adjust – *n., a.* igo, iguigo, pagigo, pagiguigo
adjustable - *kan.* kuhakuha
admire – *n., a.,* karuyag, bilib – English *believe,* pagkaruyag, pagbilib
admonish – *n., a.* waydong, susón, pahimangno, saway, pagwaydong, pagsusón, pagpahimangno, pagsaway
adopt – *n., a.* angkop, inangkop, hablos, pagangkop, paghablos
adorable – *kan.* makangurudyot, makaruruyag
adrift – *kan., kaa.* naanod
advance – *n., a.* sulong, abante - Spanish *avance* pagsulong, pagabante
adverb – *n.* kaági
advice – *n., a.* sagdon, saway, waydong, tugon, pagsagdon, pagsaway, pagwaydong, pagtugon
advisor – *n.* sanghiran
advisory – *n.* pahimangno
aeta – *n.* agta

affable – *kan.* maalikaya, masasangkayon, mahumla
affected – *kan.* naunong, apektado - Spanish *afectado*
affection – *n.* gugma, karuyag, humla
affectionate – *kan.* mahumla, mahigugmaon
affliction – *n.* kasakit, kakurian
affordable – *kan.* kaya, maparalit, barato - Spanish *barato*
afraid – *adj.* nahadlok
after tomorrow – *kaa.* kinabuwasan, sangbuwas
afternoon – *n.* kulop
afterwards – *kaa.* kataliwas, taliwas, talwas
again – *kaa.* liwat, utro - Spanish *otro*
against – *kat.* típa, kuntra - Spanish *contra*
against advice – *n., a.* pasipara, pagpasipara
agar – *n.* gulaman
age – *n.* idad - Spanish *edad*
agenda – *n.* purulungan
agent – *n.* ahinte - Spanish *agente*
aggravating – *kaa., kan.* lunlon, nadugang, naduroy
aggravation – *n.* pagduroy, samót
aggreable – *kan.* nauyon, natangdo
aggregate – *n., a.* pundok
aggrieved – *kan.* madumot, agrabyado - Spanish *agraviado*
agile – *kan.* malaksi
agitated – *kan.* aringit, nirbyuso - Spanish *nervioso*
agonize – *n., a.* hingalo, paghingalo

agree – *n., a.* abuyon,
pagabuyon, pagkasábot
agreeable – *kan.* abuyon,
naabuyon. natangdo
agreeably – *kaa.* mao
agreement – *n.* ginsabutan,
sinabutan, kaabuyunan
ahead – *kaa.* unahan, unhan
Ahoy! – *kah.* agoy
aid – *n., a.* tabang, tambulig,
bulig, ayuda - Spanish *ayuda*
air – *n.* hangin, ayre - Spanish
aire
airplane – *n.* ídro - Spanish
aereo
airport – *n.* landingan, luparan,
paluparan
Alas! – *kah.* agidaw
alcoholic – *n.* parahubog,
hubog
alcove – *n.* alkuba - Spanish
alcoba
alert – *adj.* listo - Spanish *listo*
alight – *n., a.* harón, hugdon,
pagharon, paghugdon
alive – *kan.* buhi
all – *n.* ngatanan, hurót
allegation – *n.* tahaptahap,
tuhatuha
allow – *n., a.* tugot, pagtugot
almanac – *n.* almanaki -
Spanish *almanaque*
Almighty – *n.* makagarahom
almost – *kaa., kan.* harapit,
haros, igbusay, saphid
alms – *n.* limos
alone – *kan., a.* usahan, usaan,
pagusaan, paglugaríng,
pagnawa
alphabet – *n.* kasurat, surat
already – *kaa.* na
also – *kaa.* gihap, gihapon

altered – *a., kan.* naliwat,
naiba
although – *s.* bisan
always – *kaa., kan.* gud,
kanunay, syimpre - Spanish
siempre, sigisigi
amazing – *adj.* urusahon
ambition – *n.* hangaron, inop,
ambisyon - Spanish *ambicion*
ambitious – *kan.* ambisyuso -
Spanish *ambicioso*
american – *n., kan.* kano,
amerikano - Spanish
americano
amputate – *n., a.* bigting,
pugot, pagbigting, pagpugot
amputee – *n.* pungkol
amulet – *n.* antinganting
ancestors – *n.* ginikanan,
kaapuyan
anchovy – *n.* bulinaw,
tuwakang
ancient – *n., kan.* kamaihaan,
kaniadto, kadaan, kinadaan
and – *s.* ngan, ug
angel – *n.* anghel - Spanish
angel
anger – *n.* kainiton, kairiniton,
kauriton, kasinahon
angry – *n., a.* ngalas, hangit,
sina, urit, pagkangalas, pagsina
anguish – *n.* kasakit
animal – *n.* mananap
animal kingdom – *n.*
kamananapan, kamanampan
animistic ritual – *n.*
pangatubang
animosity – *n.* dumot,
kairiniton, kasinahon
ankle – *n.* bitiis
annato seed – *n.* atsuwete -
Spanish *achiote*

anniversary – *n.* kaadlawan, katuigan
announce – *n., a.* sangyaw, pagpahayag, pagpahibaro, pagpasamwak,
announcement – *n.* pahibaro, pasamwak
announcer – *n.* tagasumat, tagsumat
annoy – *n., a.* daugdaog, unggit, pagdaugdaog, pagunggit
annoying – *kan.* makairinit, makauurit, malungot, masamok, masabal, masawi
annoying sound – *kan.* mangidlis, mangulinguli
annoyingly – *kaa.* lunlon
another – *n., han., kan.* lain, utro
answer – *n., a.* baton, pagbatón
ant – *n.* tubák
anthill – *n.* bundo
anticipate – *n., a.* paábot, pagpaábot
anus – *n.* kala, bubot
anxiety – *n.* kalisang, kalisangan, karinggal, kakulba
anxious – *kan.* kinukulba, karinggalon, lisang, nirbyuso - Spanish *nervioso*
appear – *n., a.* ulpot, sulpot, pakita, sipot, pagulpot, pagsulpot, pagpakita, pagsipot
appearance – *n.* kurti, pagpakita
appease – *n., a.* patunga, patuman, pagpatunga, pagpatuman
appetite – *n.* gana, panrasa
appetizer – *n.* sumsuman

applaud – *n., a.* pakpak, palakpak
applause – *n.* palakpakan
apply ointment or lotion – *n., a.* banyos, pagbanyos
appointment – *n.* sarabot, pitsa - Spanish *fecha*
apprehension – *n.* karinggal, pangarit
apprehend – *n., a.* sabot, hibaro,pagsabot, paghibaro
apprenhensive – *a. kan.* lisang, karinggalon, ringgal
approach – *n., a.* haraní, hiraní, pagharani
approval – *kah.* mandaw, ngani
approximately – *kaa.* mga, ti
approximation – *n.* igoigo
April – *n.* Abril, Spanish *abril*
archangel – *n.* arkanghel - Spanish *arcangel*
archbishop – *n.* arsobispo - Spanish *arzobispo*
archipelago – *n.* kapurúan
architect – *n.* arkitekto - Spanish *arquitecto*
arm – *n.* butkon, bráso - Spanish *brazo*
arm length – *n.* dupa
arm wrestle – *n., a.* tagdok, pagtagdok
armed – *kan.* armado - Spanish *armado*
armpit – *n.* írok, kilikili
armpit odor – *n.,* anghit; *kan.* maanghit
aromatic banana – *n.* bangaran
arrange – *n., a.* ayos, tuhay, pagayos, pagtuhay
arrears – *n.* atraso - Spanish *atraso*
arrest – *n., a.* dakop, pagdakop

arrival – *n.* dangatan, duongan
arrive – *n., a.* abot, dangat,
dúong, ulpot, pagabot,
pagdangat, pagdúong,
pagulpot
arrogant – *kan.* hayhat, pasikat,
suplada, aroganti - Spanish
arrogante
arrow – *n.* paná
artichoke-like fruit – *n.* panaon
article – *tud.* hi, si, an, nga,
mga
artist – *n.* artista - Spanish
artista
as – *s.* sugad
ascariasis – *n.* bitukon
ascaris – *n.* bitok
ash – *n.* abó, agbo
ashen - *kan.* maabo
ashore – *kan, kaa.* baybayon,
pasugka, dagsa
aside – *s.* lábot
ask – *n., a.* pakiana, hangyo,
pagpakiana
ass – *n.* pútik, bubot, pugtot
assignment – *n.* buruhaton
assist – *n., a.* bulig, ayuda -
Spanish *ayuda,* pagbulig,
pagayuda
assistant – *n.* kabulig
association – *n.* katiguban,
asosasyon - Spanish *asociacion*
assortment – *n.* sakutsakot,
sarusarakot, dirudilain,
magkadirudilain
assurance – *n.* patápod
pahimutang, katapuran
assure – *n., a.* pahimutang,
tápod, pagpatapod
asthma – *n.* hukab, hikab
asthmatic attack – *n., a.*
kuykoy, pagkuykoy

asymmetric – *adj.* hiwihiwi,
pilidong
at least – *kaa.* purluminos -
Spanish *por lo menos*
athlete's foot – *n.* atipunga
atmosphere – *n.* hangin,
kahanginan, ayre - Spanish *aire*
atone – *n., a.* basol, pagbasol
pamalandong,
pagpamalandong
attach – *n., a.* dukot, tugkop,
pagpadukot, pagtugkop
attachment – *n.* padukot,
katugkop
attack – *n., a.* lusob, sulong,
atake - Spanish *ataque*
attend – *n., a.* sipot, tambong,
duaw, atender - Spanish
attender, pagsipot, pagduaw,
pagatender, pagtambong
attention – *kah.* oho, hoy
attention – *n.* ataman
attestation – *kah.* kayhingan
attire – *n.* badó, súlot, suklob,
bistida - Spanish *vestido*
attitude – *n., a.* pamustura,
pustura - Spanish *postura*
attractive – *kan.* makaruruyag
auction – *n., a.* subasta -
Spanish *subasta*
audacious – *kan.* garagaraan
audacity – *n.* garagara,
kagaragaraan
August – *n.* Agusto - Spanish
agosto
aunt – *n.* dadá, nanang
austere – *kan.* ministiblis,
pispis, pinispis
authentic – *kan.* uray, tuod
authority – *n.* pagdumara,
kagamhanan, kamanduhan

automobile – *n.* kotse - Spanish *coche*, awto - American *automobile*

avalanche – *n., a.* timpag, pagtimpag

avoid – *n., a.* iwas, likay, lusot, tagam, pagiwas, paglikay, pagtaga, palusot

awaken – *n.,a.* pagmata, pukaw, pagpukaw

aware – *n., a.* sabót

awareness – *n.* kalibutan, sabót, sarabutan

awe-inspiring – *kan.* urusahon

awhile – *kaa.* kanina

ax – *n.* patok, piko - Spanish *pico*

B:b

babble – *n., a.* yakyak, yakimbot, pagyakyak

baby – *n.* bata, puya, bebi - English *baby*

baby spit – *n., a.* lúsay, paglúsay

back – *n.* luyo, talikuran

back of chest – *n.* bungkog

back of shoulder – *n.* taludtod

back up – *n., a.* atras - Spanish *atras*, pagatras

backbite – *n., a.* libak, paglibak,

backbiter – *kan.* malibak, paraglibak, tsismoso/a – Spanish *chismoso/a*

backbone – *n.* butagtok

backstroke swim – *n., a.* ulalay, pagulalay

backward incline – *n., kan., a.* bangad, nabangad

backward somersault – *n., a.* baliskad, pagbaliskad

bad – *kan.* maraot

bad habit – *n.* bisyo - Spanish *vicio*

bad luck – *n.* buwisit, buyag

badlands – *n.* kabagwakan

bag – *n.* pitaka, sako - Spanish *saco*

baggage – *n.* bagahi - Spanish *bagaje*

bail – *n., a.* límas, pyansa - Spanish *fianza*, paglímas, pagpyansa

bait – *n., a.* paon, buyóng, pagpaon, pagbuyóng

bake – *n., a.* hudno, paghimo his tinapay, paghurma, paghudno

bakery – *n.* hudnuhan, pandesalan, tinapayan, panaderiya - Spanish *panaderia,*

baking pan – *n.* hurmaan - Spanish *horma*

balance – *n., a.* timbangan, timbang, pagtimbang

balcony – *n.* balkonahi, balkon – Spanish *balcon*

bald – *n., kan.* pugo, kiskis, dangas

balitaw, balitgad – *kah.* expression of doubt, disbelief, incredulity

ball – *n.* bóla - Spanish *bola*

balloon – *n.* lubo

ballot – *n.* baluta - Spanish *balota*

balustrade – *n.* barandilya - Spanish *barandilla*

bamboo – *n.* kawayan, bagakay

bamboo bench – *n.* papag

bamboo cannon – *n.* lantaka, luthang
bamboo carrier – *n.* alát
bamboo grove – *n.* kakawayanan
bamboo hooked container – *n.* kawit
bamboo shoot – *n.* ubod
bamboo tube – *n.* lakob
banana – *n.* saging
banana blossom – *n.* púso
banana bunch – *n.* sipi
banana cluster – *n.* bulig
banana mashed – *n.* linupak
banana patch – *n.* kasagingan
banana rope – *n.* abaka
bank – *n.* banko
bankruptcy – *n., a.* lugi, pagkalugi, purdoy, bankarute – Spanish *bancarrota*
banner – *n.* wagayway, bandira - Spanish *bandera*
baptism – *n., a.* pamunyag, panbunyag, pagbunyag
baptize – *n., a.* bunyag, pagbunyag
barber – *n.* paragarot, parapangarot, barbero - Spanish *barbero*
barefoot – *n., a., kan.* lasagas, paglasagas, pagtiil, nakatiil, lasagas
bargain sale – *n.* baratilyo - Spanish *baratillo*
barge – *n.* lantsa - Spanish *lancha*
bark – *n., a.* usig, pagusig
barnacle – *n.* parukat
barracuda – *n.* pahabila
barrel – *n.* baril - Spanish *barril*
barren – *kan.* hulang
barrio – *n., kan.* barangay, hurón

base – *n.* kailadman, basihan - Spanish *base*
based – *s.* mahitungod, basi - Spanish *base*
basement – *n.* sirung
bashful – *kan.* awdunon
basic – *kan.* kinahanglan, katutungaydan
basis – *n.* hinungdanan, basihan
basket – *n.* bayong, batulang, baskit - English *basket*
basket crab trap – *n.* panggal
basketball – *n., a.* baskitbol - American *basketball*
basketball court – *n.* baskitbulan
bat – *n.* kulalapnit, kabog
bat dung – *n.* gwano
bathroom – *n.* karigusan, banyo - Spanish *baño*
bathtub – *n.* batya, banyera - Spanish *bañera*
bayleaf - *n.* rikado
be careful – *n., a.* hirót, paghirót, tagam, pagtagam
be cautious – *n., a.* ikmat, pagikmat
be certain – *n., a.* sigurado, pagkasigurado
be humble – *n., a.* paubos, pagpaubos
be nostalgic – *n., a.* andoy, pangandoy
be pregnant – *n., a.* burod, pagburod
be sure – *n., a.* sigurado, pagkasigurado
beach – *n.* baybay, baybayon
beach party – *n.* pamarigo, barakasyon
bean noodle – *n.* sotanghon
bean sprout – *n.* tawgi

beans

beans – *n.* hantak
beans black-colored – *n.*
patani
beard – *n.* bungot, barbas –
Spanish *barba*
beat up – *n, a.* gulpi, bugbog,
pagbugbog, paggulpi
beater – *n.* muronilyo -
Spanish *molinillo,* batidor -
Spanish *batidor*
beautiful – *kan.* mabaysay,
mahusay, maanyag
beautify – *n., a.* pabaysay,
pahusay, pagpabaysay,
pagpahusay
beauty – *n.* baysay, husay,
kamabaysay, kamahusay,
kahusayan
because – *s.* dará, gikan, kay,
mahitungod, tungod
beckon – *n, a.* kampay,
sangpit, pagkampay,
pagsangpit
bed – *n.* higdáan, katri, kama -
Spanish *cama*
bed-wetting – *n., a., kan.*
yamang, pagyamang,
mayamang
bedbug – *n.* sudlot
bedfellow – *n.* dirig, kadirig,
durog, kadurog
bedroom – *n.* katurúgan
bee – *n.* buyóg
beef – *n.* unod han baka, karni
- Spanish *carne*
beehive – *n.* putyukan
beetle – *n.* bagang, salagubang
beetle horned – *n.* bágang
before – *kaa., s.* hadto, sadto,
antis - Spanish *antes*
befriend – *n. a.* sangkay,
pagsangkay, pakigsangkay

beg – *n., a.* aró, pagaró,
pangaró, pakilimos,
pagpalimos - Spanish *limosna*
beggar – *n.* mangangaro,
makalilimos, makililimos -
Spanish *limosnero*
begin – *n., a.* paggikán,
pagtikáng
beginning – *n., s.* katikangan,
tinikangan, gikán, tikáng
behead – *n., a.* pugot,
pagpugot
behind – *kan.,kaa.* luyo,
paluyo, talikuran, luyuhan,
patalikod
behind – *n., kat.* likod, luyo,
belch – *n., a.* túgab, pagtúgab,
belfry – *n.* bagtingan,
lingganayan, kampanaryo -
Spanish *campanario*
belief – *n.* tulúohan
believable – *kan.* tinuod,
matuod
believe – *n., a.* túod, pagtúod,
bilib, pagbilib - English *believe*
belittle – *n., a.* paminos,
daugdaog, pagdaugdaog,
pagminos
bell – *n.* lingganay, bagtingan
bell tower – *n.* bagtinganan,
lingganayan, kampanaryo –
Spanish *campanario*
belligerent – *kan.* makiawayon,
masamok, malungot
belly – *n.* tiyan
belly fat – *n.* búyay
beloved – *n., kan.* higugmáon,
hinigugma, hinihigugma,
pinalangga, kunsuylo - Spanish
consuelo
below – *kat., kan.* ubós, ilarom
belt - *n.* paha, sinturon -
Spanish *cinturon*

bench - *n.* lingkuran, banko - Spanish *banco*
bend – *n., a., kan.* pagbaliko, baliko
bend over – *n., a.* tuwad, pagtuwad
beneath – *kat.* sirung, ilarom
benediction – *n.* amin, bendisyon - Spanish *bendicion*, pagamin
benefit – *n., a.* tagamtam, benepisyo - Spanish *beneficio*
benevolent – *kan.* malulúyon, mahatagon
beside – *kat.* sapit, tabi, ligid, kasapit, kaligiran
bet – *n., a.* taon, pusta, pagpusta, pagtáon
betel nut – *n.* búyo
betray – *n., a.* lingo, traydor, pagtraydor – Spanish *traidor*
betrayal – *n.* paglingo, pagtraydor
betroth – *n., a.* balata, pagbalata
between – *kat.* butnga
beware – *n., a.* paghirót, pagikmat, pagtagam, paglukmay
bewilder – *n., a.* lukmay, pahiusa
beyond – *s.* lapos, labaw, dayon
Bible – *n.* Bibliya - Spanish *Biblia*
bicycle – *n.* bisikleta - Spanish bicicleta
bid farewell – *n., a.* babay, panamilit, pagbabay
big – *kan.* dako, dadakuro
big toe – *n.* tamuragko, pudhay
bike – *n.* bisikleta
bile – *n.* apdo

billiard – *n.* bilyar - Spanish *billar*
billiard hall – *n.* bilyaran
bind – *n., a.* butok, pagbutok
biological child – *n.* pursuso
bipolar – *kan.* lurong, luronglurong
bird – *n.* tamsi, maya, bálod, balinsasayaw
birds – *n.* katamsihan
birth – *n., a.* katawo, natawo, anak, pagkatawo, panganak, paganak
birthday – *n.* kaadlawan, natawhan, birtde - English *birthday*
birthplace – *n.* natawuhan, natawhan, tinubuan, gintubuan
bishop – *n.* obispo - Spanish *obispo*
bisquit – *n.* karánon, biskwit - English *bisquit*
bite – *n., a.* kagát, tukob, paak
bitter – *kan.* mapaít
bitter squash – *n.* marigoso, amariguso - Spanish *amargoso*
bitterness – *n.* paít
black – *n., kan.* itom, maitom
black berry – *n.* igot
blackboard – *n.* pisara – Spanish *pizarra*
blacken – *n., a.* itom, pagitom, pagpaitom
blame – *n., a.* basol, pagbasol
blanket – *n.* taklap
blend – *n., a.* sakot, urangop, pagsakot, naurangop
bless – *n., a.* amín, bendisyon - Spanish *bendicion*, pagbedisyon, pagamín
blind – *n., a.* búta, pagbúta, pagkabúta

blinded – *kan.* nabúta
blindness - *n., kan.* butá, pagkabúta
blink – *n., a.* pirok, pisók, pagpirok, pagpisók
blister – *n.* lupak
block – *n., a.,* sangko, sugpo, bará - Spanish *barra,* pagsangko, pagsugpo, pagbalabag, pagbará
blockage – *n.* ulang, paulangan, sangkuan
blocked – *kan.* nasangko, naulang, nakaulang
blond – *n.* bulaw
blood – *n.* dugo
blood relations – *n.* kadugo, kaparyinte
blood vessel – *n.* ugat, kaugatan
blood-sucking insect – *n.* alimpapaso, namok
bloom – *n., a.* bukad, pagbukad, pamukad
blossom - *n.* bukad
blow – *n., a.* huyop, paghuyop
blow away – *n., a.* palid, pagpalid
blow nose – *n., a.* pisnga, pagpisnga
blow whistle – *n., a.* supliti, sirbato, pagsupliti, pagsirbato - Spanish *silbato*
blue – *n., kan.* bulhog, asul - Spanish *azul*
blue crab – *n.* masag
blue marlin – *n.* malasugi
blue-eyed – *kan.* bulhog
bluff – *n.* bangín, pangpang
bluish – *kan.* maasul, bulhog
blunt – *kan.* mangarol, dupol
blurred vision – *n., kan.* labad, harap, malabad

blustering wind – *n.* laburós, madlos
boa constrictor – *n.* sawá
board game of piling shells – *n.* sungka
boast – *n., a.* dasig, pagdasig, parayaw, pagparayaw
boastful – *kan.* hambog
boat – *n.* sakayán, lantsa
body – *n.* lawas
body hair – *n.* barangas
bogus – *kan.* buaw
boil – *n., a.* laso, kaladkad, paglaso, pagkaladkad
boil fish – *n., a.* tula, tinula
boil meat – *n., a.* lága, lauya, paglága, paglauya
boiled dish – *n.* tinula, lauya, linaga
boiling hot – *kan.* nakaladkad
boisterous – *kan.* maaringasa, mangiras, marisyo
bokchoy – *n.* pitsay - Chinese *cabbage*
bomb – *n., a.* pabuto, búmba - Spanish *bomba,* pagpabuto, pagbumba
bone – *n.* bukog, túlan
bonita fish – *n.* turingan
bony – *kan.* bukugon
book – *n.* basahon, barasahon, libro - Spanish *libro*
booster – *n.* tungtungan
boots – *n.* butas – Spanish *botas*
borborygmus – *n., a.* agurok, pagagurok
bored – *kan.* maluntog, mauyam, malángag, masumo, aburido - Spanish *aburrido*
boredom – *n.* sumó, uyam, luntog, lángag

boring – *kan.* masumo,
mauyam, malangkag
borrow – *n., a.* huram, utang,
paghuram, pagutang
boss – *n.* agaron, ámo, kapatas
bother – *n., a.* samok, isturbo -
Spanish *turbar,*
pagsamok, pagisturbo
bottle – *n.* butilya - Spanish
botella
bottle cap – *n.* takóp
bottom – *n.* kahiladman
bounce – *n., a.* untol, paguntol
bouncy – *kan.* buntol,
uyonguyong
boundary – *n.* sakop,
ginsakupan, ginkasakupan
bow – *n., a.* tamod, pagtamod
bow and arrow – *n.* paná
bow-legged – *kan.* sakang
bowl – *n.* kalduhan
box – *n., a.* karton, kahon,
kaha - Spanish *caja*, pagkahon
box – *n., a.* suntok, bunal,
puag, yábo
boxer – *n.* buksingero, bakser -
English *boxer*
boxer shorts – *n.* karsonsilyo -
Spanish *carsoncillo*
boxing – *n.* suntukay,
buksingay - English *boxing*
boy – *n.* intoy, otoy
brace – *n., a.* tukod, pagtukod
brackish mud – *n.* hanang
braid – *n., a.* talunay,
pagtalunay
brain – *n.* útok
branch – *n., a.* sanga,
pagsanga
brave – *kan.* maísog, mailob,
matigás
bravery – *n.* ísog, ilob,
limbasog

brawl – *n., a.* aragway,
karamsaw
bread – *n.* karáunon, karánon,
tinapay
bread crumbs – *n.* rumok,
rugmok
breadfruit – *n.* rimas
break apart – *n., a.* pagkaplag,
watakwatak
break as dawn – *n., a.* sidlit,
punias, pagsidlit, pagpunias
break day – *n., a.* purak,
pagpurak, pagpunias
break in smithereens – *n., a.*
sabrang, parik, pagparik
break into pieces – *a.*
pagpinitpinit, pagrumok
break open – *n., a.* buák,
pagbuák
break thing – *n., a.* bári, wasak,
pagbári, pagwasak, pagruba,
pagbúong
break waves – *n., a.* pagpurak
breakfast – *n., a.* pamahaw,
panmahaw
breast – *n.* súso
breath – *n., a.* ginhawa,
hangos
breath air – *n.*gininhawaan
breath heavily – *kaa.* nahangos
breathe – *n., a.* ginhawa,
pagginhawa
breathe out – *n., a.* buga,
pagbuga
breathing difficulty – *n., a.*
hapo, hangos
breech – *n.* suhí
breeze – *n.* huyop, harupoy,
huyuhoy
bribe – *n., a.* hukip, paghukip,
pagsulsol
bribery – *n.* sulsol, hukip
bridge – *n.* tulay

bright – *kan.* malamrag,
masilaw, maanyag,
brightness – *n.* hayag, kahayag,
lamrag, kalamragan
brilliance – *n.* anyag, ranggat,
kaanyag, karanggat
brilliant – *kan.* maanyag,
maranggat
bring – *n., a.* dará, pagdará
brittle – *kan.* marupok
broadcast – *n., a.* samwak,
pasamwak, pasangyaw
broadcaster – *n.* tagsumat,
parasamwak,paragsamwak
broil – *n., a.* sugba, pagsugba
broiled fish – *n.* sugba, sinugba
broken glass – *n.* buóng
broken in several parts – *kan.*
gubaguba
brook – *n.* sapa
broomstick – *n.* silhig, siphid,
batad
broth – *n.* pinakaladkad,
sabaw
brother – *n.* bugto nga lalaki
brother-in-law – *n.* bayaw
brown – *n., kan.* bulaw,
mabulaw,
brown jellyfish – *n.* mutó
brown pig – *n.* bulaw
brown rice – *n.* lakha
bruise – *n., a.* búnog, pasá
brush – *n., a.* pamaspas,
paspas, brutsa - Spanish
brocha
brush teeth – *n., a.* sipelyo,
tutbras - English *toothbrush,*
pagstutbras
bubble – *n.* bura
bucket – *n.* kabo, baldi -
Spanish *balde*
bud – *n.* biyúos, saringsing
bud of banana – *n.* púso

budding – *n.* ubod, saringsing
budge – *n., a.* dúsog, úsog,
pagdúsog,
budget – *n.* panggastos
build – *n.,a.* tindog, himo,
pagtindog, paghimo
build house – *n., a.* balay,
pagbalay, pagtindog hin balay
builder – *n.* magtirindog,
parahimo, paraghimo
building – *n.* balay
bulging – *kan.* butol, nabutol
bulging eyes – *n.* budlot
bullet – *n.* bala - Spanish *bala*
bulletin – *n.* pahayagan
bully – *n., a.* manlulupig,
mapanarhog, pagdaugdaog
bully – *kan.* malupiglupig,
madaugdaog
bullying victim – *n.*
lupiglupigon, daugdaogon
bulwark – *n.* balawarte,
balwarte - Spanish *baluarte*
bump – *n., a.* untog, pudol,
paguntog, pagpudol
bump head – *n., a.* rantok,
pagrantok
bumps – *n.* butol, butik,
burikbutik
bumpy – *kan.* butulbutol,
batsihon, batubato
bunch of banana – *n.* sipi,
bulig
bundle – *n., a.* butok,
pagbutok
bureau – *n.* sandigan,
departamento - Spanish
departamento
buried piece of wood – *n.*
tuód, pundasyon
burn – *n., a., kan.* sunóg,
pagsunog, tubod, pagtubod,
páso, napáso

106

burn vegetation – *n., a.* tápong, pagtápong
burnt – *kan.* tubód, natúbod
burnt smell – *n., kan.* angtod, maangtod
burp – *n., a.* túgab, pagtúgab
burst – *n., a.* burit, putok, buto, pagburit, pagputok, pagbuto
burst in flames – *n., a.* lurab, paglurab
burst to powder – *n., a.* aprak, pagaprak
bury – *n., a.* lubong, paglubong
business – *n., a.* pakabuhi, hiagi, negosyo - Spanish *negocio*
businessman – *n.* negosyante - Spanish *negociante*
busy – *kan.* sagipo, nagkagaramo
but – *s.* lugáring, kundi, pero - Spanish *pero*
butch – *n.* palakínon, tumboy – English *tomboy*
butcher – *n.* paraihaw, paragihaw, parapangihaw, matansero - Spanish *matanzero*
butt – *n.* pugtot, pútik
butt naked – *kan.* hubo
butter – *n.* mantika, mantikilya - Spanish *mantequilla*
butterfly – *n.* alibangbang
buttocks – *n.* pugtot, pútik
button – *n.* butonis - Spanish *boton*
buttonhole – *n.* ohales - Spanish *ojal*
buy – *n., a.* palit, kumpra, pagpalit, pangumpra
by – *kat.* kan, kanan, ligid, pára -Spanish para

by the way – *a., s., kaa.* panulibangko, sulibangko, ngáyan

C:c

cab – *n.* sakayan, taksi – English *taxi*
cabbage – *n.* ripolyo - Spanish *repollo*
cacao – *n.* kakaw - Mexican *cacahuatl*
cackle – *n., a.* kutak, pagkutak
calcium powder – *n.* apog
calendar – *n.* kalindaryo - Spanish *calendario*, almanaki - Spanish *almanaque*
calf – *n.* bitíis
call – *n., a.* tawag, sangpit
calligraphy – *n.* badlit, katinkatin
callus – *n., kan.* kubal, kubalon
calm – *kan.* malinaw, mahuyo, kalmado, kalma - Spanish *calma*
camouflage – *n., a.* urangop, pagurangop
camp – *n.* kampo - Spanish *campo*
can – *a.* puyde – Spanish *puede*
can opener – *n.* abrilata - Spanish *abrelata*
canal – *n.* hubang, kali
cancer – *n.* kanser - English *cancer*
candle – *n.* kandila - Spanish *candela*
candy – *n.* minatámis, kalamay, dulse - Spanish *dulce*

cane – *n.* sungkod, tungkod, baston - Spanish *baston*, tubó
cannon – *n.* lantaka, kanyon - Spanish *cañon*
cantankerous – *kan.* sumpungon, tarantado, makiawayayon
cap – *n., a.* takóp, pagtakóp
capability – *n.* kakayahan
capable – *a., kan.* kaya
capital (business) – *n., a.* puhunan, kapital - English *capital*
capitalize – *n., a.* puhunan, pagpuhunan
capitol – *n.* kapitolyo - Spanish *capitolio*
capricious – *kan.* liwatliwat, liwanliwan
capsize – *n., a.* taób, pagtaób, pagbalikad
captive – *n.* bihag
capture – *n., a.* bihag, dakop, pagdakop, pagkabihag
car – *n.* awto, kotse
care – *n., a.* ataman, panginano, pagataman
care provider – *n.* mangno paraataman, paramangno, paragtimangno
carefree – *kan.* waray la, waraywaray
careful – *kan.* hírot, mahirot
carefully – *kaa.* hinayhinay
careless – *kan.* amasang, kalamira, lisang, kimas, samurang
carelessness – *n.* amasang, kaamasang, kalamira, kalisangan, kakimasan
caress – *n., a.* haplas, harapihap, paghaplas

cargo – *n.* kargamento - Spanish *cargamento*
caring – *kan.* maataman, maatamanon, maaruga
carnival – *n.* karnabal - Spanish *carnaval*
carpenter – *n.* karpintero - Spanish *carpintero*
carriage – *n.* karuwahi – Spanish *carruaje*
carrier – *n.* padaráan, paradara
carry – *n., a.* dara, hakot, bitbit, sabak, pagdara, paghakot, pagbitbit, pagsabak, pagpásan
carry in the arms – *n., a.* kugos, pagkugos
carry over head – *n., a.* tukdo, pagtukdo
carry over shoulder – *n., a.* pásan, pagpásan
cart – *n.* karitilya, kariton - Spanish *carreta*
cartwheel – *n., a., kaa.* karukaliding, pagbalintong
cascade – *n.* palanas
case – *n.* baol, kaha- Spanish *caja*
case (legal) – *n.* kaso - Spanish *caso*, asunto - Spanish *asunto*
casket – *n.* baol, lungon
cassava – *n.* bilanghoy
castaway – *n., kan.* naanod, nadagsa
cast spell – *n., a.* darahog, bárang, pagdarahog, pagbarang
castigate – *n., a.* latob, kastigo - Spanish *castigar*, paglatob, pagkastigo
castrate – *n., a.* písit, pagpísit
casually – *kaa.* putingad

cat – *n.* kuying, misay, uding, kuting
cat scratch – *n.* kamras
catch – *n., a.* saló, dakop, pagsaló, pagdakop, panakop
catch crab – *n., a.* panggal, pamanggal, panmintol
catch fire – *n., a.* pagdukot, pagsurit
catch fish – *n, a.* pangisda, pangawil
catch up – *n., a.* apas, lanat, pagapas, paglanat
catch with beak or claws – *n., a.* dagit, pagdagit
catering – *n.* panluto, parapanluto
caterpillar – *n.* basol
catfish – *n.* hito, pantat
catholic – *n., kan.* katoliko - Spanish *catolico*
caldron – *n.* baóng
cause – *n.* hinungdan, sanhi, tungod, gintikangan
caution – *n., a.* .hírot pahimangno, paghirot, pagpahimango
cautious – *kan,* mahirot
cave, cavern – *n.* lungib
ceiling – *n.* alkuba
celebrate – *n., a.* pagsaurog, pag salínurog, pagrisyo
celebration – *n.* karisyo, salinurog, pasundayag
cement – *n.* simento - Spanish *cemento*
cemetery – *n.* lubungan, lubnganan, simeteryo - Spanish *cementerio*, pantyon - Spanish *panteon*
centavo – *n.* kusing, sentimo
center – *n.* butnga
centipede – *n.* ulalahipan

century – *n.* siglo - Spanish *siglo*
certain – *kan.* piho, sigurado
certainly – *kaa.* gud, agod, manggod, alang
chain – *n.* kadina - Spanish *cadena*
chaff – *n., a.* tahop, pagtahop
chair – *n.* lingkuran, silya – Spanish *silla*
chalk – *n.* tisa - Spanish *tiza*, tsuk - English *chalk*
challenge – *n., a.* ayat, pagayat, pangayat
change – *n., a.* líwan, saliwan, balyo, pagliwan, pagbalyo
change clothes – *n., a.* liwán, pagliwán
change coin – *n., a.* sukli, sinsilyo – Spanish *sencillo*, pagsukli, pagpasinsilyo
changeable – *adj.* liwatliwat
channel – *n.* sulangan
chaos – *n.* gubot, saramok
chaotic – *kan.* amasang, masamok
chaperone – *n., a.* upod, kaupod, kabunyog
chapter – *n.* yugto, bahin
character – *n.* kinaiya, batasan
charcoal – *n.* uring
charm – *n.* saot, antinganting, birtod, satamsatam
charming – *kan.* makangurudyot, kyut - English *cute*
chase – *n., a.* bukod, lanat, apas, pagbukod, paglanat
chatter – *n., a.* bungisngis, kinasabang, yawyaw
cheap – *kan.* barato

cheat – *n., a., kan.* limbong, lipat, paglimbong, paglipat, malimbong, limbungan

check – *n., a.* pagtigaman, tseki - American *check*

cheerful – *kan.* malipayon, matawa, mahiyumhiyom

cheese – *n.* keso - Spanish *queso*

cheese carabao milk – *n.* kisiyo

cherish – *n., a., kan.* mayuyo, minayuyo, pagmayuyo

chest – *n.* dughan, bungkog

chew – *n., a.* kisam, nguya, pagkisam, pagnguya

chew beetle nut – *n., a.* búyo, mama, pagbuyo, pagmama

chick – *n.* pisó, siwo

chicken – *n.* manok

chicken pox – *n.* hangga

child – *n.* anak, báta, puya

child caregiver – *n.* yaya

chills – *n.* kurog

Chinese person – *n.* intsik, intsika

chip – *n., a., kan.* tinggib, tipak, gusak, gibang, natipakan, pagtinggib, pagtipak, paggusak, paggibang, pagtipak

chipped tooth – *kan., n.* ngihab, kangihaban

chisel – *n., a.* tigib, pagtigib

chocolate – *n.* tabliya, tsokolate - Mexican *choktl*

chocolate beater – *n.* batidor, muronilyo - Spanish *molinillo*

chocolate rice porridge – *n.* sampurado

choke – *n., a..* lakog, paglakog

choose partner – *n., a.* purot, pagpurot

chop – *n.,a.* tadtad, siak, pagtadtad, pagtudtod, pagsiak

chopping block – *n.* tadtaran

choppy – *kan.* mabalod, habagat

chortle – *n., a.* hagikhik, nahagikhik, nahingas

christening – *n.* bunyag, pagbunyag, pamunyag, panbunyag

Christmas – *n.* pasko, pagkatawo han Ginuo

christmas gift – *n.* pamasko

chuckle – *n., a.* hiyom, paghiyom

church – *n., a.* singba, singbahan, singbahan, pagsingba

churchgoer – *n.* parasingba, maniringba

cicada – *n.* purat, ganghis

cigar – *n., a.* tustos, pagtustos, panustos

cinema – *n.* sinehan – English *cinema*

cinnamon – *n.* kaningag

circle – *n.* lidong

circular – *kan.* malidong

circumcise – *n., a., kan.* pagturi, pagpaturi, turí

circus – *n.* sirko - Spanish *circo*

city – *n.* siyudad - Spanish *ciudad*

city dweller – *n.* tagasyudad, syudadano, syudadnon

claim – *n., a.* tagiya, pagangkon, pagtagíya, panagiya

clairvoyant – *kan.*paabatón

clam – *n.* pangtion, punaw, buranday, piyong

clamp – *n*. kimpit, turnilyo -
Spanish *tornillo*
clap – *n., a*. pakpak, palakpak,
pagpakpak, pamalakpak
clarity – *n*. kapawaan,
kapáwan, kalinawan
class – *n*. kalahi, kalidad -
Spanish *calidad*
classmate – *n*. klasmet –
English *classmate*
claw – *n., a*. kagát, pagkagat,
pangagat
clay – *n*. lagay, lapok
clay pot – *n*. daba
clay red coloring – *n*. purog,
barok
clean – *kan*. mahamis,
malimpyo - Spanish *limpio*
clean surroundings – *n., a*.
hawan, paghawan
cleanliness – *n*. kahamisan,
kamalimpyo
clear – *kan*. malinaw, huyayag
clear up vegetation – *n., a*.
hawan, dalos, paghawan,
pagdalos
cleaver – *n*. uták
cleft lip – *n*. bungí, kabungian
cliff – *n*. bangín, pangpang,
panhulugan
climb – *n., a*. saka, saklang,
pagsaka, pagsaklang
cling – *n., a*. kábit, kapyot,
pagkapyot, pagkabit
clip – *n., a*. kimpit, ipit,
pagkimpit, pagipit
clitoris – *n*. tinggil
clock – *n*. orasan, relo -
Spanish *reloj*
close – *n., a*. sira, pagsará,
pagsira - Spanish *cerra*
close – *kan*. apiki, hirani,
harani, kasapit

close eyes – *n., a*. píyong,
pagpíyong
close fist – *n., a*. kumo,
pagkumo
close mouth – *n., a*. tákom,
pagtákom
close-knit - *kaa*. dikitdikit,
sapitsapit, dukutdukot
cloth – *n*. dugnit, tila – Spanish
tela
cloth cover – *n*. tahob
clothes – *n*. badó, súlot, suklob
clothes line – *n*. palaypay,
palaypayan
clothes pin – *n*. kimpit
clothing – *n*. dugnit, panapton,
saplot
tila
cloud – *n*. dampog
cloudiness – *n*. dalumdom,
kadampugan
cloudy – *kan*. madampog,
madalumdom, madágom
club – *n*., a. balbag, baston,
pagbalbag
clumsy – *adj*. tikwugon,
kalamira
coarse – *kan*. butulbutol,
masapara, gusakgusak,
gurakgusak, bastos - Spanish
basto
coarse skin – *n*. kupos,
bukulbukol, burikbutikon
cobweb – *n*. lawalawa
coccyx – *n*. kigol
cockatoo – *n*. abukay
cock crow – *n., a*. tugaok,
panugaok, pagtugaok
cockfight – *n., a*. purok,
búlang, pagpurok, pagbúlang
cockfighting arena – *n*.
búlangan

cockfighting outside arena –
n., a. tupada, pagtupada
cockle clam – *n.* piyóng
cockpit – *n.* bulangan
cockroach – *n.* bangka
cocoa – *n.* kakaw
coconut – *n.* lubi
coconut climber – *n.*
mananggiti, mananangot,
manaranggot
coconut grater – *n.* kaguran
coconut husk – *n., a.* bunót,
pagbunot
coconut leaf – *n.* lukay
coconut milk – *n., a.* hatok,
tunó, paghatok
coconut milk dish – *n.*
hinatukan, tinunuan
coconut milk taro delicacy – *n.*
lidgid, iraid, binagol, sagmani
coconut sapling – *n.* tumos
coconut scoop – *n.* hungot
coconut seed – *n.* búwa
coconut sheath – *n.* gunot,
bunúot
coconut shell – *n.* bagol
coconut sprout – *n.* daol
coconut syrup – *n.* latik
coconut toddy – *n.* tuba
coconut wine maker – *n.*
paragtuba, manananggot,
manaranggot
coffee – *n.* kape - Spanish *café*
coffin – *n.* lungón
cogon grass – *n.* kugon,
kakugnan
cohabit – *n., a.* lúngon,
paglungon
coherent – *adj.* tultol
coiled hair – *n., a.* pungos,
kurong, pagpungos, pagkurong

coin – *n.* kwarta – Spanish
cuarta, sinsilyo – Spanish
sencillo
coincide – *n., a.* kadungan,
dungan, pagdungan, katungod,
pagkatungod
coincidentally – *kaa.* kadungan
coitus – *n., a.* iyot, himaga,
putík, pagiyot, pagputik,
paghimaga
cold – *kan.* mahagkot,
mataghom
coldness – *n.* hagkot, taghom,
kataghuman, kahagkutan
colds – *n.* sipon
colic – *n.* kabag
collapse – *n., a.* rúnog,
pagrúnog
collect – *n., a.* tirok, tipon,
tígob, pagtirok, pagtipon,
pagtígob
collect debt – *n., a.* sukot,
pagsukot
collide – *n. a.* bulang, bangga,
bunggo, purok, pagbúlang,
pagbunggo, pagpurok,
pagbangga, pagtagpo
collision – *n.* banggaay,
bunggúay, purok, búlang
colorful – *kan.* maribhong
colorpaper trimmings – *n.*
karaykay, ngaraykaray
comb – *n., a.* surod, sudlay,
pagsurod, pagsudlay
come – *n. a.* kadi, pagkadi,
pagsingadi
come apart – *n. a.* bulag,
pagbulag, pagburublag
come closer – *a., kaa.* harani,
daraon, pagdaraon, paghiraní,
paharaní,
come down – *n., a.* lusad,
paglusad, paglugsong

come face to face – *n., a.*
asdangay, atubangay,
pagasdangay, pagatubang,
pangatubangay
come in – *n., a.* paguswag,
pagsulód
come last – *n., a.* pukis, urhi,
pagpapukis, pagpaurhi
come up – *n., a.* saka, uswag,
pagsaka, paguswag
come what may! – *kah.* bahala
na!
comedian – *n.* kinkoy,
kumidyante - Spanish
comediante
comedy – *n., kan.* patawa,
katawanan, swirte, maswirte,
pataráwan
comfortable – *kan.* naayon,
mahimurayaw
command – *n., a.* sugo,
kamanduhan, mandato,
mando - Spanish *mandar*
commandment – *n.* sugo,
surundon, kasuguan
commemorate – *n., a.* saurog,
salínurog, pagsaurog,
pagsalínurog
commemorate dead person –
n., a. tagbo, patagbo,
pagpatagbo
commit suicide – *n., a.*
pagpakamatay, pagtigok
commodities – *n.* kumpra,
baligya
common good – *n.* kaupayan
han ngatanan
commotion – *n.* aringasa,
karigudigo, saramok
communal work – *n., a.*
pintakasi, pagpintakasi

communion – *n., a.*
kumunyon, pangumunyon,
pankumunyon
community – *n.* mulupyo,
katilingban, kumunidad -
Spanish *comunidad*
compact – *kan.* súok, sìkon
compact – *n., a.* sumpa,
sumpáan, ginsabutan,
pagsumpa
companion – *n.* upod, kaupod,
padis, kapadis
companionship – *n.* kaupuran,
kabunyog
compassion – *n., a.* paíd,
pagpaíd
compete – *n., a.* aarig, aragaw,
rumba, pagaarig, pagaragaw,
padasigay, pagrumba
competition – *n.* aarig, aragaw,
dasigay, paprumba
complacent – *kan.*
waraywaray, hubya
complain – *n., a.* reklamo -
Spanish *reclamo*, araba,
pagaraba, pangaraba
complainer – *n.* reklamador -
Spanish *reclamador*
complete – *n., a., kan.* buó,
lukop, paglukop, pagbuó,
pagkumpleto – Spanish
completo
complicate – *n., a.* sangkot,
kuri, pagkuri, pagpakuri,
pagsangkot
complicity – *n., kan.*
kasangkot, kakampi, nasangkot
comply – *n., a.* sunod, sugot,
pagsugot, pagsunod
computer – *n.* pangihapan,
kompyuter - American
computer

113

computer keyboard – *n.* kibord
- American *keyboard*
computer mouse – *n.* maus -
American *mouse*
comrade –*n.* kasangkayan,
kumpanyero - Spanish
compañero
con – *n., a.* uwat, panguwat
con artist –*n.* manguruwat,
mangunguwat,
conceal – *n., a.* tágo, urangop,
pagtago, pagurangop
concealed – *kan.* tagó, tinago,
naurangop
concentrate – *n., a.* titig, tutok,
pagtitig, pagtutok
concentrated – *kan.* hútok
concentration – *n.* tinutukan,
tinitigan, kahibangkaagan
concern – *kah.* buyag, ada
takay!
concern – *n., a.* ataman,
panginano, pangataman
conch shell – *n.* budyong
concoction – *n., a.* kutil
condescension – *n.* súro
condition – *n.* kahimtang,
kahimtangan
condolence – *n.* duyog,
pakiduyog, naduyog
confession – *n., a.* kumpisal,
pangumpisal, pankumpisal
confidante – *n.* tinapuran
confide – *n., a.* tapod,
pagtápod
confidence – *n.* tápod, tagya
confine – *n., a.* tuob, pagtúob
confined space – *kan.*
maalinsúob, alimúot
confinement – *n.* túob, natúob
confirmation – *n.*
pangumpirma, pankumpirma

confirmed – *kan.* ámo, máo,
tama
conflict – *n., a.* agaw, aragaw,
pagagaw
conform – *a., kan.* abuyon,
uyon, nauyon
confront – *n., a.* sukmat, bukó,
pagsukmat, pagbukó,
atubangay, asdangay
confront falsehood – *n., a.*
bukó, pagbukó
confrontation – *n.* atubangay,
aragtubang, asdangay
confuse – *kan., a.* gupóng,
lipat, wurok, wara, paggupong,
paglipat, pagwurok, pagwara
confusion – *n.* kagupong,
kalipatan, kawurokan
congested – *kan.* bugíot
congressman – *n.* diputado,
kongresista - Spanish
congresista
conjunction – *n.* sumpay,
kasumpay, kadugtong
connect – *n., a.* dugtong,
sumpay, tugkop, pagdugtong,
pagsumpay, pagtugkop,
pagkatinkatin
connection – *n.* kadugtong,
kasumpay, katugkop,
katinkatin
conned – *kan.* nadára, nauwat
connivance – *n.* kasabot,
kakonsabo, kakampi
connive – *n., a.* kampi,
pagkampi, konsabo,
pagkonsabo
conscience – *n.* buót
conscientious – *kan.* buótan,
mahirot
consciousness – *n.* buót,
kaburúton, kalibutan

consecutively – *kaa.* sunudsunód
consequence – *n.* dinangatan, kahingadtuan, nahingadtuan
consequentially – *kaa.* mirisi, tibway
consonant – *n.* katunog
constant – *kan.* sigidas, kanunay
constant companion – *n.* upodupod, kalungon
constipation – *n.* tinutubol
constituents – *n.* mulupyo
consult – *n., a.* sanghid, sagdon, pasagdon, pananghid, pagpasagdon
consume – *n., a.* úbos, ímod, puyas pagúbos, pagímod, pagpuyas
consumed – *kan.* naúbos, naimod, napuyas
container – *n.* garapon, surudlan, batulang
contamination – *n., a.* tapón, tapuntapon, pagtapón, pagtapuntapon
contempt – *n.* pakaalo, pagpakaalo
contest speed – *n., a.* rumba, parumba, paprumba, latusay
continuation – *n.* kadugtong, kasunod, kasumpay
continue – *n., a.* dayon, sigi, padayon, pagdayon, pagpadayon, pasigi
continuous – *kan.* sigisigi
continuously - *kaa.* sigidas, pasigi, sunodsunod
contribute – *n., a.* amot, aragmot, pagamot, pagaragmot
control – *n., a.* pugong, pigil, pagpugong, kuntrol - English *control*, pagkuntrol

contusion – *n.* búnog, pasá
conversation – *n.* yakanay, himangraw, karukayakan, hiruhimangraw, pulungay,
converse – *n., a.* yakan, himangraw, pagpulong, pagyakan, paghimangraw, pagkarukayakan, pagpulongpulong
conviction – *n., a.* dígon, pangatadungan, pagdígon
convinced - *kan.* abuyon, kumbensido - Spanish *convencido*
convulse – *n., a.* kurog, kirig, pagkirig, pagkurog
convulsion – *n.* kirig, kurog
cook – *n.* paragluto, parapanluto, kusinero, kusinera - Spanish *cocinera*
cook – *n., a.* lúto, paglúto, pagtúon
cook coconut taro – *n.,a.* , tabudlo, pagtabudlo
cook coconut sweet rice – *n., a.* sahog, biko, pagsahog, pagbiko, suman
cook fish in vinegar – *n., a.* paksiw, pagpaksiw
cook porridge – *n., a.* lugaw, paglugaw
cook rice – *n., a.* túon, paglúto, pagtúon
cookie – *n.* karáunon, karánon
cooking – *n.* panluto
cooking ingredients – *n.* panakot
cooking oil – *n.* lana, asyite – Spanish *aceite*
cooking pot – *n.* lutúan
cooking with salt vinegar – *n.* pinaksiw

115

cooking with shrimp sauce – *n.*
hinipunan
cool – *kan.* matugnaw,
mabugnaw
coolness – *n.* tugnaw, bugnaw
cooperate – *n., a.* bulig, kampi,
pagbublig, pagburublig,
pagkampi
coordinated – *kan.* angay,
bagay, dungan
copra – *n., a.* lugit, lukad,
paglugit, paglukad
copulate – *n., a.* putík,
himaga, pagputik, paghimaga
copy – *n., a.* subad, kupya -
Spanish *copia*, pagsubad,
pagkupya
copycat – *kan.* masubad
coral rock – *n.* malabinagong
core – *n.* daol, butnga, kasing
corn – *n.* maís
corner – *n.* kanto, iskina -
Spanish *esquina*
corpse – *n.* patáy, minatay
correct – *n., a., kan.* asya,
mao, tama, tultol, tádong,
matádong pagtádong
correspond – *n., a.* katugma,
pagtugma
corruption – *n.* tinuyaw,
panikas, linurong
cost – *n., a.* pirá, tagpira, balor
costly – *kan.* mahal
costume – *n., a.* suklob, bistida
- Spanish *vestido*
cotton – *n.* gapas
cough – *n., a.* batók, ubó,
pagubó, pagbatók
cough vigorously – *n., a.*
kuykoy, pagkuykoy
council – *n.* sanghiran,
konseho - Spanish *concejo*

counsel – *n., a.* sagdon,
pagsagdon
count – *n., a.* ihap, pagihap
count with the fingers – *n., a.*
tinamban, pagtinamban
counter – *n., a.* tugbang,
pagtugbang
counter table – *n.* pasamano
counterpart – *n., kan.*
katungod, kalingit, katugbang
country – *n.* nasod
couple – *n.* magtiayon,
magasawa
couple dance – *n.* amenudo,
kuratsa
couple dance – *n., a.*
amenudo, kuratsa, paado,
pagamenudo, pagkuratsa,
pagpaado
courage – *n.* ísog
court – *n., a.* kunsuylo,
pangunsuylo
courtship dance – *n.* kuratsa
cousin – *n.* patod, igsyapa
covenant – *n.* sumpáan, saad,
panaaran
cover – *n., a.* taklób, takóp,
tabón, pagtaklób, pagtakóp,
pagtabón
cover with cloth – *n., a.* tahob,
pagtahob
cow – *n.* baka - Spanish *vaca*
cowrie, cowry – *n.* buskay
crab – *n.* alimango, kinis,
masag
crabby – *kan.* aringit
cramps – *n., a.* bikog,
pagbikog
crane – *n.* tikling
crash – *n., a.* bunggo, bangga,
bagsak, pagbunggo,
pagbangga, pagbaksak

crave – *n., a.* lihi (pregnancy), ipa, paglihi, pangipa
crawl – *n., a.* kamang, pagkamang
craziness – *n.* lurong, kato, kalurongan, katuyawan
crazy – *kan., a.* tutuyawon, tuyawtuyaw, lipóng, lurong, pagkalurong, pagkatuyaw
crease – *n., a.* kunot, pilo, pagkunot, pagpilo
create – *n., kan., a.* larang, himo, hinimo, paglarang, paghimo
create chaos – *n., a.* samok, pagsamok
create hole – *n., a.* buho, guho, pagguho, pagbuho, pagluho
creation – *n.* lalarangan, kaladngan, paglarang, kahimo, tinuha
creek – *n.* sapa, liro
crewmember – *n.* katrabaho, tripulante - Spanish *tripulante*
cricket – *n.* burlo, ganghis
cripple – *n., a.* piang, piáy
crispy – *kan.* maragumok
critical – *kan.* gulpi
criticize – *n., a.* pagsusón
critters – *n.* mananap
crochet – *n., a.* gantsilyo - Spanish *gancho*, paggantsilyo
crocodile – *n.* buwaya
crony – *n.* batos
cross – *n., a.* balabag, tabok, krus - Spanish *cruz*, pagbalabag, pagtabok, pangudos
cross-eyed – *kan.* duling, libát
crosswise – *kaa.* balabag, pabalabag
crotch – *n.* singit, hita

crouch – *n., a.* kirugtol, biruksot, pagkirugtol, pagbiruksot
croup – *n.* kuykoy
crow – *n.* uwak
crow as rooster – *n., a.* tuktugaok, pagtugaok, panugaok
crowd – *n.* katawuhan, katáwhan, kadamuan, kadáman
crowded – *kan.* bugíot, masuok
crown – *n., a.* pudong, pagpudong
crucifix – *n.* krusipiho - Spanish *crucifijo*
cruel – *kan.* madarahog, masungit
cruelty – *n.* darahog, kasungitan
crumble as bread – *n., a.* rumok, pagrumok,
crumble as pile – *n., a.* timpag, pagtimpag
crumbs – *n.* rumok
crumple – *n., a.* kurumos, kunot, pagkunot, pagkurumos
crumpled – *kan.* pirikot, kunot, nakunot, kurumos, nakurumos
crunch – *n., a.* ragumok, pagragumok
crunchy – *kan.* maragumok
crush – *n., a.* rumok, rugmok, pagrumok, pagrugmok
crusted drool – *n.* buray
crutch – *n.* sungkod, tungkod
cry – *n., a.* tuók, tangis, pagtuók, pagtangis
cry loudly – *n., a.* kuyahaw, ngurahab, pagkuyahaw, pagngurahab
crybaby – *kan.* matuok

crystal clear – *kan.* matínaw
cucumber – *n.* pipino
cuddle – *n., a.* hangkopay, kupkopay, paghangkopay, pagkupkopay
cuddle with legs – *n., a.* tangday, pagtangday
cult – *n.* tuluuhan
cup – *n.* tasa - Spanish *taza*
cupboard – *n.* aparador - Spanish *aparador*
cure – *n., a.* tambal, bulong, pagtambal, pagbulong
curl hair – *a., kan.* pagkurong, balagúnon
curly – *kan.* balagúnon, kurungon
current – *n.* sulog, kuryinte - Spanish *corriente*
curse – *n., a.* baráng, buyag, paggaba, pagbaráng, pabuyag,
curse words – *n., a.* buyayaw, pagbuyayaw
cursive – *n., a.* badlit, katinkatin, pagkatinkatin, pagbadlit
curved – *kan.* baliko
custom – *n.* panurundon, batasan, kabatasanan, kustumre - Spanish *costumbre*
customer – *n.* mamaralit, kustomer - English *customer*
cut – *n., a.* utod, tabas, tudlis, busbos, pagutod, pagtabas, pagbusbos, pagtudlis
cut cloth – *n., a.* tabas, pagtabas
cute – *kan.* makangurudyot
cut grass – *n., a.* dalos, haras, pagdalos, pagharas
cut hair – *n., a.* arót, pagarót, pagpaarót

cut into pieces – *n., a.* utudutod, pagutudutod
cutlass – *n.* sundang
cutting board – *n.* tadtaran
cuttlefish – *n.* kulambutan
cut with saw – *n., a.* sirutso, pagsirutso
cut with scissors – *n., a.* gunting, paggunting
cynical – *kan.* marauton, madumot, matapubre

D:d

dagger – *n.* pisaw, punyal – Spanish *puñal*
daily – *kaa.* kadaadlaw, adlawan, adlawadlaw,
damage – *n., a.* hibang, kahibang, piruwisyo - Spanish *perjuicio,* pagkahibang
damages – *n.* danyos - Spanish *daño*
damsel – *n.* daragita
dance – *n., a.* sayaw, pagsayaw
dance between bamboo pools – *n., a.* tinikling, pagtinikling
dare – *n., a.* ayat, pagayat
daring – *kan.* maungod, manlibasog
dark – *kan.* maitom, masirom
darkness – *n.* sirom, dulom, kasisidman
dart – *n., a.* sumpit, pagsumpit
date – *n.* adlaw, pitsa - Spanish *fecha*
daughter – *n.* anak nga babayi
daughter-in-law – *n.* umagad, umagad nga babayi

dawn – *n.* kaagahon,
panugaok, punías
day – *n.* adlaw
day after tomorrow – *n.*
sangbuwas, kinabuwasan,
sarusangbuwas
day before yesterday – *n.*
kasangkulop
daybreak – *n., a.* punías,
kaagahon, panugaok, pagsidlit,
pagpunías
daytime – *n.* kaadlawon
deaf – *n.* bungól
deafened – *kan.* nabungól
deafness – *n.* kabungulan
dealer – *n.* negosyante -
Spanish *negociante*
dear – *kan.* mahal, pinalangga,
hinigugma
death – *n.* kamatayan
death anniversary – *n., a.*
tagbo, tapos, patagbo, patápos
debt – *n., a.* utang, pagutang,
pangutang
debt collector – *n.* manurukot,
paragsukot
decade – *n.* katuígan, dekada -
Spanish *decada*
deceitful – *kan.* malimbong,
malingo, madaya
deceive – *n., a.* paglimbong,
pandaya, paglingo, pagtuyaw,
paginggayar - Spanish *engañar*
December – *n.* Disyembre -
Spanish *diciembre*
decide – *n., a.* larang, buót,
tuig, pagbuót, paglarang,
pagtuig
decision – *n.* burútan, larang,
kaladngan, desisyon - Spanish
decision
deck of playing cards – *n.*
baraha - Spanish baraja

declaration – *n.* pahayag,
deklarasyon – Spanish
declaracion
declare – *n., a.* pahayag,
pasabot, pagpahayag,
pagpasabot
decorate – *n., a.*
panrayandayan, pagadurno -
Spanish *adorno*
decorated cart procession – *n.*
karro - Spanish *carro*
decoration – *n.* rayandayan,
adurno, dekorasyon - Spanish
decoracion
deep – *kan.* halarom, hilarom
deep breath – *n., a.* hangos,
paghangos, nahangos
deep forest – *n.* kagurangan,
kagugúban, kabagwakan
deep red – *n.* bulagaw,
mapulapula
deep sorrow – *n.* kabidúan
deep violet – *n.* tagom
deep voice – *n.* garhob
deep water – *n.* kahalaruman,
kahaladman
deer – *n.* bugsok
defecate – *n., a.* tatái, uro,
pagtai, paguro
defend – *n., a.* sagang, ugop,
pagsagang, pagugop,
pagdepensa
defense – *n.* sagang,
panagangan, depensa -
Spanish *defensa*
deficient – *kan.* kulang,
dugangan, durugangan
deficit – *n.* kulang, kakulangan
definitely – *kaa.* manggod
deflate – *n., a.* hiyos, hungaw,
pagpahiyos, pagpahungaw
deformity – *n.* pilidong,
kapilidong

delay – *kan., a.* urhi, paurhi,
langan, langanlangan, sáag,
pagpaurhi, pagkasáag,
paglanganlangan
delayed – *kan.* naurhi
delicacy mashed sweet potato
– *n.* linupak
delicacy sweet rice, coconut
and chocolate – *n.* muron
delicacy sweet taro in coconut
milk – *n.* tabudlo
delicious – *kan.* marasa
deliver – *n., a.* dúlong, padara
deluge – *n., a.* lunop, dugyok
demand – *n., a.* araba, reklamo
- Spanish reclamo, demanda -
Spanish *demanda*
demented – *kan.* lipóng,
malipong,
democracy – *n.* demokrasya -
Spanish *democracia*
demon – *n.* demonyo
denial – *n., kah.* diwara,
ambot, waray ngani
dense – *kan.* sìkon, súok
dentist – *n.* manggagabot,
dentista - Spanish *dentista*
denture – *n.* posteso - English
prothesis
deny – *n., a.* diwara,
pagdiwara, likaw, paglikaw
depart – *n., a.* iwas, larga,
lakat, pagiwas, paglarga,
paglakat,
department – *n.* departamento
- Spanish *departamento*
depend – *n., a.* tápod, sarig,
pagtápod, pagsarig
dependable – *kan.* tultol,
tapuran, matatapuran
dependence – *n.* pagtápod
dependent – *kan.* tapód

deposit money – *n.* pagtipon,
deposito - Spanish *deposito*
depot (fuel) – *n.* deposito -
Spanish *deposito*
deprived – *kan.* kabos
depth – *n.* kahilaruman,
kahiladman, kahaladman
deride – *n., a.* tamay,
pagtamay
descend – *n., a.* lugsong,
lusad, paglugsong, paglusad
descendants – *n.* kaapuhan,
sumurunod
design – *n.* disenyo - Spanish
diseño
desire – *n., a.* hingyap, tukso,
ungara, paghingyap,
pagkatukso, pagungara
desirous – *kan.* makaiipa
mahibulong, mahiblong, ,
makahiringyap,
desktop computer – *n.* destap-
American *desktop*
despite – *s.* lábot
dessicate – *n., a.* ugá, pagugá
dessicate by smoking - *n.* luon
dessicated – *kan.* ugá
dessicated coconut meat - *n.*
kupras, lugit, lukad
destiny – *n.* hingadtuan,
kahangturan, kapalaran,
kalaradngan
destroy – *n., a.* bungkag, guba,
ruba, pagbungkag, pagguba,
pagruba
detach – *n., a.* lukba, bulag,
paglukba, pagbulag
determination – *n.*
panlimbasog
determined – *kan.* manlibasog
determiner – *tud.* mga, nga, an
devil – *n.* panulay, yawa,
demonyo - Spanish *demonio*

devour – *n., a.* lámoy, pag
lámoy
devour by fish – *n., a.* sibad,
pagsibad
dewdrop – *n.* túnog
dialect – *n.* yinakanan,
yinaknan
diarrhea – *n., a.* urúuro,
pagtatai
dictionary – *n.* puplungan,
purulungan, pangahulugan
die – *n., a.* patay, hanaw,
paghanaw, namatay
diease organism – *n.* kagaw,
bayrus
differ – *n., a.* ibá, pagibá
different – *kan.* iba, ibáibá,
lain, kakaiba
differently – *kaa.* lugod
difficult – *kan.* makuri
difficulty - *n.* kuri, kakurian
dig – *n., a.* hukay, ukab,
paghukay, pagukab
dig ditch – *n., a.* hubang,
pagubang
dig hole – *n., a.* ukab, buho,
pagukab, pagbuh,
dig out – *n., a.* hukay, ukab,
pagukab, paghukay
digging – *n.* inukab, hinukay,
binukad
dilute – *kan.* lapsaw
diminished – *kan.* naminos
diminished size or quantity -
kan. nagutiay
dimple – *n.* kalundiis
dining room – *n.* karáunan
dinner plate – *n.* plato -
Spanish *plato*
dirt – *n., a.* húgaw, lamiri
dirt on skin – *n.* kagíd
dirty person - *kan.* amóg,
buringon, buringot, kagiron

dirty place – *kan.* mahugaw,
malamiri
dirty stain – *n.* kagíd
dirty water – *kan.* malubog,
malamiri disabled person – *n.*
piáy disagree – *n., a.* típa,
pagtípa
disagreeable – *kan.* natipa
disappear – *n., a.* wara,
bugkot, hanaw, pagwara
disappointment – *kah.* odayka,
purbida
disapproval – *kah.* baa
disarray – *kan.* hiwihiwi,
amasang
disaster – *n.* rimalaso
discolor – *n., a.* lubád,
paglubád
discomfort – *n.* sagabal,
makabubudlay
discontinuous – *kan.* utudutod
discover – *n., a.* agí, hikay,
diskubre - Spanish *discubre*,
pakaagí, paghikay,
pagdiskubre
discover secret – *n., a.* buking,
bisto - Spanish *vista*,
pagbuking, pagbisto
discovered – *kan.* natadan,
nadiskubrihan
discuss – *n., a.* himangraw,
purulungan, hisgot, saysay,
pulungpulong, pagsaysay
pagpurulungan, paghisgot,
paghimangraw
discussion - *n.* saysay,
himangraw, hisgotay
hiruhimangraw, karukayakan
disease – *n.* sakit
disease and poverty – *n.*
kasakitan, kapubrihan
disembark – *n., a.* háwas,
paghawas

disgrace – *n.* disgrasya - English *disgrace*
disgusting – *n.* piristihon
dish premarinated pork – *n.* humba, adubo
disharmony – *kan.* yabag
disheveled – *kan.* buringot, nagpaparagpag
disintegrate – *n., a.* burublag, pagburublag
disinterested – *kan.* siridngon
dislike – *n., a.* diri, pagdiri
dislocate – *n., a.* lugas, paglugas
dislocate joint – *n., a.* lisó, piang, paglisó, pagpiang
dislodge – *n., a.* hurós, harós, ligas, paguros, pagligas, paghurós, pagharós, pagligas
dismantle – *n., a.* bungkag, pagbungkag
dismount – *n., a.* háwas, pagháwas
disorderly – *kan.* lisang, sarawayon, samurang
disoriented – *kan.* linga, lipat
disown – *n., a.* salikway, pagsalikway
display – *n., a.* laray,latag, paglaray, paglatag
display ostentatiously – *n., a.* sangyaw, pasundayag, pagsangyaw, pagpasangyaw, pagpasundayag
displeasure – *n.* kabudlay
disposition – *n.* kaburúton
disrespectful – *kan.* waray respite, sarawayon
distance – *n.* distansya - Spanish *distancia*
distant – *kan.* harayo, hirayo
distasteful – *kan.* maluwad
distorted – *kan.* birikis, pirikot

distribute – *n., a.* sarahid, panhatag, bahinbahin, baragayaw, barabhin
district – *n.* barangay, baryo, purok, distrito - Spanish *distrito*
disturb – *n., a.* alburoto, isturbo - English *disturb*
disturbance – *n., a.* samok, alburuto – Spanish *alboroto*
disturbed – *kan.* bigit, hangit
disturbing – *kan.* masamok
ditch – *n.* hubang
dive – *n., a.* layog, lurop, paglayog, paglurop
diversion– *n.* kalingawan
divide – *n., a.* bahinbahin, tunga, pagbahinbahin, pagtunga
dividend – *n.* kabahin, kabahinbahin
division – *n.* bahinbahin, pagbahinbahin
divorce – *n., a.* bulag, pagbulag
dizziness – *n.* hílo, lípong
dizzy – *a., kan.* lípong, malipong
doe – *n.* libay
do not – *n., a.* ayáw pagbuhat
doctor – *n.* mananambal, manarambal, doktor - English *doctor*
doctrine – *n.* panutduan, duktrina – Spanish *doctrina*
dog – *n.* ayam, ido
dog copulating – *n.* tawil, pagtawil
dogma – *n., a.* panutduan
don't know – *kah.* ambot!
done – *kan.* human, tapós
donkey – *n.* asno - Spanish *asno*

door – *n.* suluran, sudlanan, purtahan - Portuguese *porta*
door panel – *n.* sada
doormat – *n.* pahiran
doorway – *n.* agían purtahan
double – *kan.* duha, duble - Spanish *doble*
double vision – *n.* duling, libat, kadulingan, kalibatan
doubt – *kah.* balitaw, balitgad, okong
doubt – *n., a.* kahulop, ruhaduha, duhaduha, duda - Spanish *duda*
dove – *n.* sarapati, limukon
down – *n., kat.* barahibo, ubos
downpour – *n., a.* bunok, buhos, pagbunok, pagbuhos
downstream – *n.* palawod
dozen – *n.* dosena - Spanish docena
drag – *n., a.* danas, hila, pagdanas, paghila
draggy – *kan.* masapnot
dragonfly – *n.* tarimbubunay
drain – *n., a.* sayurong, basyahan - Spanish *vaciar*, pagbasya
draw – *n., a.* badlis, pagbadlis
dreadful – *kan.* makalilisang, makaharadlok
dream – *n., a.* inóp, paginóp
dress – *n., a.* bádo, panapton, pagbádo
dressmaker – *n.* mananahi, manarahi, paragtahi
dried – *kan.* ugá
dried fish – *n.* bulad
dried snot – *n.* ngánga
drift – *n., a.* anod, anas, paganod, paanod, paganas
driftwood – *n.* batang

drinking glass – *n.* baso - Spanish *vaso*
drinking spree – *n.* tagaytagay, irignom
drip – *n., a.* turo, pagturo
drive away – *n., a.* tabog, iwas, layas, pagtabog, pagpaiwas, pagpalayas
drizzle – *n., a.* tarahiti, tarithi, pagtarahiti, pagtarithi
drop – *n., a.* hulóg, taktak, paghulóg, pagtaktak
drop by – *n., a.* hapit, paghapit
drop forcefully – *n., a.* pusdak, pagpusdak
droplet – *n.* turo
drop off – *n.* hulugan, hinulogan, panhulugan
drown – *n., a.* lumos, lunod, pagkalumos
drowsiness – *n.* piraw, kapirawan, katurugon
drowsy – *kan.* piraw, nahingaturog
drugs – *n.* druga
drugstore – *n.* butika – Spanish *botica*
drum – *n.* bumbo - Spanish *bombo*
drunk – *kan.* hubog
drunkard – *n.* parahubog
drunkenness – *n.* kahubugan
dry – *kan.* mamara
dry – *n., a.* ugá, pagugá
dry season – *n.* huraw
dry under the sun – *n., a.* bulad, pagbulad
dry up – *n, a.* mara, hubas, pagmara, pagpahubas
dryland – *n.* sagka, sugka, kamádan
duck – *n.* itik, pato - Spanish *pato*

due to – *s.* gikan, nahiunong

dues – *n.* amot, aragmot

dugout canoe – *n.* balúto, barúto

dull – *kan.* masapnot, mangarol, dupol, bulok (as mental capacity)

dumb – *n.* ngúla

dunk – *n., a.* tulnob, tiksop, pagtulnob, pagtiksop

durable – *n.* madigon

duration – *n.* kaiha

during – *s.* samtang, durante - Spanish *durante*

dusk – *n.* kakurulpon

dust – *n.* taputapo

dust devil – *n.* alipuros

dusty – *kan.* mataputapo

dutiful – *kan.* tangkod

duty – *n.* katungdanan, serbisyo - Spanish *servicio*

dwarf – *n.* diwindi

dwarf coconut tree – *n.* lingkuranay

dyke – *n.* palakínon, tumboy – English *tomboy*

dynamite fishing – *n.* badil

E:e

each – *kan.* matag, tag, kada – Spanish cada

each – *n., kaa.* tagusa, tagsa

eagle – *n.* agila

ear – *n.* talinga

ear wax – *n.* atuli

earlier – *kan., kaa.* kanina, karukanina, tirutemprano

early – *kan., kaa.* agap, temprano - Spanish *temprano*

early morning - *n.* kaagahon, panugaok

earn – *n., a.* tipig, ipon, pagtipig, pagipon

earnest – *kan., kaa.* hingpit, tímos

earrings – *n.* ariyos - Spanish *arreos*

earth – *n.* kalibutan, tuna

earthen jar – *n.* tibod

earthly – *adj.* kinalibutanon

earthquake – *n.* linog

earthworm – *n.* wati

ease – *n.* sayon

easy – *kan.* masayon

easily – *kaa.* hayahay

easily laughing – *kan.* matawa

easily scammed – *kan.* uruwaton

easily upset – *kan.* tarantado, pungtanon

east – *n.* sirangan, sinirangan, kasirangan

east wind – *n.* kanaway

easy – *kan.* masayon

eat – *n., a.* kaon, pagkaon

eat between meals – *n., a.* miryenda - Spanish *merienda*

eat with bare hands – *n., a., kan.* kamot, pagkamot, pagkinamot, kinamot

eaves – *n.* saruyong

echo – *n., a.* aningal, haráging

eclipse – *n.* bakunawa

ecstasy – *n.* karayhakan

edema – *n., a.* hupong, paghupong

edge – *n.* ganggang, pangpang

edible – *kan.* makaraon

edible fern – *n.* pakó

edible slimy fish – *n.* parutpot, lawayan

educated – *kan.* maaram, tinunan, idukado - Spanish *educado*

eel – *n.* kasili
effeminate – *n.* babayínon, bayot
effort – *n., a.* tikos, tinguha, talinguha, pagtikos, paningkamot, panlimbasog
egg – *n.* bunay
eggplant – *n.* tarong
egotistical – *adj.* makiiyaiya, bilib ha kalugaringon
eight – *num.* waló, otso - Spanish *ocho*
eighteen – *num.* dyesiotso - Spanish *dieciocho*
eighty – *num.* kawaluàn, otsenta - Spanish *ochenta*
elapse – *n., a.* hagos, labay, paghagos, paglabay
elastic – *kan.* maunat
elbow – *n., a.* síko, pagsikó
elderly – *n.* kalagasan, kalagsan
elderly-like – *kan.* lagaslagasoy
elect – *n., a.* pili, pagpili
election – *n.* pinilíay
electric fan – *n.* bintilador - Spanish *ventilador*
electric meter – *n.* kuntador - Spanish *contador*
electricity – *n.* kuryente - Spanish *corriente*
elegance – *n.* garbo
elegant – *kan.* garbuso
eleven – *num.* onse - Spanish *once*
elope – *n., a.* tabag, buyóng, pagtabag, pagbuyóng, pagilop- English *elope*
else – *kaa.* lugod
embarrass – *n., a.* pakaálo, kaawód, pagpakaalo,
embarrassment – *n.* álo, awód, kaarawdan

ember – *n.* bagá
embrace – *n., a.* hangkop, kupkop, paghangkop, pagkupkupay
embroider – *n., a.* burda - Spanish *borda*
embroider mat – *n., a.* pahot, pagpahot, pamahot
embroidery – *n.* burda, pinahutan
embroil – *n.* intriga
emerge – *n., a.* ulpot, pagulpot
empathetic – *kan.* mahumla, maluluyon
empathic expression – *kah.* odog
empathize – *n., a.* paid, pagpaìd, pagduyog, pagkaluoy, naalopan
empathy – *n.* duyog, kaluoy, alop, kapaìd
employee – *n.* impleyado - Spanish *empleado*
empty – *n., a., kan.* basya, basiyo - Spanish *vacio*, pagbasya, pagubós, ubúsúbos
empty out food – *n., a.* hukad, paghukad
encantation – *n., a.* hudimhudim, yakyak, pahudimhudim, pagyakyak
enchanted being – *n.* diwata
encounter – *n.,*tapo, kita, pagtapo, pagkita
encounter by chance – *n., a.* hagilap,tara,paghagilap, nataraan
encourage – *n., a.* aghat, abiabi, pagaghat, pagabiabi
encouragement – *n.* kaaghat, pagaghat

end – *n., a.* tapós, taliwas, talwas, pagtapós, pagtaliwas, pagtalwas

end bondage – *n.* kataliwasan, katalwasan

end-point – *n.* katapusan, tumoy

endear – *n., a.* aring, buyóng, pagaring, pagbuyóng

endearment – *n.* buyóng, aringaring

ending – *n.* tubtob, katapusan, kahangturan

endorse – *n., a.* undong, pagundong

endurance – *n.* katatagan, ilob, pagilob, pagantos, pagtikos, talinguha, tinguha

endure – *n., a.* ilob, antos, tikos, agwanta - Spanish *aguantar,* pagilob, pagantos, pagtikos, pagagwanta

enduring – *kan.* mailob, matatag

enemy – *n.* kaaway

engage – *n., a.* awil, pagawil

engine – *n.* makina - Spanish *maquina*

engine oil – *n.* asyite - Spanish *aceite*

engross – *n., a., kan.* awil, pagawil, naawil

enjoin – *n., a.* abiabi, gagad, pagabiabi, paggagad

enjoying – *kan.* naayon, narayhak

enjoyment – *n.* rayhak

enlarge – *n., a., kan.* dako, padako, pagdako, nadako

enlargement of scrotum – *n.* búyong, buyungon

enlighten – *n., a.* hayag, kahayag, pahayag, paghayag

enlightenment – *n.* kapáwa, kapawaan, kapáwan, kahayag

enough – *kan., kaa.* sadang, husto

enslave – *n., a.* uripon, paguripon, suhito - Spanish *sujeto*

entangle – *n., a.* sagapot, pagsagapot, nasagapot

entangle as thread – *n., a.* gumok, paggumok, nagumok

enter – *n., a.* sulód, pagsulód

entertain – *n., a.* liaw, lingaw, pagliaw, paglingaw

entertaining – *kan.* makawiwili, makaliliaw, nakakaliaw

entertainment – *n.* kaliawan, kalingawan, pasundayag

entice – *n., a.* ugay, pagugay

entrails – *n.* tinai

entrance – *n.* suluran, sudlanan

entrust – *n., a.* halad, tubyan paghalad, pagtubyan, pagintrigá

envelope – *n.* subri - Spanish *sobre*

envious – *kan.* náawa, naiipa

environment – *n.* kaligiran

envy – *n., a.* kaawa, kaípa, pagkaawa, pagkaípa

epilepsy – *n.* buntog, buntugon

equal – *n., a..* tupong, pagtupong

equally shared – *kan.* saradang, barabhin

equip – *n., a.* gamit, paggamit

equipment – *n.* gamit, garamiton, kagamitan

equivocate – *n., a.* ruhaduha, duhaduha, alang, alangalang,

pagruhaduha, pagalang,
pagalangalang
erase – *n., a., kan.* pára,
pagpára, pagbora, napára
eraser – *n.* pará, panbora, bora
- Spanish *borrador*
erode – *n., a.* timpag,
pagtimpag
errand – *n., a.* sugo, pagsugo
escape – *n., a.* lusot, búhi,
púga - Spanish *fugar,*
nakalusot, nakabúhi, pagpúga
escapee – *n.* púga
especially - *kaa.* labi
essence – *n.* uray,
katutungaydan
estimate – *n., a.* igoigo,
pagigoigo
etch – *n., a.* badlis, pagbadlis
eternity – *n.* dayon, kadayunan
etiquette – *n.* batasan
eunuch – *n.* pisít
evaporation – *n.* alisngaw
even – *kan.* patas
even though – *s.* bisan,
bisanla, bisla
events – *n.* nahihinabo,
nahitatabo
eventuality – *n.* hingadtuan,
kahangturan, kahingadtuan,
nahingadtuan
every – *kan.* tag, matag, kada -
Spanish *cada*
everyone – *n., han.* tagusa,
tagsa, kada usa
everything – *n., han.* hurót,
ngatanan, kadabutang
evil – *kan.* manunulay,
karautan, maligno
evil spirit – *n.* maligno,
panulay, demonyo - Spanish
demonio

exacerbate – *n., a.* tulos,
pagtulos
exact – *kan.* igo, tama
exaggerate – *n., a., kah.* súro,
pasubra, pagsúro, pagpasubra,
harumamay
exaggeration – *n.* harumamay,
pasubra - Spanish *sobra*
examine – *n., a.* usisa, suri,
iksamen - Spanish *examen,*
pagusisa, pagsuri, pagiksamen
example - *n., a.* pananglitan,
panurundon
exasperate - *n., a.* budlay,
kabudlay
exasperation - *kah.* agoy
excavate - *n., a.* ukab, hukay,
pagukab, paghukay
excavation – *n.* inukab,
hinukay, buhó
except – *s.* lábot
excess – *n., a.* sapaw, subra -
Spanish *sobra,* pagsubra,
pasubra
excessive – *kan.* uráura, subra,
duro
exchange – *n., a.* balyo,
balyúan, balyuay
excise – *n., a.* busbos, busni,
pagbusbos, pagbusni
exciting – *kan.* makawiwili,
makaruruyag
excrement – *n.* tái
excuse – *n., a.* baribad, tabi,
pamaribad, pagpalusot, panabi
execute by hanging – *n., a.*
bitay, pagbitay
exert effort – *n., a.* tinguha,
pagsiguro, pagtinguha,
pagtalinguha, paniguro
exhale – *n., a.* buga, pagbuga
exhaust – *n., a.* gúol, hawol,
pagkagúol

exhausted – *kan.* mahawol, maguol, makapoy

exit – *n.* gawasan, garawasan, garawsan

expasperating – *kan.* mabudlay

expenditure, expenses - *n.* gastos, panggastos

expensive – *kan.* mahal

experience – *n.* kinaadman

expert – *kan.* makarit, maabtik

expertise – *n.* karit, kakaritan, kaabtik

expired air – *n.* gininhawaan

explain – *n., a.* saysay, hisgot, pagsaysay, paghisgot

explode – *n., a.* butó, putok, aprak, pagbutó, pagputok, pagaprak.

explosive – *n.* pabuto, paputok

export – *n.* iksport - English *export*

expose – *n., a.* huwaw, paghuwaw

exposed – *kan.* dayag

express affection – *n., a.* aring, pagaring, pagaringaring

exterior – *n.* gawas

extra – *n.* sapaw, subra - Spanish *sobra*, pasubra

extract coconut milk – *n., a.* pugá, pagpugá

extract tooth – *n., a.* gabot, paggabot

extrasensory perception – *n., a.* paabat, pagpaabat

extreme – *n.* kasagsagan

extricate – *n., a.* lukba, paglukba

extrovert – *kan.* makiaangayon

exuberant – *n., kan.* rayhak, narayhak

eye – *n.* matá

eye cataract – *n.* bulhog

eyebrow – *n.* kiray

eyeglass – *n.* salaming, antiyuhos - Spanish *anteojos*, antipara - Spanish *anteparras*

eyelash – *n.* pirok

F:f

façade – *n.* atubangán

face – *n.* bayhon, dagway, kahimó, nawong

face – *n., a.* atubang, pagatubang

face covering – *n.* bangot, maskara, mask - English *mask*

face each other – *n., a.* atubangay, pagatubangay

face front – *n., a.* atubáng, pagatubáng

face towel – *n.* labakara – Spanish *lava cara*

face-to-face meeting – *n., a.* atubangay, aragtubang, pagatubangay, pagaragtubang

facet – *n.* hitsura - Spanish *hechura*

factory – *n.* himuan, hirimuan, talyer - Spanish *taller*

fad – *n.* uso, nauso

fade – *n., a.* lubád, papas, hanaw, paglubád, pagpapas, paghanaw

faded – *kan.* lúbad, nalubad, pará

faggot – *n.* butok

fail business - *n., a.* purdoy, bankarute - Spanish *bancarrota*

fail test or examination – *n., a.* hulóg, pagkahulog, waray pasar

faint – *n., a.* himatay, hílo, pasma, pasmado

fairy – *n.* diwata, kahuynon
faithful – *kan.* tangkod, tuptop, matinuuhon, matinumanon
fake – *kan.* buáw
fall – *n., a.* pagkahulóg, pagtagak, pagkataktak, pagkatumba
fall apart – *n., a.* rumpag, pagrumpag
fall as structure – *n., a.* rúnog, pagrúnog
fall backward – *n., a.* baliskad, pagbaliskad
fall flat – *n., a.* hulampag, paghulampag
fall forcefully – *n., a.* umpag, pagkaumpag
fall forward – *n., a.* balintong, pagbalintong
fall in line – *n., a.* paglinya
fall on bottom – *n., a.* napauntog, pagkauntog
fall on ground – *n., a.* paglaparag
false – *n., kan.* buwa, binuwabuwa
false accusation – *n., a.* tuhatuha, butangbútang, tahaptahap, pagtuhatuha, pagbutangbútang falsehood – *n.* buwa, panhimuwa
falter – *n., a.* ruhaduha, pagruhaduha
fame – *n.* bantog, kabantugan
family – *n.* panimalay, pamilya - Spanish *familia*
family name – *n.* apelyido - Spanish *apellido*
famine – *n.* gútom, kagutom, katgutom
famish – *n., a.* gutóm, pagkagutóm, paggutom

famous – *kan.* sikát, bantugan, dungganan, dungugan
fan – *n., a.* paypay, abaniko - Spanish *abanico*, pagpaypay
fan palm – *n.* buri
far away – *kaa.* harayo, hirayo
fare – *n., a.* bayád, pasahi - Spanish *pasaje*, pagbayad, pamasahi
farewell – *n.* panamilit
farm – *n., a.* uma, paguma
farmer - *n.* paragúma, parauma
fart – *n., a.* utot, pagutot
fast – *kan., kaa.* nahírit, madagmit, matulin, paspas
fat – *n., kan.* tambok, mantika, matambok
fat belly – *kan.* búyayon
fate – *n.* kapalaran
father – *n.* amay, tatay, itay, padre, papa
father-in-law – *n.* ugangan nga lalaki
fathom – *n., a.* dupa, tugkad, pagtugkad
fatigue – *n. kan.* butlaw, kapoy, kaguol, mabutlaw, makapoy, maguol
fatten – *n., a.* patambok, pagtambok, pagpatambok
fatty – *kan.* tambokon, mantikaon
faucet – *n.* gripo - Spanish *grifo*
fault – *n.* sayop
favor – *n.* alayon, pabor - Spanish *favor*
favored – *kan.* pinaurog
favorite – *n.* kagustuhan, pinaurog, paburito - Spanish *favorito*
fear – *n.* hadlok, kahadlok, kulba, kakulba
fearful – *kan.* hadlukon

fearless – *kan.* maísog, kahadlukan
feather – *n.* barahibo
February - *n.* Pebrero - Spanish *febrero*
feces – *n.* tái
fee for service – *n.* suhol, bayaran
feed animal – *n., a.* túbong, pagtúbong
feed by hand – *n., a.* timo, pagkamót, pagtimo
feel – *n., a.* abat, pagabat,
feel awful – *n., a.* kanugon, panganugon
feel dizzy – *n., a.* hílo, pagkahílo
feel self-pity – *n., a.* úba, paguba
feel thirst – *n., a.* uhaw, pagkauhaw
feeling of fullness - *n.* luwad, pagkaluwad
feeling snubbed – *kan.* nauba
feet – *n.* siki, tiíl, singkadol
feline excrement – *n.* tarig
fell a tree – *n., a.* pulod, pagpulod
fellow – *n., kan.* kausa, igkasi
fellowmen – *n.* igkasitawo
female – *n.* babayi
female teacher – *n.* manunutdo nga babayi, magturutdo, maistra - Spanish *maestra*
fence - *n.* alad, alasid, kudal
fern plant – *n.* harupay
fertilizer – *n.* gwano - Spanish *guano*
fetch water – *n., a.* alog, pagalog
fever – *n.* hiranat
few – *adj.* gutíay

fickle – *kan.* liwatliwat, ruhaduhaan
fiction – *n.* himohimo
fiesta – *n.* patron, piyesta - Spanish *fiesta*
fifteen – *num.* napulo kag lima, kinse - Spanish *quince*
fifty – *num.* kalimaan, kalíman, singkwenta - Spanish *cincuenta*
fight – *n., a.* away, aragaway, aragway, ato, dulóng, pagaway, pagato, pagdulong, pagaragway
fight by horns – *n., a.* sungay, pagsungay
fight by sticks – *n., a.* balbagay, arnisay, pagbalbagay, pagarnisay
fight by stones – *n., a.* batakay, batuhay, pagbatakay, pagbatuhay
fight over – *n., a.* aragaw, pagaragaw
file – *n., a.* kilkig, pagkilkig
file complaint – *n., a.* kiha, demanda - Spanish *demanda,* pagkiha, pagdemanda
fill in – *n., a.* tákop, pagtákop
fill up – *n., a.* punó, pagpunó
filler word – *kah., a., kan.* kúan, anó, pagkúan, paganó
filter – *n., a.* sára, pagsára
final – *kan.* katapusan, kasagsagan, ultimo - Spanish *ultimo*
finality – *n.* katapusan
finally – *kaa.* manta, tibway
financial difficulty – *n.* gipit
find – *n., a.* agí, biling, hikay, tara, pagagí, pagbiling, paghikay, pagtara

fine – *n., a., kan.* sirot, pino -
Spanish *fino*
fine-toothed comb – *n., a.*
sudlay
finger – *n.* tudlo
fingernail – *n.* kuló
finish – *n., a.* tapos, talwas,
human, sangpot, pagtapos,
pagsangpot, paghuman
finish line – *n.* tubtob,
katapusan, tinubtuban
fire – *n.,* a. kalayo, súnog,
pagsunog
fire ants – *n.* hamtik
firefighter – *n.* bumbero -
Spanish *bombero*
fire from work – *n., a.* tanggal,
pagtanggal
firefly – *n.* bukatkat, aninipot
firewood – *n.* sungó
fireworks – *n.* butubutó, kwitis
firm – *n., kan.* karígon,
madígon
first – *kan.* syahan, una, syapa
fish – *n., a.* isda, kinawilan,
pangisda, pangawil
fish by dynamite – *n., a.* badil,
pagbadil, panmadil
fish hook – *n., a.* kawil,
pangawil, pagkawil
fish pen – *n.* bunúan, bintulan
fish sauce – *n.* patis
fish scale – *n.* hingbis
fish trap – *n.* bintol
fishbone – *n.* bukog
fisherman – *n.* labasiro,
mangingisda, mangirisda,
manaragat
fishing net – *n.* pukot, laya
fishy – *kan.* malangsa,
malángig, mairuisda
fist – *n.* kamaúo, kumo, suntok

fistfight – *n., a.* suntukan,
suntukay, puniti, purupniti
fisticuffs – *n., , a.* suntukan,
suntukay, puniti, purupniti
fit – *n., a., kan.* pagtugma,
pagígo, ígo, igsakto - Spanish
exacto
five – *num.* lima, singko -
Spanish *cinco*
fix – *n., a.* ayad, pagayad
flag – *n., a.* wagayway, bandira
- Spanish *bandera,*
pagwagayway
flagstone – *n.* palanas
flamboyant – *kan.* garbuso
flame – *n.* kalayo
flare – *n.*pamahungpahong
flare up – *n., a.* lurab, suklab,
paglurab, pagsuklab
flare up wound – *n., a.*
rangrang, pagrangrang
flat – *kan.* yapad
flat basket – *n.* nigo
flat fish – *n.* palád
flat nose – *n., kan.* pingak
flat terrain – *n., a.* patag,
pagpatag
flatland – *n.* patag
flatlands – *n.* kapatagan
flatten plant stem – *b., a.*
tultog, palpag, pagtultog,
pagpalpag
flatten dough – *n., a.* pisá,
pagpisa
flatten land – *n., a., kan.*
pánas, patag, pagpánas,
pagpatag
flatulence – *n.* kabag, utot
flatulent – *kan.* mautot
flaw – *n.* sayop
flea market – *n.* tábo
flee – *n., a.* layas, paglayas,
pagpalayas

fleeting – *kan.* dalikyat,
lumalabay
flesh – *n.* unod, kaunuran
flexibility – *n.* lubay,
kalubayan
flexible – *kan.* malubay
flick – *n., a.* kablit, latik, pitik,
pagkablit, paglatik, pagpitik
flight – *n.* kalupad, kalpad
flimsy - *kan.* manipis
fling – *n., a.* waklit, wirik,
pagwaklit, pagwirik
flip backward – *n., a.* baliskad,
pagbaliskad
flip forward – *n., a.* balintong,
pagbalintong
flirt – *n., a.* bílad, pikat,
pagbílad, pagpikat
flirtatious – *kan.* nabilád,
napikat, pitikbirik
float – *n., a.* abayan, lutaw,
paglutaw
flood – *n., a.* baha, lunop,
dugyok, pagbaha, naglunop
floor – *n.* salóg, andana
floor scrub – *n., a.* lampaso,
paglampaso
flotsam – *n.* batang
flounder – *n.* palád
flour noodle – *n.* miki
flow – *n., a.* lanay, awas, ági,
paglanay, pagawas, pagági
flower – *n.* bukad
fluke – *n.* palád
flummox – *n., a.* gupong,
pagkagupong, pagwurok,
nawurok
flush – *n., a.* buhos, pagbuhos
fly – *n., a.* lupad, paglupad,
pagkalupad, pagkalpad
fly – *n.* langaw

fly kite – *n., a.* magugbanog,
pagbanugbanog,
pagmanugbanog
flying – *n ., a.* pagkalupad,
pagkalpad
flying lemur – *n.* kagwang
foam – *n.* bura
fog – *n.* burong
foggy – *kan.* burungon
fold – *n., a.* pilo, tígob,
pagpilo, pagtígob
fold clothes – *n., a.* lukot, pilo,
paglukot, pagpilo
fold umbrella – *n., a., kan.*
tiklob, tikyuob, pagtiklob,
pagtigyuob
folk dance – *n.* sarayawon
follow – *n., a.* bunyog, dúyog,
sugad, sunod, subaybay,
pagsunod, pagbunyog,
pagsugad
follow blindly – *a., kaa.*
sunúdsúnod, pasunúdsúnod
follow hurriedly – *n., a.* apas,
pagapas
follow orders – *n., a.* sugot,
pagsugot
follow the way – *n., a.* susog,
pagsusog
follow-up – *n., a.* subay,
pagsubay, pagsubaybay
follower – *n.* batos,
sumurunod, kabunyog
following day – *kaa.*
kinabuwasan
fond – *kan.* mahilig
fondle – *n., a.* harapihap,
kaham, pagharapihap,
pagkaham
fontanel – *n.* bubon
food – *n.* pagkáon, karáunon,
karánon
food particles – *n.* mumo

fool – *n.* tuyawtuyaw, pusong, lango, tunto
fool around – *n., a.* tuyaw, linurong, pagtuyaw, paglurong
foolish – *kan.* tuyawtuyaw, langulango, tunto, pusong, bungaw
foolish person – *n.* salipungog, lango, luronglurong
foolishness – *n.* kalukuhan, katuyawan, kabungawan, katuntuhan, kalangulanguhan
foot – *n.* tiil, siki, singkadol
foot bridge – *n.* latayan
footprint – *n.* tapak, tamak
for – *kat.* han, san, pan, pára
forbid – *n., a.* pugong, pagpugong,
forbidden – *kan.* igindidiri, pinudngan
forcast – *n., a.* panakna
force – *n., a.* kusóg, pirit , pugos, lugos
forceful – *kan.* kusugan, kusgan
forcefully – *kaa.* husog
forcibly – *kaa.* husogan
forehead – *n.* agtang
foreign – *kan.* dayo, langyaw
foreign body on eye – *n.* puling
foreigner – *n.* langyaw, banyaga, dayuhan
foreman – *n.* kapatas - Spanish *capataz*
forest – *n.* guba, kaguguban, kakahuyan
foretell – *n., a.* panakna
forever – *n., kaa.* dayon, kadayunan, kahangturan, dayuday
forget – *n., a.* limot, pangalimot, paglimot

forgetful – *kan.* limutanon, limtanon
forgive – *n., a.* pasaylo, pagwara
forgotten – *kan.* napará, kalimtan
fork – *n.* tinedor - Mexican *tenedor*
formula – *n.* timpla
fortunate – *kan.* mapalad, maswirte
fortune – *n.* bahandi, karikuhan, swirte - Spanish *suerte*, purtona - Spanish *fortuna*
forty – *num.* kaupatán, kwarenta - Spanish *cuarenta*
forward – *kaa.* uswag
forward incline of boat – *kan.* natuwad
forward somersault – *n.* balintong
foster child – *n.* hinablusan, minangnuan
foul-smelling – *kan.* malangsa
found – *kan.* natadan, nabilngan
founder – *n.* nagtindog
fountain – *n.* burabod, tubód
four – *num.* upat, kwatro - Spanish *cuatro*
fourteen – *num.* katorse - Spanish *catorce*
fraction – *n.* pinit
fracture as bone – *n., a.* piang, bari, pagpiang, pagbari
fragment – *n.* kapinit
fragrance – *n.* hamot
fragrant – *kan.* mahamot
frail – *kan.* lupaypay
frank – *kan.* mahilwason
fraud – *n.* buwa, buáw. kabuwaan, kalimbungan

fraudulent – *kan.* buáw, malimbong, buwáon

fray – *n., a.* badbad, bákad, pagbadbad, pagbákad,

free – *kan.* buhi

freedom – *n.* katalwasan, kataliwasan

frequent – *kan.* masukot

frequently – *kaa.* agsob, kasagaran

fresh (fish) – *kan.* lábas

fresh water – *n.* tábang

Friday – *n.* biyernes - Spanish *viernes*

fried sesame balls – *n.* kabak

fried smashed banana – *n n.* baduya

friend – *n., a.* sangkay, sambi, , kasangkayan

friend trusted – *n.* tinapuran

friendly – *kan.* makisangkay, makiaangayon, makisasangkayon

fright – *n.* hadlok

frighten – *n., a.* hadlok, ugmad, paghadlok, pagugmad

frightened – *adj.* nahadlok, naugmaran

frightful – *kan.* hiribhirib, makahiribhirib, makaharadlok

frigid – *n., kan.* hagkot, mahagkot

frigidity – *n.* kataghuman, katugnawan, kabugnawan

frivolous – *kan.* pasikat

frog – *n.* pakla

from – *n kat.* tìkang

front – *n.* atubangán, printe - Spanish *frente*

frontage – *n.* atubángan

frown – *n., a.* kurisom, simangot, pangurisom

fruit – *n., a.* bunga, prutas - Spanish *fruta*, pagbunga, pamunga

fruit bat – *n.* kulalapnit

fruitless – *kan.* hulang

fry – *n., a.* sanglag, prito - Spanish *frita*, pagprito, pagsanglag

frying pan – *n.* karaha

fulfill – *n., a.* tuman, pagtuman

full – *kan.* punó

full after eating – *kan.* busog

full moon – *n.* kadayaw

full shaven head – *n.* kiskis, pugo

fullness – *n.* hurak, kahurakan

fully bearded – *kan.* bunguton

fully loaded boat – *kan.* tugob

fume – *n.* utbo, bahó - Spanish *vaho*

fun – *kan.* marisyo

funds – *n.* kíta, puhunan

funeral – *n.* lamay, minatay, taguminatay

funeral procession – *n., a.* taguminatay, bunyog, pagtaguminatay, pagbunyog

fungal skin infection – *n.* atipunga, buni, alapap

funny – *kan.* katawanan, pataráwan

fuss – *n., a.* busyo, pagbusyo

fussy – *kan.* aringit, aburido, busyuhon

futile – *kan.* kanugon, kawang

future – *n.* kabubwason

fuzz – *n.* barahibo, bulbol

fuzzy – *n.* barahibuon, bulbulon

134

G:g

gain – *n.* gahin, ganansya - Spanish *ganancia*
gall bladder – *n.* apdo
gallivant – *n., a.* lakwatsa, sudoysudoy, ligoyligoy, paglakwatsa, paligoylogoy
galvanized roofing – *n.* sim
gamble – *n., a.* pusta, sugal, huygo, huygo - Spanish *juego*
gambler – *n.* sugarol, hugador - Spanish *jugador*
gang – *n., a.* barkada
gangster – *n.* kabarkada
gap – *n.* látang
garbage – *n.* sighot, siot, hugaw, basura - Spanish *basura*
garbage bin – *n.* basurahan
garbled voice – *kan.* basag
garden – *n.* tanaman, katanuman, katanman
gargle – *n., a.* limugmog, paglimugmog
garlic – *n.* lasuna, ahos - Spanish *ajo*
garlic-flavored fried rice – *n.* sanglag, sinanglag
garment – *n.* dugnit, súlot
garrulous – *kan.* mayakan, kinasabang, mayakimbot
gasoline – *n.* gasolina - Spanish *gasolina*
gather – *n., a.* tirok, pundok, pagtirok, pagpundok
gather around table – *n., a.* hampang, pagharampang
gather crowd – *n., a.* tipon, tirok, pundok, pagtitirok, pagpurundok, pagtiripon
gathering – *n.* harampang, kadamó, katitirok, tipuntipon

gay – *n.* bayot, babayínon
gaze – *n., a.* kulaw, pagkulaw
gecko – *n.* tiki, tuko, haló
gelatin – *n.* gulaman
generic – *kan.* waraywaray
generous –*kan.* mahatagon
genitalia – *n.* atubangán, ikinatawo, buras
genuflect – *n., a.* luhod, pagluhod
genuine – *kan.* uray
geoduck clam - *n.* tiwil
germ – *n.* kagaw, mikrubyo
gestating swine - *n.* anáy
get – *n., a.* kuha, pagkuha
get attention – *n., a.* bílad, pagbílad
get bored – *n., a., kan.* uyam, sumo, nauuyam, sinusumhan
get colds – *n., a.* sipon, sinisipon
get dirty – *n., a.* hugáw, paghugáw
get dizzy – *n., a.* lípong, pagkalípong
get mad – *n., a.* budlay, pagkabudlay
get married – *n., a.* asawa, pagasawa, pangasawa
get up – *n., a.* buhát, bangon, pagbuhát
get upset – *n. a.* init, kasina, pagkataranta
gettogether – *n.* harampang, kirigta hiruhimangraw, pagkatitirok, tipuntipon
ghost – *n.* kalag, murto - Portuguese *morto*
giant – *n.* kapri, higante - Spanish *gigante*
gift – *n.* pahalipay, regalo - Spanish *regalo*
giggle – *n., a.* piyait, pagpiyait

ginger – *n.* lúya
girl – *n.* oday
girlfriend – *n.* uyab
give – *n., a.* hatag, duhol
give a name – *n., a.* bunyag, pagbunyag
give birth – *n., a.* anak, paganak, nanganak
give excuses – *n., a.* baribad, pamaribad
give gift – *n., a.* hatag, pasko, pamasko, pagpamasko
give thanks – *n., a.* salamat, pasalamat, pagpasalamat
give up priority to another – *n., a.* paumaya, pagpaumaya
gizzard – *n.* batikulon
glance – *n., a.* siplat, pagsiplat
glans penis – *n.* uló
glare – *n., kan.* silaw, masilaw
glass – *n.* salaming
glass jar – *n.* garapon
glitter – *n., a.* inggat, ranggat, pagranggat
glittering – *kan.* mainggat
glorious – *kan.* himaya
glory – *n.* kahimayaan
glue – *n., a.* papilit, pilit, dikit, dukot, pagpapilit
glutinous rice – *n.* pilit
gluts – *n.* pugtot
gluttony – *n.* kabusugan
gnarly – *kan.* balikawot, buhulbuhol
gnat – *n.* tagnok
gnawing pain – *n.* ngutngot
gnawingly painful – *kan.* mangutngot
go – *n., a.* kadto, pangadto, pagkadto, pagsingadto
goad – *n., a.* surugsurog, pagsurugsurog
goat – *n.* kanding

go against – *n., a.* apras, pagapras
go closer – *n., a.* daraon, harani, pagdaraon, pagharani
goggles – *n.* antipara - Spanish *anteparras*
go incognito – *n., a.* tagutago, pagtagutago
go outside – *n., a.* gawas
go through – *n., a.* lapos
go to – *n., a.* ngadto, pagkadto
go under – *n., a.* sirung, pagsirung, pagpasirung
go up – *n., a.* saka, pagsaka, pagsaklang
God – *n.* Diyos - Spanish *Dios*
God forbid! – *kah.* simbako!
godbrother – *n.* ugto nga lalaki
godchild – *n.* pinanganak, inaanak
godfather – *n.* padrino - Spanish *padrino*
godmother – *n.* madrina - Spanish *madrina*
godsister – *n.* ugto nga babayi
gold – *n.* bulawan
gold-coated tooth – *n.* bansil
golden – *kan.* bulawanon
good – *kan.* maupay
good intention – *kah.* kalaw
goodbye – *n., a., kah.* panamilit, pagbabay, babay!
goodness – *n.* upay, kaupayan
goods – *n.* baligya, kumpra
goose – *n.* gangsa - Spanish *ganso*
goose bumps – *n.* marihayaw
Gosh! – *kah.* harumamay, palá
gossip – *n., a.,* libak, hurobhurob, huribhurib, tsismis – Spanish *chisme*, paglibak, pagtsismis

gossipy – *kan.* malibak, tsismoso/a - Spanish *chismoso/a*

gourd – *n.* karubasa - Spanish *calabaza*

government – *n.* gubyerno - Spanish *gobierno*

government official – *n.* opisyal - English *official*

grab – *n.,* a. agaw, aragaw, pagagaw

graceful – *kan.* mahinhin, mahiyumhiyom, garbuso - Spanish *garboso*

gracefulness – *n.* garbo - Spanish *garbo*

gracious – *kan.* baráan

grade – *n.* grado - Spanish *grado*

grain – *n.* grano - Spanish *grano*

grandchild – *n.* apo, (*pl*) kaapuhan

grandfather – *n.* lolo

grandmother – *n.* lola

grandparent – *n.* apoy, (*pl*) kaapuyan

grant – *n., a.* hatag, paghatag

grapefruit – *n.* suha, aslom

grapes – *n.* ubas - Spanish *uva*

grasp – *n., a.* kapot, kuhida- Spanish *cogida*

grass – *n.* banwa

grass cuttings – *n.* dinalos, sighot, siot

grasshopper – *n.* apan

grate coconut – *n., a.* kinagod, kagod

gratitude – *n.* salamat

grave – *kan.* malala, grabe - Spanish *grave*

grave – *n.* lubungan, lubnganan

gravel – *n.* bato, graba - Spanish *grava*

graveyard – *n.* pungtod, lubungan, lubnganan

gray – *n., kan.* abó, agbo, maabo

gray hair – *n., kan.* uban, ubanon

grayish – *kan.* maabo

grease – *n.* lana, grasa - Spanish *grasa*

greasy – *kan.* madulas

great – *kan.* makarit

greatness – *n.* karit, kakaritan

greed – *n.* imot, kahalutan, kalamutan, kahangulan

greedy – *kan.* awaanon, hakog, halot, lamot, maimot, hangol

greedy in eating – *kan.* makaon, maharaw

green – *n., kan.* luhaw, lunghaw, birde - Spanish *verde*

green onion – *n.* prisya

green pepper – *n.* hulabtog

greenish – *kan.* mabirde

greeting – *n., a.* kumusta - Spanish *como esta,* pangumusta

grievance - *n.* uba, hinanakit, atraso, agrabyado, Spanish *agraviar*

grill – *n., a.* sugba, sugbaan

grimace – *n., a.* hingit, paghingit

grin – *n., a.* ngisi, ngirit, pagngisi, pagngirit

grind – *n., a.* giling, garing, paggiling, paggaring

grinder – *n.* gilingan, garingan

grind grain in stone mill – *n., a.* garing, paggaring

grinning – *n.* nagngingirisi

gritty – *kan.* masapara,
barason,matagudtod as in rice
groin – *n.* hita
groom – *n., a.* buyóng,
pagbuyóng
gross – *n. kan.* ngirhat,
mangirhat, makangingirhat
ground floor – *n.* sirung
group – *n.* kampi, grupo –
Spanish *grupo*
grouper – *n.* tingag
grow as person – *n., a.* tubó,
pagtubó
grow as plant – *n., a.* túbo,
pagtúbo, pagturók
grow roots – *n., a.* gamot,
paggamot, panggamot
growing – *kan.* nadako,
dumako, tumubo
growl – *n., a.* ngurudo,
pagngurudo
gruesome – *kan.* ngirhat,
makangingirhat
grumble – *n., a.* ngurudo,
ngurutob, alburoto - Spanish
alboroto
guard – *n., a.* bantay, mangno,
gwardya - Spanish *guardia*,
pagbantay, pagmangno,
paggwardya
guardian – *n.* mangno,
magmarangno, gwardyan -
Spanish *guardian*
guess – *n., a.* tigó, pagtigo
guessing game – *n.* tigutigo,
tigutigúay
guest – *n.* dayo, dayuhan,
bisita - Spanish *visitor*
guest room – *n.* ruwang, sála
guide – *n., a.* tigaman,
pantigaman, pagtigaman
guide animal – *n., a.* tugway,
pagtugway

guidelines – *n.* surundanon
guilt – *n., a.* basol, pagbasol
guitar – *n., a.* sista, gitara -
Spanish *guitarra*
gullible – *n., kan.* uwat,
uruwaton, matuoron
gum – *n.* buyó
gumamela – *n.* takuranga
gunbattle – *n.* púpsilay,
purupsilay
gunfight – *n., a.* pusilay,
púpsilay, pagpusilay,
pagpúpsilay
gurgling sound – *n., kan.*
karalkaral, makaralkaral
gusty – *kan.* madlos
gutter – *n.* saruyong

H:h

habit – *n.* batasan
habitual – *kan.* sabid kasabid,
hiara
hack with cleaver – *n., a.*
bagtak, pagbagtak
hack with cutlass – *n., a.*
tigbas, pagtigbas
hair – *n.* buhok
hair stylist – *n.* paraarot,
parapangarot
hair whorl – *n.* alimpupuro
haircut – *n., a.* arót, pagarot,
pagpaarot
hairless part of scalp – *n.*
pahak, kapahakan
hairy – *kan.* buhukon,
barangason
half – *n., a.* tunga, pagtunga,
katunga
half-breed – *n.* mestiso -
Spanish *mestizo*
half-naked – *kan.* lubas

halibut – *n.* palád
hall – *n.* ruwang
ham – *n.* hamon - Spanish *jamon*
hammer – *n., a.* pukpok, martilyo - Spanish *martillo*, pagpukpok, pagmartilyo
hammock – *n., a.* duyan, pagduyan
hand – *n.* kamot
hand washing clothes – *n., a.* laba, kurukuso, paglaba, pangurukuso
handcuff – *n., a.* pusas - Spanish *esposas*
handful – *n., kan.* harop, kumo
handgun – *n.* pusil
handicap – *n.* piáy
handkerchief – *n.* panyolito - Spanish *pañuelo*
hands full – *kan.* kagaramo
handsome – *kan.* gwapo - Spanish *guapo*
hang – *n. a.* bitay, sablay, patunton, pagbitay, pagsablay
hang as suicide – *n., a.* hikog, tigok, bitay, paghikog, pagtigok, pagbitay
hang clothes – *n., a.* palaypay, pinalaypay, pagpalaypay, pamalaypay
hang on – *n., a.* kábit, kapyot, pagkábit, pagkapyot
hang over shoulder – *n., a.* saklay, pagsaklay
haphazard – *kan.* amasang
haphazardly – *kaa.* inamasang, gusakgusak, gurakgusak
happen – *n., a.* hitabó, hinabó, paghitabó, panhinabó, pagpapas
happenings – *n.* nahitatabó, nahihinabó, karigudigo

happiness – *n.* lipay, kalipayan
happy – *kan.* malipay, makalilipay, malipayon
harbor hatred – *n., a.* pungot, pagkapungot
harboring bad feelings – *kan.* madumot
hard – *kan.* matíga, madígo, marígon, makuri
hard chew – *kan.* matignos
hard stick – *n.* balbag
hard touch – *kan.* matíga
hard wood – *n.* narra, *Pterocarpus species*
hard word – *n.* paniguro, paningkamot
hardly – *kaa.* inarikawot, apinas - Spanish *apenas*
hardness – *n.* tiga, kadígon
hardship – *n.* kakurian
harelip – *n.* bungí
harm – *n., a.* hibang piruwisyo – Spanish *perjuicio*, paghibang
harmonica – *n.* silindron
harmonize – *n., a.* angay, pagangay, pagpaangay
harmony – *n.* kaangay, naangay
harpoon – *n.* bangkaw
harrass – *n., a.* tarhog, pagtarhog, pagtiupay
harrassment – *n.* panarhog
harvest rice – *n., a.* barí, pagbarí
harvest time for rice – *n.* katbari
hat – *n.* kalo
hateful – *kan.* ngalsanon, pungtanon
hatred – *n.* kangaralson, kabudlay, kainiton, kairiniton, kangalason, kangaralson, kapungot

hatred – *n.* sina, kasinahon
haul down – *n., a.* ariya -
Spanish *arriar*, pagariya
have – *a.* may, mayada
have difficulty – *n., a.* kuri,
pagkuri
hawk – *n.* banog
hazelnut – *n.* pili
he – *han.* hiya, siya
head – *n.* úlo
head scarf – *n.* panyo
headdress – *n.* pudong
headline news – *n.*
larayulohan
heal – *n., a.* upay
healer – *n.* tambalan
hear – *n., a.* báti, dungog,
pagbáti, pagdungog, památi,
hearing – *n.* pandungog,
pagbáti
heart – *n.* kasingkasing,
kurason - Spanish *corazon*
heartbeat – *n., a.* kutob, pitig,
putok, pagkutob
heartfelt – *kan., kaa.*
kinasingkasing, húlos
heaven – *n.* langit
heavenly – *kan.* langitnon
heavens – *n.* kalangitan
heavy – *kan.* mabúgat
heavy breathing – *kan.*
nahangos
heel – *n.* tikod
height – *n.* taas, kahataas,
tindog
heir – *n.* tinuínan
heirloom – *n.* tinipigan,
hinumduman
helm – *n.* timon
helmsman – *n.* timonil
help – *n., a.* tabang, tambulig,
bulig, ayuda - Spanish *ayuda,*
pagtabang, pagbulig, pagayuda

helper – *n.* kabulig, surugúon
helpful – *kan.* mabuligon
helpless – *kan.* puliki,
sagipo
hem – *n.* sidsid
hemline – *n.* sidsid
hemorrhoid – *n.* almuranas
hemp – *n.* abaka
hen – *n.* ugáng
henchman – *n.* batos,
tawutawo, tawuhan
her – *han.* iya
herbal medicine – *n.* arbularyo
- Spanish *herbolario*
herbalist – *n.* arbularyo
here – *kat., kaa.* nganhi, ngadi,
didi, dinhi, aadi
heritage – *n.* panurundon
heron – *n.* atalabong
herring fish – *n.* tamban
hesitant – *kan.* alangalang
hesitate – *n., a.* ruhaduha,
alangalang, duhaduha,
kahulop, pagalangalang,
pagruhaduha, pagkahulop,
pagduhaduha,
hibiscus – *n.* takuranga,
gumamela *Hibiscus rosa–
sinensis*
hiccup – *n., a.* siklo
pagsiklo
hidden – *kan.* tagó
hide – *n., a.* himos, hipos,
tágo, paghimos, paghipos,
pagtago
hide and seek – *n.* tigbutigbuay
hide-out – *n.* taguan, taraguan
high – *kan.* hitaas, hataas
high blood pressure – *n.* alta
presyon
high tide – *n.* táob
high-pitched – *n., kan.* ngidlis,
mangidlis, tipli

high-pitched metallic sound –
n. tagingting
high-pitched piercing sound –
n., a. piyait, napiyait, pagpiyait
highness – *kan.* harangdon
highway – *n.* agían, aragian,
haywe – English *highway*
hike – *n., a.* baktas, pagbaktas
hilarious – *kan.* katawanan
hill – *n.* tayod
hilly – *kan.* bukidbukid
hinder – *n., a., kan.* ulang,
sangko, pagulang, pagsangko
hindrance – *n.* sagabal,
makauulang, sangkúan,
hindsight – *n., a.* pustrira -
Spanish *postrero*
hinge – *n.* bisagra - Spanish
bisagra
hinterlands – *n.* hurón
hinterlands – *n.* kagugubaan,
kagugúban
hinterlands – *n.* kagurangan
hips – *n.* hita, pígi
hirsute – *kan.* barangason
his – *han.* iya
history – *n.* kasumatan,
kasumatan
hit – *n., a.* bunggo, puag,
gulpi, pagbunggo, paguag
hit a snag – *n., a.* sangit,
pagsangit
hit a target – *n., a.* tama, igo,
pagtama, pagigo
hit head with knuckle – *n., a.*
kidni, dagol, pagkidni,
pagdagol
hit head with stone or object –
n., a. lagtak, paglagtak
hit with fist – *n., a.* bunal,
pusak, pagbunal, pagpusak
hit with stick or club – *n., a.*
balbag, pagbalbag

hoarse – *n., kan.* pagaw, paás,
basag
hobby – *n.* kalingawan
hog feed – *n.* tubóng
hold – *n., a.* kapot, bitbit,
pagkapot, pagbibit
hold around waist – *n., a.*
háwak, pagháwak
hold breath – *n.,a.* utók,
pagutók
hold hands – *n., a.* agbay,
pagagbay
hold over shoulder – *n., a.*
sagubay, sagbay, pagsagubay,
pagsagbay
hole – *n.* guhó, luho, buhó
hole in the ground – *n.* buhó
hollow tube drum – *n.*
karatong
holy – *kan.* baráan, langitnon
holy mass – *n.* misa - Spanish
misa
home – *n.* balay, panimalay
home care – *n.* atimangno
homosexual – *n., kan.* bayot,
babayínon, palakínon, tumboy
– English *tomboy*
hone sharp tool – *n., a.* báid,
pagbáid
honest – *kan.* tangkod, buotan,
tuptop
honey – *n.* dugos
honk – *n., a.* putpot, pagputpot
honor – *n., a.* dungog,
pagpasidungog
honor – *n.* dungog
honorable – *kan.* tinahod
dungganan, dunguganan,
harangdon
honorific for rich woman – *n.*
donya - Spanish *doña*
honorific for an older woman –
n. mana

honorific for father of a
godchild – *n.* padí, parí
honorific for majesty – *kan.*
harangdon
honorific for mother of a
godchild – *n.* madi, mari
honorific for older man – *n.*
mano
honorific for Roman Catholic
nun – *n.* madre - Spanish
madre
honorific for Roman Catholic
priest – *n.* padre - Spanish
padre
honorific for the deceased
person – *kan.* hat
honorofic for rich man - *n.*
don - Spanish *don*
hoofs – *n.* pakdol
hook – *n.* kawil
hook – *a.* sabit, sangit,
pagsabit, pagsangit
hook, line and sinker – *n.*
kawil
hooked – *kan.* balikawot,
nasangit
hop – *n., a.* piktaw, pagpiktaw
hope – *n., a.* láom, paglaom
hopefully – *kaa.* kunta, unta
hopscotch – *n.* patintiro
horn – *n., a.* sungay,
pagsungay
hornbill – *n.* kalaw,
Penelopides samarensis
hornet – *n.* hamumuong
horny – *kan.* uragon, uuragon,
himamagon
horrendous – *kan.*
makaharadlok, makarimadima
horrible – *kan.* makarimadima
horse – *n.* kabayo - Spanish
caballo

horseback ride – *n., a.*
pangabayo, pagkabayo
horse drawn carriage - *n.*
tartanilya
hospitable – *kan.*
maatamanon, maaruga
hospital – *n.* ospital - English
hospital
hospitality – *n., a.* ataman,
pagataman
hot – *kan.* mapaso, masirak,
madagaang
hot and humid – *kan.*
maalinsuob
hour – *n.* oras
house – *n.* balay
house clothes – *n., a.* timasa,
pagtimasa
house lizard – *n.* taguto, tiki,
túko, tabili
house stilt – *n.* tukó, harigi
household – *n.* panimalay,
tagbalay
housemaid – *n.* binatá,
suruguon
how – *kaa.* unanhon, unanon
how much – *kaa.* tagpira
human body – *n.* lawas,
kalawasan
human race – *n.* lahi
humble – *kan.* ubsanon,
mapinaubusanon,
mapinaubsanon, kinablas,
kablasanon
humid – *kan.* maalinsuob,
maalisngaw
humidity – *n.* alinsuob, tuob
humiliate – *n ., a.* tamay,
pagtamay
humility – *n.* pinaubsanon,
kamapinaubsanon
hump – *n., a.* babá, pagbabá
hunch – *n.* kutob

hunchback – *n.* buktot
hundred – *num.* gatós, syin -
Spanish cien(to)
hunger – *n.* gútom, kagutom,
katgutom
hungry – *n kan.* magutom,
gutóm, ginugutom
hunt – *n., a.* hanting, pamusil,
paghanting
hunting – *n.* hanting - English
hunting
hunting knife – *n.* hanting
hurl – *n., a.* lábay, waklit,
pilak, paglábay, pagwaklit,
pagpilak
hurriedly – *kaa.* dalían,
kadagmitan, madali, apurado
hurry – *n., a.* dalí, dagmit,
apura - Spanish apurar,
pagdalí, pagdagmit, pagapura
husband – *n.* bana
husband and wife – *n.*
magasáwa, magtiayon
husk coconut – *n., a.* bunót,
pagbunót
husk rice – *n., a.* bayó,
pagbayó
husked rice – *n.* bugas
hut – *n.* payag
hyperactive – *kan.* maabtik,
makiwa
hyperactivity – *n.* kaabtik,
kamakiwá
hyperbole – *kah.* harumamay
hypertension – *n.* alta presyon
- Spanish *alta presion*
hypoglycemia – *n., kan.*
pasma, pasmado, kagutom

I:i

I – *han.* ako, ko
ice – *n.* yilo - Spanish *hielo*
ice cream – *n.* ayskrim -
American *ice cream*
ice cream cone – *n.* apa
ID card – *n.* sidula
idiot – *kan.* bungaw, paog,
paugpaog
idle talk – *n.* yawyaw,
yakimbot, pagkinasabang
if – *s.* kun, pag
ignite – *n., a.* dagkot, surit,
pagdagkot, pagsurit
ill-mannered – *kan.* bastos,
waray batasan
illegal gambling – *n.* masyaw
illegal numbers game – *n.*
huweteng
illness – *n.* sakit
image – *n.* ladawan
imagination – *n.* panhunahuna
imitate – *n., a.* subad, sugad,
susog, sunod, pagsubad,
pagsugad, pagsusog, pagsunod
imitating – *kan.* masunod,
masubad
immediately – *kaa.* dalían,
kadagmitan, dalikyat,
immobilize – *n., a.* gapos,
paggapos
immoral – *kan.* salbahi
impassive – *adj.* malimbasog
impatient – *kan.* mabudlay,
budlayon
imperative – *adj.* suguon,
kasuguan
impetuous – *kan.* aringit,
putong, tarantado, makuti,
sumpungon, budlayon
impious – *kan.* irihis

implicate – *n., a.* sangkot,
pagsangkot
important – *kan.*
mahinungdanon
impoverished – *kan.* kablas,
kabos, pubre - Spanish *pobre*
improve – *n., a.* upay,
pagupay, pagpaupay,
pagpakaupay
impudence – *n.* kagaragaraan
impudent – *kan.* garagaraan
in – *kat.* ha, sa, tungod
inadequate – *kan.* kulang,
inarikawot
in accordance with – *s.*
mahitungod
in continuation of – *s.*
kadugtong
in front of – *kat.* atúbang,
atúbangan
in name only – *kan.* hangaran,
kangaranngaran
in order to – *s.* agod, basi
in place of – *s.* imbis
in regards to – *s.* bahin
in the middle of – *kat.* butnga
in the name of – *kat.* hangaran
in what manner or way – *kaa.*
unanhon, unanon
inadequate – *kan.* kulang,
ministiblis, inarikawot
inarticulate – *kan.* yano,
hinurunanon
incantation – *n.* orasyon,
satamsatam, yakyak
incarnate – *n., a.* katawo,
pagkatawo
incentive – *n., a.* aghat,
pagaghat
incinerate – *n., a., kan.* ugtang,
pagugtang, naugtang
incise – *n., a.* tudlis, pagtudlis

inclination- *n.* hilig,
bakilid(side),bangad(backward)
, tuwad(forward)
inclined – *kan.* mahilig, maki,
bakilid(side), nabangad
(backward), natuwad (forward)
include – *n., a.* sakop, upod,
pagsakop, pagupod
including – *s.* pati, kaupod,
kasakop
income – *n., a.* kíta, kuhida,
hiagi
incomplete – *kan.* sáphid,
kulang
increasing quantity – *kan.*
nadamo
increasing size – *kan.* nadako
increasingly – *kaa.* nadugang,
natikadako, natikadamo
incredibly – *kaa.* harumamay
incredulous – *kah.* balitaw,
balitgad
indecision – *n.* kahulop,
ruhaduha, duhaduha
indecisive – *kan.* alangalang,
ruhaduhaan, hulpanon
Indian national – *n.* Bombay
indifference – *kah.* saho
indigo – *n.* tagom
indulge – *n., a.* ungay,
pagungay
industrious – *kan.* maabtik,
maduruto, makugi, kugihan
inedible crab – *n.* kagang,
kayamas
inept – *kan.* tagdal
inexpensive – *kan.* barato -
Spanish *barato*
infect somebody – *n., a.* tapón,
pagtapón
inferior – *kan.* lupig
infertile – *kan.* baog, hulang

infest with flies – *n a., kan.*
langaw, langawon
infest with termites – *a., kan.*
ánay, anayon
infinitive – *n.* pag + (verb)
inflate – *n., a.* lubo, paglubo,
pagpalubo
inflated ego – *kan.* suplada -
Spanish *soflado*
inflect wound on someone –
n., a. samad, pagsamad
influenced – *kan.* padára
inform – *n., a.* pahibaro,
pasabot, sayod, sumat,
pagpahibaro, pagpasabot,
panginsayod, pagsumat,
information – *n.* sumat,
kasayuran, pasabot
informer – *n.* sayod
ingrate – *n.* bungalos
inguinal fold – *n.* singit
inguinal hernia – *n.* luslos
inherit – *n., a.* supo, pagsupo,
panunod
inheritance – *n.* supo,
tagubilin, panurundon
inherited – *kan.* sumupo,
sinupuan, sinundan
initiative – *n.* limbasog,
panlimbasog
inject – *n., a.* túrok, pagtúrok,
pagpatúrok
injure – *n., a.* hibang,
karimalaso, pagkahibang
injury – *n.* kahibang, rimalaso
ink – *n.* tinta - Spanish *tinta*
inland – *kaa.* iraya, suba
inner thigh – *n.* hita
innovation – *n.* tinuha
inquire – *n., a.* pakiana,
pagpakiana
insane - *kan.* tuyawtuyaw
insanity - *n.* kato

incense – *n.* dapadapo,
sahumeryo – Spanish
sahumerio
insensitive – *kan.* mailob
insert – *n., a.* suksok,
pagsuksok
inside – *kat.* súlod, sakob
inside out – *kan.* balikad
insight – *n.* kinaadman
insignificant – *kan.* mutukoy,
pirapira
insistence – *n.* saritsarit,
paningkamot
insolence – *n.* kagaragara
insolent – *kan.* garagaraan
inspect – *n., a.* buslong, kita,
kulaw, pagbuslong, pagkulaw,
pagkita
installment – *n.* hulogan
instance – *n.* kamutangan,
kaso - Spanish *caso*
instead – *kaa.* imbis,
lugod
instruction – *n.* tutdo,
tagubilin, surundon
instructor – *n.* magturutdo,
manunutdo
insufficiency – *n.* kakulangan
insult – *n., a., kan.* álo,
pakaálo, insulto - Spanish
insultar, agrabyado - Spanish
agraviado
insurance – *n.* panigurado
integrate – *n., a.* pagsakop,
pagbuó
intelligence – *n.* hibaro,
kahibaro, kinaadman,
kabaltukan, kaabtikan
intelligent – *kan.* baltok,
maaram, maabtik
intensely – *kaa.* duro
intention – *n.* dupot

interconnected – *kan.* durugtong, katinkatin, surumpay
interest – *n.* gusto, dupot, karuyag, kagustuhan
interference – *n.* labot, panginlabot
interior – *n.* sakob
internal ear infection – *n.* búog, buugon
interrogative exclamatory word – *kaa.* ba
interrupt – *n., a.* baráw, supla, pagbaráw, pagsupla
interrupt convensation – *n., a.* sagbang, pagsagbang
interrupted – *kan.* utudutod
intertwined – *kan.* linubid
interval – *n.* látang
intervene – *n., a.* labót, paglabót, panginlabot
interwoven straw – *n.* batulang, alat, baskit – English *basket*
intestines – *n.* tinái
intimate – *n., a.* sambi, pakisambi
intimidate – *n., a.* tarhog, pagtarhog, pagpugos, paglugos
intimidation – *n.* tarhog, panarhog
intrepid – *kan.* maísog, matigás, maungod
intrigue – *n.* indigan, intriga - Spanish *intrigar*
introduce – *n., a.* pakilala, intrigá, pagpakilala, pagintrigá
introspection – *n.* pamalandong
introvert – *kan.* maalin
intrude – *n., a.* sugod, pagsugod
intuition – *n.* kitakita

invade – *n., a.* lusob, sugod, paglusob, pagsugod
invader – *n.* mananakop
invented falsehood – *n., a.* himohimo, tahaptahap, paghimhimo, pagtahaptahap
invention – *n.* tuha, tinuha, tuhatuha
inventive – *n.* matinguhaon
inverse – *kan.* balikad
invert – *n., a.* balikad, tuwad, pagbalikad, pagtuwad
inverted *kan.* tuwad
investigate – *n., a.* suri, usisa, imbistiga - Spanish *investigar*, pagsuri, pagusisa, pagimbistga
investigative – *kan.* mabusisi, mausisa
invincible – *kan.* mabaskog, maísog, matigás
invistigate – *n., a.* usisa, pagusisa
invitation – *n.* pagabiabi, imbitasyon - Spanish *invitacion*
invite – *n., a.* abiabi, imbitar - Spanish *invitar*, pagabiabi, pangimbitar
involve – *n., a., kan.* labót, ungay, awat, gagad, paglabot, paggagad, pagawat, pagungay
involvement – *n.* panginlabot, pagungay, pakaawat, paggagad
iron – *n.* puthaw, yirro - - Spanish *hierro*
iron clothes – *n., a.* plantsa - Spanish *plancha*, pagplantsa
irreverent – *kan.* irihis
irritable – *kan.* ngalsanon, aringit, sumpungon, inít, pungtanon

irritate – *n., a.,* unggit,
pagunggit
irritating – *kan.* masawi
makangangalas, malungot,
makangaralas, makairinit,
makauurit, masamok, masabal
irritating pain – *kan.* kirot,
mahapdos
irritating sound – *kan.*
mangulinguli
island – *n.* puró, isla - Spanish
isla
it – *han.* hiya, siya
itchiness – *n.* katol, girhang,
ngarangara
itchy – *kan.* makatol,
magirhang, mangarangara
its – *han.* iya

J:j

jab – *n., a.* bundol, pagbundol
jail – *n., a.* priso, prisuhan
January – *n.* Inero - Spanish
enero
jaundice – *n.* darag
jaws – *n.* ngawingawi
jealous – *kan.* maabugho,
náawa
jealousy – *n., a.* abugho,
kaawa, pagkaawa,
pangabugho
jeans – *n.* maong
jeep, jeepney – *n.* dyep -
American *jeep*
JesusMaryJoseph – *kah.*
Susmariyosep!
jewelry – *n.* alahas
job – *n.* buruhaton
join – *n., a.* duyog. pagduyog

join conversation – *n., a.*
hampang, himangraw,
paghampang, paghimangraw
joints – *n n.* kaluluthan
joke – *n., a.* patawa, intrimis,
swirte - Spanish *suerte,*
pagpataw, pagintrimis,
pagswirte
joker – *kan.* maswirte,
kumidyante - Spanish
comediante, dyoker –
American *joker*
journey – *n.* sakayón, lakaton,
biyahe -Spanish *viaje,* nabigar
- Spanish *navigar*
joy – *n.* lipay, kalipayan
judge – *n., a.* hukom, huwes -
Spanish *juez*
jug – *n.* tibod
July – *n.* Hulyo - Spanish *julio*
jumble – *n., a., kan.*
karambula, pagkarambula
jump – *n., a.* lukso, pitik,
ambak, paglukso, pagpitik,
pagambak
June – *n.* Hunyo - Spanish
junio
just – *kaa.* daw
justice – *n.* hukom
justification – *n.*
pangatadungan

K:k

kalachuchi flower – *n.*
kalatsutsi
kaleidoscope – *n., kan.*
dirudilain, durudilain,
magkadirudilain, sarusarakot
kamias – *n.* íba
karma – *n.* gaba

keel — *n.* kilya - Spanish *quilla*
keep – *n., a.* himos, hipos, paghimos, paghipos
keep quiet – *n., a.* hilom, paghilom
keep still – *n., a.* puruko, pagpuruko
keep upright – *n. a.* tiso, tigdong, tindog, pagtiso, pagtigdong, pagtindog
keepsake – *n.* hinumduman, rekwerdo- Spanish *recuerdo*
kerosene – *n.* pitrolyo - Spanish *petroleo*
kettle — *n.* takuri, kaldero - Spanish *caldera*
key – *n.* yabe
keyboard – *n.* kibord - American *keyboard*
kick – *n., a.* banyak, sikad, sipa, tindak
kick ball – *n.* sipa
kidnap – *n., a.* tabag, buyong, pagtabag, pagbuyóng
kill – *n., a.* pátay, pagpátay
kill oneself – *n., a.* unay, pakamatay, pagunay, pagpakamatay
king – *n.* hadi
kingdom – *n.* ginhadían, kahadian
kingfish – *n.* tangigi
kiss – *n., a.* harok, pagharok
kitchen – *n.* lutúan, kusina - Spanish *cocina*
kite – *n.* banugbanog, manugbanog
kitten – *n.* iring, misay
knee – *n.* tuhod
kneel – *n., a.* luhod, pagluhod
knife – *n.* pisaw, kutsilyo - Spanish *cuchillo*

knock – *n., a.* tuktok, pagtuktok
knock head with knuckles – *n., a.* dagol, kidni, pagdagol, pagkidni
knot – *n.* buhol
knotty – *kan.* buhulbuhol
know – *n., a.* hibaro, arám, sabot, paghibaro, pagarám, pagsabót
know-how – *n.* kaaráman, kinaádman
knowing – *kan.* kamaaram
knowledge – *n.* áram, hibaro, kinaádman, kaaráman, kaádman, sabót
knowledgeable – *kan.* kamaaram, maaram
knucklehead – *kan.* sarawayon

L:l

laborer – *n.* hurnal, trabahador - Spanish *trabajador,* obriro – Spanish *obrero*
lack – *n., a.* kakulangan, puwaki, pagkulang
lacking – *kan.* kulang, dugangan, durugangan, ubúsúbos, puwaki
ladle – *n.* luwag, sandok
lady – *n.* daraga
lagoon – *n.* liro, sapa, danaw
lake – *n.* sapa, danaw, lawak
lamp – *n.* suga, lampara - Spanish *lampara*
land – *n.* tuna
land a boat – *n., a.* duong, pagduong

land flight – *n. a.* hugdon, haron, paghugdon, pagharon
land ownership – *n.* katunaan
land tenant – *n.* saop, parauma, paraguma
land turtle – *n.* baó, hangag
landing place – *n.* duungan, duruungan, pantalan, landingan - English *landing*
language – *n.* yinaknan, kayakan, purulungan, pinulungan, lingguahi - Spanish *lenguaje*
lantern – *n.* suga, parol - Spanish *farol*
laptop – *n.* laptap - American *laptop*
lard – *n.* tambok, mantika - Spanish *manteca*
large – *kan.* dako, dadakuro
large anchovy – *n.* tuwakang
large basket – *n.* batulang
large bat – *n.* kabog
large bell – *n.* kampana
large clay jar – *n.* tadyaw
large house lizard – *n.* tiki, túko
large jellyfish – *n.* bukya
large straw bag – *n.* bayong
larva, butterfly – *n.* basol
larva, mosquito – *n.* wutok
larynx – *n.* bútol
lascivious – *kan.* uragon
last – *kan.* pukis, urhi, ultimo – Spanish *ultimo*
last night – *n.* kagábi
late – *kan.* urhi, atrasado - Spanish *atrasado*
late afternoon – *n.* kakurulpon
lately – *kaa.* unina, niyan
later – *kaa.* kataliwas, niruniyan, uruunina
lather – *n., a.* bura

laugh – *n., a.* tawa, pagtawa, pagkatatawa
laugh with snorting sound – *n., a.* hagikhik, hingas, panhagikhik
laughable – *kan.* pataráwan
laughter – *n.* tawa, katatawa
launch – *n.* lantsa
launch – *n., a.* undong, pagundong
launch journey – *n., a.* gikan, paggikan, pagpagikan
launder – *n., a.* laba, paglaba - Spanish *lavar*
laundry – *n.* linabahan, labada - Spanish *lavada*
laundry woman – *n.* paraglaba, parapanlaba, labandera - Spanish *lavandera*
laurel leaf – *n.* rikado
law – *n.* baláod
lawyer – *n.* abugado Spanish *abogado*
lay eggs – *n., a.* pagbunay
laziness – *n.* kahubya, kahubyaan
lazy – *kan.* hubya, hubsak, siridngon
lead an animal – *n., a.* tugway, pagtugway
lead prayer – *n., a.* pamatbat, mamaratbat
leader – *n.* púno, punúan, lider- Spanish *lider*
leadership – *n.* pamunuan, liderato – Spanish *liderato*
leaf – *n.* dahon
leaf of coconut – *n.* lukay **leak of air or gas** – *n., a.* hungaw, paghungaw
lean on – *n., a.* sarig, sandig, pagsandig, pagsarig

leap – *n., a.* lukso, piktaw, ambak, paglukso, pagpiktaw, pagambak
leap as a frog – *n., a.* pitik, pagpitik
learn – *n., a.* hibaro, santop, tigaman, arám, pagkahibaro, pagsantop, pagtigaman, pagarám
learn a lesson – *n., a.* maan, pagmaan
learn a skill – *n., a.* arám, pagarám
learning – *n.* hibaro, santop, pagtuón
leasurely walk – *n.* sudoysudoy, lakwatsa
leave – *n., a.* pagbaya, pagíwas, paglayas
leave behind – *n., a.* pabilin, pagpabilin
leave nothing – *n., a.* puyas, ímod, pagpuyas, pagímod
leave unfinished – *n., a.* salin, pagsalin
leaves of Moringa oleifera tree – *n.* kamalungay
left – *n.* wala
leftover – *n.* bahaw, salin, tabigi, subra - Spanish *sobra*
leg – *n.* bitíis
lemon – *n.* hiris, sidras, limon – Spanish *limon*
lemon grass – *n.* tanglad
lesbian – *n.* palakínon, tumboy – English *tomboy*
lesson – *n.* tuúnan, turúnan, santop, tigamnan, tirigamnan
let go – *n., a.* búliw, pagbúliw
letter – *n.* surát, litra – Spanish *letra*
level – *n., a.* patag, panas, pagpatag, pagpanas

lever – *n.* ligwat, lukba, panligwat, panlukba
liar – *n., kan.* buwáon
liberty – *n.* katalwasan
libidinous – *kan.* uragon, himamágon
libido – *n.* urag
library – *n.* barasahan
lice – *n.* kuto
license plate – *n.* plaka, Spanish placa
lick – *n., a.* diláp, mulmol, pagdilap, pagmulmol
lid – *n., a.* takóp, pagtakóp
lie – *n., a.* buwa, pagbuwa
lie down – *n., a.* higda, hundaray, lunay, lukot, paghigda, paghundaray, paglunay, paglukot
lie on back – *n., a.* huyang, paghuyang
lie on belly – *n., a.* kulob, hapa, dapa, pagkulob, paghapa, pagdapa
lie on one side – *n., a.* kilikid, pagkilikid
life – *n.* kinabuhi
life vest – *n.* abayan
lift – *n., a.* angat, alsa - Spanish *alzar,* pagangat, pagalsa
light – *kan.* magaan, mapawa, nasiga
light – *n., a.* kapawaan, kapáwan, kahayag, lága, lamrag
light a fire – *n., a.* surit, dagkot, dukot, pagsurit, pagdagkot, pagdukot
light a lamp – *n., a.* suga, siga, pagsuga, pagsiga
light bulb – *n.* bumbilya - Spanish *bombilla*

light candle – *n., a.* tayok,
pagtayok
light weight – *kan.* magaan
lighted – *kan.* nasiga
lighthouse – *n.* parula -
Spanish *faro*
lightning – *n., a.* kikidlat,
lilipak, lilinti, pagkikidlat,
paglilipak, paglilinti
likable – *kan.* karuyagon,
makaruruyag
like – *kan., s.* bagá, bagay,
angay, sugad, alagidagid,
sama, sugad, pariho - Spanish
pareja
like – *n., a.* ayón, gusto -
Spanish *gustar*, karuyag,
pagayón, pagayón,
pagkagusto, pagkaruyag
likely – *kaa.* sugadsugad
likeness – *n., a.* alagidagid,
pagkalagidagid, kaliwat
liking – *n., kan., kaa.*
kagustuhan, naayón, maki
limber – *kan.* malubay
lime – *n.* kidya, kalamansi
line – *n.* bagis, linya - Spanish
linea
lip – *n.* imim
listen – *n., a.* báti, pamati,
pagbati, pagpamati
listing – *kan.* kiling, nakiling
litter – *n.* sighot, siot
little – *adj.* gutíay
little finger – *n.* tamuyingking
livelihood – *n.* panginabuhi
lively – *kan.* maribhong,
marisyo
liver – *n.* atay
lizard – *n.* taguto, tabili, tiki,
tuko
loathesome – *kan.*
makangangalas, makangaralas

lobster – *n.* banagan, tapusok
locate – *a.* pagtungod,
pagbiling
location – *n.* tungod
lock – *n., a.* kandado, yabe -
Spanish *llave*, pagkandado
locust – *n.* duron
log – *n.* truso - Spanish *troza*
loin – *n.* baláwang, baywang
loin cloth – *n.* bahag
long – *kan.* halaba, hilaba
long life – *n., kan.* hilawig nga
kinabuhi
long wave – *n.* humatol
longtime dwellers – *n.*
tuminungnong
look – *n., a.* kulaw, kita,
pagkulaw, pagkita
lookalike – *kan.* kaliwat, supo
look back – *n, a.* lingi, paglingi
look for – *n., a.* biling,
pagbiling
look like forebear – *n., a.* supo,
pagsup, sumupo
look out – *n., a.* tánaw,
tanawan, tangbo, dungaw,
tangbuan, pagtánaw,
pagtangbo, pagdungaw
look up – *n., a.* hangad,
paghangad
lookout – *n.* lantawan
looks – *n.* hitsura, kurti
loose – *kan.* halúag, haluhago,
huwang
loose ends – *n.* tawidil
loot – *n., a.* kawat, kinawatan,
agaw, inagaw, pangawat,
pangagaw
lopsided – *a., kan.* pihing,
pagangihas, bintulawo,
naangihas, hiwí, pilidong
Lord – *n.* Ginúo

lose – *n., a.* wara, pirde -
Spanish *perdido*, wagtang,
pagwara, pagpirde
lose game – *n., a.* latak, lupig,
pagpalupig
loud cry – *n.* ngurahab
louse – *n.* kuto
louse-infested hair – *n., kan.*
kutuon
lovable – *kan.* makaruruyag,
makangurudyot,
love – *n., a.* gugma, mahal,
paghigugma, pagmahal
love affair – *n.* higugmaay,
paghigugmaay
love potion – *n.* lumay
loved one – *n.* higugmáon,
hinihigugma
low tide – *n.* hubas
low-grade fever – *n.* sinat
low-pitched dragging sound –
n. karadol
low-pitched reververating
sound – *n., a.* ugong,
pagugong, naugong
lower – *n., a.* ariya, turos,
tunod pagariya, pagturos,
pagtunod
lower – *kaa.* ubós
lower in status – *n., a.* paubos,
pagpaubos
lower place – *n.* ubós, ilarom
lowly – *kan.* mapinaubusanon,
mapinaubsanon
luck – *n.* kapalaran, swirte -
Spanish *suerte*
lucky – *kan.* mapalad,
madaog, buynas – Spanish
buenas, maswirte - Spanish
suerte
lukewarm – *kan.* malanhod
lump – *n.* bukol, hubag
lump in throat – *n.* hibol

lumpy – *kan.* búkulbúkol
lunatic – *kan.* lurong
lunch – *n.* paníngudto,
paníudto
lung – *n.* bága
lustful – *kan.* uragon
luxuriant – *kan.* marampag
luxury – *n.* lúho, rangya,
karangyahan

M:m

mabalod – *kan.* wavy, choppy
machine – *n.* makina - Spanish
maquina
mackerel – *n.* buraw, hasahasa
mad – *kan.* hangit, bigit, lurong
made of – *kan.* kuha, hinimo
madness – *n.* kahangit, kabigit,
kalurong
magazine – *n.* pahayagan,
basahon, barasahon
maggot – *n.* ulod
magnet – *n.* batúbarani
maiden – *n.* daragita
mail – *n.* surát
maintain – *n., a.* mantinir –
Spanish *mantener*, pagmantinir
majority – *n.* kadamuan,
kadáman, urog, kaudgan
make – *n., a.* himo, hinimo,
paghimo
make amends – *n., a.* basol,
pamalandong, pagbasol
make better – *n., a.* upay,
pagupay
make dirty – *n., a.* hugáw,
paghugáw
make knot – *n., a.* buhol, higot
pagbuhol, paghigot
making – *n.* hinimo, paglarang

male homosexual – *n*. bayot, babayinon
male teacher – *n*. magturutdo, maistro - Spanish *maestro*
malfeasance – *n*. tinuyaw, linurong
mallet – *n*. pukpok, palpag
maltreat – *n., a*. darahog, pagdarahog
man – *n*. tawo, lalaki
manacle – *n., a*. pusas, pagpusas
manage – *n., a*. dumara, pagdumara
management – *n*. pamaagi, kadumara
mankind – *n*. katawhan, kadáman
mandate – *n*. mandato - Spanish *mandato*
maneuver – *n*. maniubra – Spanish *maniobra*
mango – *n*. mangga
mangrove – *n*. bakhaw, kabakhawan
manhandle – *n., a*. bugbog, kastigo, pagbugbog, pagkastigo – Spanish *castigar*
manhood – *n*. pagkalalaki
manners – *n*. batasan, kinaiya
many – *kan*. damo, dadamuro
marathon – *n*. maraton – English *marathon*
marble – *n*. hulins, marmol – Spanish *marmol*
March – *n*. Marso - Spanish *marzo*
march – *n., a*. martsa - Spanish *marcha*, pagmartsa
marginal – *kan*. ministiblis
marinate fish – *n., a*. kilaw, kinilaw, pagkilaw

marinate or cook with vinegar – *n., a*. kilaw, suoy, pagkilaw, pagsuoy
mark – *n., a*. tigaman, timre, bagis, pagtigaman
mark with line – *n., a*. linya, paglinya
marker – *n*. tigaman
market – *n*. tabuan, merkado - Spanish *mercado*, tiyangge - Mexican *tianguis*
married couple – *n*. magasáwa
marry – *n., a*. asawa, kasal - Spanish *casar*, pangasawa, pagpakasal
Mary and Joseph! – *kah*. susmariyosep
marshland – *n*. kalagayan, kahanangan
masculine female – *n*. palakínon
mash – *n., a*. dugmok, pisa, pagdugmok, pagpisa
massage – *n., a*. hilot, paghilot
masseur – *n*. hilot, manhihilot nga lalaki
masseuse – *n*. hilot, manhihilot nga babayi
master – *n*. agaron, ámo
masturbate – *n., a*. salsal, pagsalsal
mat embroiderer – *n*. magparahot, mamarahot
mat weaver – *n*. maglalara, manlalara
match – *n*. puspuro - Spanish *fosporo*
matchmaking – *n., a*. tugpo, padis, pagtugpo, pagpadis
match stick – *n*. palito
mate – *n*. káusa, kaupod, kapadis

mattress – *n.* kultson - Spanish *colchón*

mature coconut – *n., kan.* lahing, butóng

maturity – *n.* kalahingan

maul – *n., a.* bugbog, kastigo, pagbugbog, pagkastigo – Spanish *castigar*

May – *n.* Mayo - Spanish *mayo*

mayhem – *n.* samok, saramok, karamsaw

mayor – *n.* mayor, mayora - English *mayor*

me – *han.* akon, ak, nakon

meal – *n.* karáunon, karan'on, pagkáon

mean – *kan.* masungit, istrikto – Spanish *estricto*

meaning – *n.* kahulugan, pangahulugan, hinungdan

measles – *n.* tipdas, tigdas

measure – *n., a.* sukol, takos, pagsukol, pagtakos

measurement – *n.* dangaw, dupa, sukol

meat – *n.* unod, karni – Spanish *carne*

meat boiled vegetables – *n.* linaga, lauya

medication – *n.* bulong, tambal

medicinal lotion – *n.* banyos, panbanyos

medicine – *n.* tambal, bulóng, medisina, English *medicine*

meet – *n., a.* tapo, kita, pagtapo, pagkita

meeting – *n.* harampang, kirigta hiruhimangraw, pagkatitirok, tipuntipon

melancholia – *n.* kasubo, pangandoy,

melancholic – *kan.* nangangandoy

mellow sound – *n., kan.* lanoy, nalanoy

melt – *n., a.* tunaw, pagtunaw, pagpatunaw

member – *n.* kakampi, kagrupo, miyembro – Spanish *miembro*

memento – *n.* hinumduman

memorize – *n., a.* santop, hunahuna, dumdom, pagsantop, pagdumdom

memory – *n.* dumdom hinumduman, hinumdum

menace – *n.* samok

mendacious – *kan.* buwáon

mendacity – *n.* pagkabuwáon

mend – *n., a.* sursi, tahi, pagsursi, pagtahi

menial – *kan.* pinubre

menstruation – *n.* kabulanan, rigla - Spanish *regla*

mentally retarded – *n., kan.* kulangkulang, linga

mention – *n., a.* hilwas, luwas, hisgot, paghilwas

merchandise – *n.* baligya

merchant – *n.* negosyante

merciful – *kan.* malulúyon

mercilessly – *kaa.* gulpi - Spanish *golpe*

mercury – *n.* asoge - Spanish *azoque*

mercy – *n.* kaluoy

mermaid – *n.* kataw

mesentery – *n.* rayaraya

mess – *n., a.* samok, kasamukan, pagsamok

message – *n.* tugon, minsahe - Spanish *mensaje*

messy – *kan.* buhulbuhol, masamok, gumok

meteorite – *n.* bulalakaw
method – *n.* paagi, pinaagi
meticulous – *kan.* makuti,
mabusisi, mauyatom
microbe – *n.* kagaw
middle – *n.* butnga
midnight – *n.* katutnga
midrib of coconut leaf – *n.*
gihay
midwife – *n.* parapanganak,
partira - Spanish *partera*
might – *n.* gahom
miliaria – *n.* hulashulas
military parade – *n.* martsa
milk – *n.* gatas
milkfish – *n.* bangus
milled rice – *n.* bugas
million – *num.* libo, ribo
millipede – *n.* bayod
mind – *n., a.* hunahuna,
panhunahina, paghunana
mine – *han.* akon, ak, nakon
minuend – *n.* kaíban
minion – *n.* batos, tawutawo,
tawuhan
minute – *n.* takna, minuto -
Spanish *minuto*
miraculous – *kan.* urusahon,
milagruso - Spanish *milagroso*
mirror – *n.* salaming, ispiho -
Spanish *espejo*
miscellaneous – *kan.*
magdirudilain, durudilain,
ibáibá, magkasarusarakot
mischief – *n.* lungot,
kamalabad, kalabaran
mischievous – *kan.* malabad,
malungot, pilyo, maiyotiyot
miser – *n.* barat, kuripot
miserly – *kan.* kuripot
misfortune – *n.* buwisit,
dimalas, kakurian, rimalaso

mishmash – *a., kan.* pagkusat,
kusat, kusatkusat
mislead – *n., a.* warawara,
pagwarawara
miss – *n., a.* iliw, pagiliw
misshapen – *kan.* pilidong
missing tooth – *n.* ngihab
mist – *n.* túnog, taburos
mistake – *n., a.* salá, sayop
mistress – *n.* kabít, kerida –
Spanish *querida*
mite – *n.* tungaw, kagaw
mitigate – *n., a., kan.* iban,
pagiban, naiban, naminos
mix – *n., a.* sakot, timpla, ukay,
hálo, pagsakot, pagtimpla,
pagukay, paghálo
mix with soup – *n., a.* bahog,
sabaw, pagbahog
mixed – *kan.* sarakot
mixed-up – *kan.* buhulbuhol
mixture – *n., a.* sarakot, timpla
- Spanish *templar*, pagsarakot,
pagtimpla, pagsarakot
modest – *kan.* kinablas,
mahinhin, mahiyumhiyom
moist – *kan.* humog, mahulos
moisten – *n., a.* hulós, humog,
paghulos, paghumog
molar – *n.* bágang
mold – *n., a.* hurmaan, hurma -
Spanish *horma*, paghurma
mold (fungus) – *n., a.* alamag,
pagalamag
mold with hand – *n., a.* gumo,
paggumo
moldy – *kan.* alamagon,
maamhok
mole – *n.* árong
moment – *n.* takna
Monday – *n.* lunes - Spanish
lunes

155

money – *n.* salapi, kwarta – Spanish *cuarta*
money box – *n.* alkansiya
moniker – *n.* sangbay, angga
monitor lizard – *n.* halo
monkey – *n.* ulot, amó, tamoy, unggoy
monosodium glutamate – *n.* bitsin - Chinese *bi chin*
monotonous – *kan.* masumo, maluwad
monsoon – *n.* habagat
month – *n.* bulan
monthly – *n., kaa.* kabulanan
mood – *n.* kaburúton
moon – *n.* bulan
moonlit – *kan.* bulanon
morals – *n.* batasan, kinaiya, álo
more – *kan., kaa.* mas - Spanish *mas*
moribund – *kan.* masakiton
morning – *n.* aga
morning mist – *n.* túnog
morsel – *n.,* pinit, mumo
mortar – *n.* almiris - Spanish *almirez*
mosquito – *n.* namok
mosquito net – *n.* muskitero - Spanish *mosquitero*
mosquito-infested – *kan.* manamok
moss – *n.* lumot
mossy – *kan.* lumuton, malumot
most – *kaa.* pinaka
mostly - *kaa.* urog
moth – *n.* kakanog
mother – *n.* inay, iroy, nanay, mama,
mother-in-law – *n.* ugangan nga babayi

motion – *n., a.* kiwa, bantad pagkiwa, pagbantad
motionless – *n., a.* dupay, pagdupay
motive – *n.* hinungdan, rason - Spanish *razon*
motorized outrigger – *n.* pambot – American *pump boat*
mount spur in cockfight – *n., a.* taod, pagtaod
mountain – *n.* bukid
mountain dweller – *n.* bukidnon
mountain range – *n.* kabudkiran
mountainous – *kan.* bukidbukid, budkiron
mourn – *n., a.* lutó, paglutó
mouse – *n.* maus - American *mouse*
mouse – *n.* yatot
mouth – *n.* bába
move – *n., a.* bantad, kiwa, pagbantad, pagkiwa
moveable – *kaa.* makiwa, dusuduso
movement – *n.* kiwa, bantad
movie theater – *n.* kirítan, sinehan – English *cinema*
movies – *n.* kiríton, sine
Mr. – *n.* mano, mister –English mister, senyor – Spanish *señor*, don
Mrs. – *n.* mana, mistress – English mistress, senyora – Spanish *señora*, donya – Spanish *doña*
mucus – *n.* muhog, sípon, lako
mud – *n.* lagay, lapok
mud crab - *n.* kagang
muddy – *kan.* malagay, malapok

muddy brackish water – *n.*
kahanangan
muddy water – *n.* hanang
mullet fish – *n.* balanak
multiplication – *n.* damudamo
multiplier – *n.* kadámo
multiply – *n., a.* damo,
pagdamo
multitask – *n., a.* sugabin,
pagsugabin
multitude – *n.* kadamuan,
kadáman, katawuhan,
katawhan, katilimban,
katilingban
mumble – *n., a.* ngurutob,
pagngurutob
mumps – *n.* bikag
mundane – *kan.* kinalibutanon
municipality – *n.* bungto
murder – *n., a.* pátay, pagpátay
murkiness – *n.* lubog,
kamalubog
muscles – *n.* unod
muscles and tendons – *n.*
kaunuran, kaundan
muscular – *kan.* kusugan,
kusgan
mushroom buttonlike – *n.*
ulaping
mushy – *kan.* mayaguta
music – *n., a.* tugtog, tukar,
musika - Spanish *musica*,
pagtugtog, pagtukar
mussel – *n.* tahong
must – *n., a.* kinahanglan,
pagkinahanglan
mustache – *n.* bigote - Spanish
bigote
mustard – *n.* mustasa - Spanish
mostaza
mute – *n.* ngúla
my – *han.* akon, ak, nakon

mythical mermaid – *n.* úkoy,
sirena – Spanish *sirena*

N:n

nab – *n., a.* dakop, pagdakop
nagging – *kan.* maabugho
nail – *n., a.* raysang, paris
naked – *kan.* hubo
name – *n., a.* ngaran, tawag,
pagngaran, pagtawag
namesake – *n.* kangaran,
tukayo - Spanish *tocayo*
nape – *n.* bátok, taludtod
narcotics - *n.* narkotiko -
English *narcotics*, druga -
Spanish *droga*
narrow – *kan.* haligot, hiligot
narrow plank – *n.* latayan
nasal secretions – *n.* muhog,
sipon, lako
nation – *n.* nasod
nature – *n.* kinaiya, naturalisa,
Spanish *naturaleza*
naughty – *kan.* pilyo, sutil
nauseous – *kan.* masukasuka
navel – *n.* pusod
navigate – *n., a.* nabigar,
Spanish *navegar*, pagnabigar,
pagsakayon
near – *kaa., kat.* haraní, hiraní,
apiki
nearby – *kan.* haráni, hiráni
nearly – *kaa.* harapit
neat – *kan.* maayos
necessities – *n.* kinahanglan
neck – *n.* liog
necklace – *n.* kwintas
necktie – *n.* kurbata - Spanish
corbata

need – *n., a.* kinahanglan, pagkinahanglan
needle – *n.* dagom, túrok
needy – *kan.* kablas, tapód, tagdal, kablasanon, makinahanglanon
negate – *n., a.* diri, pagdiri
negative – *n.* waray, diri, negatibo - Spanish *negativo*
negative anticipation or surprise – *kah.* diripala, dipala
negative head gesture – *n.* pilingpiling
neglect – *n., a.* pasibayá, pagpasibaya
negligence – *n.* pasibayá
negotiate – *n., a.* negosyo - Spanish *negocio*
negrito – *n.* agta
neighbor – *n.* anyaw
nephew – *n.* umangkon
nervous – *kan.* nirbyuso
nervousness – *n.* nirbyos
nest – *n.* salag
neuter – *n., a.* písit, pagpisit
neutered animal – *n.* pisít
nevus – *n.* árong
new – *kan.* bágo
new moon - *n.* kawara, dulom
newly wed – *n.* kinasal news – *n.* mga sumat, susumaton, surumaton, nyus - English *news*
news broadcast – *n.* pasamwak
newscaster – *n.* parasamwak,paragsamwak
newsman – *n.* tagasumat, tagsumat
newspaper – *n.* pahayagan, nyuspepor - English *newspaper*
next *kan., kaa.* sapit, sunod kasunod, kasapit

nibble – *n., a.* timitimi, kutkot, kitkit, pagkutkot
nice – *kan.* sapak
nickname – *n.* sangbay, annga
niece – *n.* umangkon nga babayi
night – *n.* gábi
night before last – *n.* kasanggabi
night blindness – *n.* harap
nightmare – *n., a.* ngarat, ugmad, bangungot, pagngarat, pagugmad, pagbangungot
nimo, nim – *pron.* you, your, yours
nighttime – *n.* kagabíhon
nine – *num.* siyám, noybe - Spanish *nueve*
nineteen – *num.* napulo kag siyam, dyesinoybe - Spanish *diecinueve*
ninety – *num.* kasiyaman, nobenta
ninth – *num.* ikasiyam
nipa palm fruit – *n.* pungo
nipa palm leaves – *n.* nipa
nipa shingle – *n.* páwod
nipa wine – *n.* dalisay
nipple – *n.* yupyupan
no – *n.* diri
nod – *n., a.* tangdo, pagtangdo
node – *n.* bukó
noise – *n.* aringasa, ngiras
noisy – *kan.* maaringasa, mangiras
nonchalant – *kan.* putingad
none – *n.* waray
noon – *n.* udto
north wind – *n.* amihan nose – *n.* irong
nose bleed – *n., a.* kunggo, sunggo, pangkunggo, pagsunggo

nose ring – *n.* baklaw
nostalgia – *n.* kahidlaw,
kamingaw, pangandoy
nostalgic – *kan.* madidlaw,
mamingaw, makahiridlaw,
namimingaw, nangangandoy
nothing – *n.*, *kan.* waray
notice – *n.* pahibaro,
pahimangno
noun – *n.* ngaran
nourishment – *n.* sustansya
November – *n.* Nobyembre -
Spanish *noviembre*
now – *kaa.* yana
nude – *kan.* hubo
numb – *kan.* mabanhod
number – *n.* ihap, numero –
Spanish *numero*
numbers game – *n.* huweteng -
Chinese *jue teng*
numbness – *n.* banhod
nun – *n.* madre – Spanish
madre
nurse – *n.* nars - English *nurse*
nutrition – *n.* sustansya

O:o

oar – *n.* bugsay
oath – *n.*, *a.* sumpa, pagsumpa,
panumpa
obedient – *kan.* buotan,
masugot, matinumanon
obese – *kan.* buntol
obey – *n.*, *a.* sugot, sunod,
pagsugot, pagsunod
obfuscate – *n.*, *a.* lipat,
warawara, pagwarawara,
paglipat
obligation – *n.* katungdanan
oblige – *n.*, *a.* angay,
pakiangay, pagpakiangay

obscene – *kan.* maláway
obscenity – *n.* láway,
kaláwayan, kabastusan
obscure – *n.*, *a.* salipod,
pagsalipod
obsequious – *kan.* masugot,
matinumanon
observe – *n.*, *a.* kitakita,
pagkitakita
obstinate – *kan.* makauulang,
sagabal
obstruct – *n.*, *a.* sangko, ulang,
pagsangko, pagulang
obstruction – *n.* sangkúan,
sagabal
obstructive – *kan.* sangkuan,
makauulang, nakabara
obvious – *kan.* dayag, huyayag
occasion – *n.* higayon
occupation – *n.* hiagi,
pakabuhi, panginabuhi
occupy – *n.*, *a.* lukop,
paglukop
occur – *n.*, *a.* hitabo,
paghitabo, paghinabo
occurence – *n.* nahitatabo,
nahihinabo, karigudigo
ocean – *n.* lawod, kalawdan
October – *n.* Oktubre - Spanish
octubre
octopus – *n.* kugita, pugita
odor – *n.* báho
of – *kat.* hit, hiton, kan
offended – *kan.* naubós,
agrabyado
offensive – *kan.* masungot,
maláway
offer – *n.*, *a.* halad, tubyan
paghalad, pagtubyan,
pagintrigá
offering – *n.* halad, tubyan
office – *n.* opisina - Spanish
oficina

often – *kan., kaa.* agsob,
masukot
oil – *n.* lana
oil lamp – *n.* paagahan, suga,
lampara
oily – *kan.* mantikahon,
mantikáon
Okay! – *kah.* Ayós!
old – *kan.* daan, lagas
old folk – *n.* kalagasan,
kalagsan
old person – *n.* apoy, lagas,
tigurang
old times – *n.* kamaihaan,
kadaan
old-fashioned – *kan.* kinadaan,
kamaihaan
older – *kan.* magurang
older sibling – *n.* magurang
nga bugto
oldest daughter – *n.* suhag nga
babayi
oldest son – *n.* suhag nga lalaki
omnipotent – *n.* makagarahom
on – *kat.* tungod
on the edge – *kan.* tagilid,
takilid
once – *kaa.* ikagusa, ugsa,
usahay
one – *num.* usá, uno - Spanish
uno
one finger breadth – *n., a.*
dangaw
one hundred – *num.* usa
kagatos, syin - Spanish *cien*
oneself – *n.* kalugaringon
onion – *n.* prisya, sibuyas -
Spanish *cebolla*
only – *kaa.* la, gudla, manta
only child – *n.* bugtong nga
anak
only that – *s.* lugáring

onset – *n.* katikangan,
tinikangan
onset – *n.* tinikangan,
katikangan
open – *n., a.* buka, bukás, abri,
pagbuka, pagbukás, pagabri -
Spanish *abrir*
open mouth – *n., a.,* ngangá,
pagngangá
open seas – *n.* kadagatan,
kalawdan
open space – *n.* kalarakan
opening – *n.* bungsaran
operate – *n., a.* busbos,
pagbusbos
operation – *n.* maniubra -
Spanish *maniobra*
opportunistic – *kan.* singabot,
patakas
opportunity – *n.* higayon
oppose – *n., a.* tipa, atubang,
tugbang, pagtipa, pagatubang,
pagtugbang
opposite – *kan.* bali,
kaatubang, katugbang
or – *s.* o
oral thrush – *n.* singaw
orange color – *n.* dúrog
orderliness – *n.* murayaw,
kamurayaw, katuhayan,
kamurayawan
order – *n., a.* sugo, ayos,
mando, surundon, tuhay
orderly *kan.* maayos, tuhay,
mahimyang
orderly – *n.* kabulig
ordinary – *kan.* ordinaryo -
Spanish ordinario, yano -
Spanish *llano*
organization – *n.* katiguban,
katitirok, kaurusa

organize – *n., a.* tigob, tirok, ayos, pagtigob, pagtirok. pagayos
orgasm – *n., a.* himaga, nahihimaga, paghimaga
origin – *n.* katikangan, tinikangan, gintikangan
original inhabitants – *n.* tuminungnong
ornaments – *n.* rayandayan
ostentatious – *kan.* marangya
other – *n.* lain, iba
Ouch! – *kah.* agidoy, agi
our, ours – *han.* áton, at, naton, amon, namon
out of breath – *n., a., kan.* punga, hingal, hangos, nahangos
out of tune – *kan.* yabag, sintunado - Spanish *sintonizar*
outerspace – *n.* kalarakan
outfit rooster with spur - *a.* tadí
outgrow – *n., a.* tinubuan, gintubuan
outline – *n., a.* laray, paglaray
outrigged boat – *n.* balúto, barúto
outrigger – *n.* katig
outside – *n.* gawas
oven – *n.* hudno - Spanish *horno*
over – *kat.* labaw, igbaw, bawbaw
overbearing – *kan.* maisog, maabugho
overcast – *n., kan.* madágom, dalumdom, madalumdom,
overcritical – *kan.* masuson
overcrowded – *a., kan.* bugíot, masuok, suksok
overflow – *n., a.* salwak, laswak, paglaswak
overripe – *kan.* dunot

overshoot – *n., a.* lahos, lapos, paglahos, paglapos
overwhelmed – *kan.* kagaramo
owl – *n.* bukaw
own – *n., a.* arog, mayada, pagrog, pagtagíya
owner – *n.* tagíya, mayada
ownership - *n.* panagíya, kalugaringon, kamáyada pangalugaringon,
oyster – *n.* sisi, talaba, tipay, tilang

P:p

pack – *n., a.* dasok, pagdasok
pack in coconut shell – *a., kan.* bagol, binagol
package – *n.* padará
paddle – *n., a.* bugsay, pagbugsay
padlock – *n.* kandado
page – *n.* paypay
pail – *n.* baldi
pain – *n.* ulol, sakit
painful – *kan.* maúlol, masakit
paint – *n.* pintura
painter – *n.* pintor - Spanish *pintor*
pair – *n.* lingit, padis
palace – *n.* palasyo - Spanish *palacio*
pale – *n., kan.* duás, nabughat
palm – *n.* pálad
palm flour – *n.* arasip
palm frond – *n.* buri, talipot, *Corypha umbraculifera*
palm leaf – *n.* palwa - Spanish *palma*
palm reading – *n.* panhimalad
palm scoop – *n.* harop, hakop

palmetto – *n.* anahaw
palpitate – *n.* kulba, pagkulba
palpitation – *n.* kakulba
pamper – *n., a.* palabilabi, palangga, paura
pancreas – *n.* udilas
pancreatitis, alcoholic – *n.* bangungot
pandemic – *n.* pandemya
pantry – *n.* bangira
pants – *n.* saruwal
papaya – *n.* kapaya
paper – *n.* papil - Spanish *papel*
paper bag – *n.* supot
paper wrapper – *n.* putos
parasite – *n.* huthot, singabot
parasite infested – *n.* bitukon
parasitic worm – *n.* bitok
parcel – *n.* padará
parent – *n.* káganak, ginikangan
parish – *n.* parokya
parents of son-in-law – *n.* balayi
parrot – *n.* pikoy
part – *n.* bahin, sangkop, parti - Spanish *parte*
partake – *n., a.* baragayaw, sahid, bahinbahin, pagbaragayaw, pakibahin, pagsahid
participate – *n., a.* awat, bulig, ungay, panginlabot, paawat, pagbulig
partner – *n.* padis
partnership – *n.* kaupod, kabunyog
party – *n.* kadamó, sarusaro, partido - Spanish *partido politico*
pass – *n., a.* ági, dayon, pagági, pagdayon

pass an exam or grade - *a.* pasar - Spanish *pasar*
pass beyond – *n., a.* lapos, lahos, paglapos, paglahos
pass by – *n. a.* labáy, paglabay
pass in time – *n., a.* hagos, paghagos
pass out – *n., a.* himatay, paghimatay
pass the ball – *n., a.* pása - Spanish *pase,* pagpasa
pass under – *n., a.* suhot, sirung, pagsuhot, pagsirung
passage – *n.* agían, aragian, dalan
passenger – *n.* pasahero - Spanish *pasajero,* sákay
passerby – *n.* lumalabay
past – *kan.* hagos
past – *kat.* hadto, sadto
past – *n.* kasanhi, kaliwas, naglabay, kasanhi, naghagos
paste – *n., a.* papilit, padukot, pagpapilit, pagpadukot
pastime – *n.* kalingawan
patch – *n., a.* sarop, tangkop, pagsarop, pagtangkop
path – *n.* dalan, agian
pathetic – *kan.* makaluluoy
patience – *n.* pasyinsya - Spanish *paciencia*
patient – *n.* maysakit, pasyinte - Spanish *paciente*
patron saint – *n.* patron, patrona
pattern – *n.* kahímo
pay – *n., a.* bayad, pagbayad
pay attention – *n., a.* pamati, pagkita
pay by installment – *n., a.* húlog, hulogan, paghulugan
payment – *n.* bayád, suhol
peace – *n.* kamurayawan

peace and order – *n.* himurayaw, kahimurayawan
peace of mind – *n.* kahimutangan, kahimtang
peaceful – *kan.* mamingaw, mahimyang, kamingawan
peak – *n.* tuktok, talimpukayan
peal – *n., a.* ripike - Spanish *repique*, pagripike
pealing of bells – *n.* ripike
peanut – *n.* mani
pearl – *n.* mutya
pebble – *n.* suliot
peck as chicken – *n., a.* tuktok, pagtuktok
peddle – *n., a.* sudoy, baligya, pagsudoy, pagbaligya
peel – *n., a.* parot, pánit, pagpánit, pagparot
peep – *n.,* a. hiling, paghiling, panhiling
peg – *n.* tusok, tugsok
penalize – *n., a.* sirot pagsirot
penalty – *n.* sirot
pencil – *n.* badlis, lapis - Spanish *lapiz*
penetrate – *n., a.* tusok, turok, tugsok, pagtusok, pagturok, pagtugsok
penetrating – *kan.* madulot, matarom
penile erection – *n.* utóg
penile splint – *n.* kalawat
penis – *n.* utin, silinggoy
penmanship – *n.* ági, kasurat
people – *n.* katawuhan, katawhan
pepper – *n.* haráng, pamyenta - Spanish *pimientos*
perchance – *kaa.* manggad, bangin, ada, tingali
perfidy – *n.* linurong, tinuyaw
perfume – *n.* pahamot

perhaps – *kaa.* ada, bángin, manggad, tingali
period – *n., a.* tuldok
period time – *n.* kapanahunan, termino - Spanish *termino*
permission – *n.* tugot sanghid
permit – *n., a.* sarit, tugot, pagsarit, panarit, pagtugot
perplexed – *n.* lipat, pausa, pahiusa, kawurok
perseverance – *n., a.* talinguha, tinguha, pagtalinguha
persevering – *kan.* mailob, maningkamot, kanunay
persistent – *kan., kaa.* kanunay, sigidas
person – *n.* tawo
personality – *n.* bugos nga pagkatawo, personalidad – Spanish *personalid*, pamahungpahong
perspiration – *n.* balhas, singot
perspire – *n., a.* singot, pagbalhas, pagsingot
pertaining rural areas – *kan.* hurunanon
pertaining to spanish culture – *kan.* kinastila, kinatsila
pertaining the city – *kan.* syudadnon
pertaining to – *kat.* hiunong
pertussis – *n.* kuykoy
peso – *n.* piso - Spanish *peso*
petroleum – *n.* pitrolyo
petulant – *kan.* putong, makuti, aringit
petulant – *kan.* pungtanon, nakarangkang, aringit, putong, makuti, sumpungon
pharmacy – *n.* botika - Spanish *botica*
pharynx – *n.* langaglangag, tutunlan

philippine lime – *n.* kidya, kalamansi

physician – *n.* mananambal, manarambal

photograph – *n.* ladawan

piano – *n.* piyano - English *piano*

pick a fight – *n., a.* pika - Spanish *pica*, pagpika

pick up – *n., a.* purot, pagpurot

pickaxe – *n.* patok, piko - Spanish *pico*

pickle – *n., a.* kilaw, pagkilaw

pickled fish with coconut milk – *n.* kinilaw

picnic – *n.* barakasyon

picnic in water – *n.* pamarigo

picture – *n.* ladawan

piecemeal – *kan.* talaita, tinalaita, tagitagi, tinagitagi

piece of bread – *n.* pinit

pierce – *n., a.* dulot, buno, pagdulot, pagbuno

pierce though – *n., a.* tuhog, pagtuhog

piercing sound – *n.* piyait

pig – *n.* baboy, baktin

pig pen – *n.* tangkal

pig suckling – *n.* pasí

pigeon – *n.* sarapati

piggery – *n.* baktinan, babuyan

piggy bank – *n.* alkansiya - Spanish *alcancia*

piggyback – *n., a.* babá, pagbabá

piglet – *n.* baktin

pile – *n., a.* pundok, tambak, patongpatong, pagpundok, pagtambak, pagpatongpatong

pill – *n.* bulong, tablita – Spanish *tableta*

pillow – *n.* ulunan

pimple – *n.* púnggod

pin – *n., a.* pakot, alpiler - Spanish *alfiler*

pincers – *n.* kagát

pinch – *n., a.* kurot, kutol, parkurot, pagkutol

pinch ears – *n., a.* piknit, pagpiknit

pink – *n.* limbahon, limbawon

pinnacle – *n.* tuktok, talimpukayan

pioneer – *n.* panguna, tuminungnong

pistol – *n.* pusil

pit – *n.* buhó, inukab

pitch – *n., a.* itsa, pagitsa

pitiful – *kan.* makaluluoy, kairo

pittance – *n.* limos

pity – *n., a.* kaluoy, paid, pagkaluoy, pagpaid

pivot – *n.* kasing

placate – *n., a.* patunga, pagpatunga

place – *n., a.* tungod, lugar - Spanish *lugar*, paglugar, pagtungod

placenta – *n.* pinaulnan, inulunan, inulnan

plague – *n.* pandemya, pisti - Spanish *peste*

plain – *kan.* yano - Spanish *llano*

plains – *n.* patag, kapatagan

plan – *n., a.* larang, plano - Spanish *plano*

plane – *n., a.* sapyo, idro, pagsapyo

plank – *n.* damyo, latayan

plant – *n., a.* tanom, pagtanom

platform – *n.* tungtungan

play – *n., a.* mulay, uyag, laksi, pagmulay, paguyag

play basketball – *n., a.*
baskitbol – American
basketball, pagbaskitbol
play hide and seek – *a.*
tagutago, tigbutigbuay
play hopscotch – *a.* patintiro,
pagpatintiro
play music – *n., a.* tugtog,
tunóg, tukar - Spanish *tocar*
play numbers - *n., a.* masyaw
play such game - *a.* sato
play tag – *n., a.*
dakupdakupay,
pagdakupdakupay
playground – *n.* murulayan
playhouse – *n.* balaybalay,
malaybalay
playmate – *n.* kauyag, kamulay
plaything – *n.* mulayan,
uyagan
plea – *n.* araba, pangamuyo,
panginyupo
plead – *n., a.* araba,
pangaraba, panginyupo
pleasant – *kan.* makaruruyag,
matahom, mahumla,
mahiyumhiyom
please – *kaa.* pastilan, palihog
pleasure trip – *n., a.*
sakaysakay, pagsakaysakay
plenitude – *n.* kahurakan
plentiful – *kan.* damo, nahurak
plenty – *n., kan.* damo,
dadamuro, kahurakan,
pliant – *kan.* malubay
pliers – *n.* plais - American
pliers
plight – *n.* kahimutangan,
kahimtang
plow – *n., a.* arado - Spanish
arado, pagarado, paguma
plug – *n., a.* sarop, pagsarop

pocket – *n., a.* bulsa - Spanish
bolsa, pagbulsa
poem – *n., a.* siday, pagsiday
point – *n.* kataisan, kataruman,
katarman
point – *n., a.* kataisan, tudlok,
pagtudlok
pointed – *kan.* taís
pointed stick - *n.* tusok, tugsok
pointer - *n.* tudlok
poison – *n., a.* hiló, baráng,
lumay, paghiló, pagbarang,
paglumay
poison dispenser – *n.* hilúan,
barangan
poisonous – *kan.* makahihilo,
malara
poke with finger – *n., a.*
tulpok, pagtulpok
poke with pole – *n., a.* bundol,
dukdok, pagbundol
pole – *n.* tuko, pusti - Spanish
poste
policeman – *n.* pulis - Spanish
policia
political agenda - *n.*
plataporma - Spanish
Plataforma
polverize – *n., a.* dúrog,
bukbok, pagdúrog
pomelo – *n.* suha
pomano – *n.* tarukitok
pond – *n.* liruan, sapa
pool – *n.* liro
poor – *kan.* kablas,
kablasanon, pubre - Spanish
pobre
poor health – *n.* kasakitan
pope – *n.* santo papa
populace – *n.* katilimban,
katilingban, mulupyo
popular – *kan.* bantugan,
kilalado

popularity – *n.* bantog, kilala
pork – *n.* unod han baboy
pork rind – *n.* tsitsaron -
Spanish *chicharron*
porridge – *n.* lugaw
porter – *n.* hurnal, kargador -
Spanish *cargador*
positive – *n.* positibo - Spanish
positivo
possess by spirits – *a.*, *kan.*
bugkot, binugkot, sinangkayan
post – *n.* harigi, tuko, pusti -
Spanish *poste*
posterity – *n.* kabubwason
postpone – *n.*, *a.* ugsod,
pagugsod
posture – *n.* pustura
pot – *n.* daba, marihuwana
pothole – *n.* batsi
pouch – *n.* supot
poultry chickens - *n.*
kamanukan
pound – *n.*, *a.* tudtod, bayó,
pukpok, tultog, pagtudtod,
pagbayó, pagpukpok,
pagtultog
pounded toasted rice – *n.*
pilipig
pour – *n.*, *a.* ipis, huwad,
pagipis, paghuwad
pour wine – *n.*, *a.* tagay,
pagtagay
pout – *n.*, *a.* murusot, yamid,
pagmurusot
poverty – *n.* kakablasan,
kakurian, kapubrihan
powder – *n.* bukbok, pulbura,
Spanish *polvora*
power – *n.* gahom,
kagamhanan
powerful – *kan.* gamhanan
praise – *n.*, *a.* dayaw, palabi,
pagdayaw, pagpalabi

prawn – *n.* lukon, sugpo
pray – *n.*, *a.* ampo, pagampo,
pangadi
prayer – *n.* pagampo,
pangamuyo, orasyon - Spanish
oracion
prayer group - *n.* mangangadi,
mangaradi
prayer leader – *n.* mamaratbat
precious – *kan.* minayuyo,
bulawanon
precipice – *n.* ganggang,
pangpang
precise – *kan.* igo, tuptop
prediction – *n.*, *a.* tagna,
panagna
preferably – *kaa.* asay
preference – *n.* kagustuhan
pregnancy – *n.*, *a.*, *kan.* burod,
pagburod, pinaanakan,
pinangkan
preoccupation – *n.*
hibangkaagan
preparation – *n.* andam,
kaandaman
prepare – *n.*, *a.* andam,
pagandam
preposition – *n.* katungod
presence – *n.*, *a.* tambong,
pagtambong
present – *n.*, *a.* intrigá,
pagintrigá
president – *n.* punuan,
presidente - Spanish *presidente*
press – *n.*, *a.* duón, pisá,
pagduón, pagpisá
pretending – *kaa.* napaka-
(used as prefix)
pretentious – *kan.* bagá,
bagábagá
pretty – *kan.* mabaysay,
mahusay, matahom

prevent – *n., a.* likay, pugong, tagam, paglikay, pagpugong, pagtagam
prey – *n.* singabotan, biktima – Spanish *victima*
price – *n., a.* piráhon, prisyo – Spanish *precio*, tagpira
prick – *n., a.* pagtúrok, pagpaturok
pride – *n.* dasig, parayaw
priest – *n.* padi
prison – *n.* prisuhan
prisoner – *n.* priso - Spanish *preso*
prize – *n.* daóg, primyo - Spanish *premio*
probably – *kaa.* bángin, tingali
proceed – *n., a.* padayon, sigi - Spanish *seguir*, pagpadayon, pagpasigi
process – *n., a.* paagi, kaagi, pinaagi
proclaim – *n., a.* pamulong, pamahayag
proclivity – *n., kan.* hilig, maki- (used a prefix)
procrastinate – *n., a.* langanlangan, uruugsod, anganangan, buwasbuwas
prod – *n., a.* aghat, ugay, surugsurog, tukso, pagtukso, pagaghat, pagugay, pagsurugsurog
product – *n.* hinimo, producto – Spanish *producto*
profane – *kan.* maláway
profanity – *n.* buyayaw, kaláwayan
profile – *n.* dagway, kahimo, hitsura
profit – *n.* gana, gahin, ganansya - Spanish *ganancia*

program – *n., a.* programa, pasundayag
progress – *n., a.* kaupayan, kauswagan, progreso - Spanish *progreso*, paguswag, pagpaupay, pagpakaupay
progressive – *kan.* mainuswagon, maupay, progresibo - Spanish *progresivo*
prohibit – *n., a.* ayáw, dirí, pugong, pagdirí, pagpugong
prohibited – *kan.* igindidiri
prolong – *n., a., kan.* pagiha, maiha
promenade – *n.* pasyada - Spanish *paseo*
promise – *n., a.* sáad, pagsáad
prompt – *kan.* listo - Spanish *listo*
prone – *n., a., kaa.* kulob, hapa, dapa, pagkulob, paghapa, pagdapa, pagka
pronoun – *n.* hangaran
propeller – *n.* pála - Spanish *pala*
propensity – *n., kaa.* hilig, maki, pagka
prophesy – *n., a.* tagna, panagna, panakna
prophet – *n.* manaragna
prosperity – *n.* upay, kaupayan, kauswagan, progreso - Spanish *progreso*
prosperous – *kan.* maupay, mainuswagon, progresibo - Spanish *progresivo*
prostitute – *n.* burikat
prostrate – *n., a.* dapa, kulob, hapa, pagdapa, pagkulop
protect – *n., a.* panagang, dangop, pagdangop, pagproteher - Spanish *proteger*

protection – *n.* dangupan, dalaganan, panagangan, darangpan, proteksyon - Spanish *proteccion*

protest – *n., a.* araba, reklamo - Spanish *reclamo*, pangaraba, pagreklamo

prothesis – *n.* posteso - Englsh *dental prosthesis*

protracted – *kan.* maiha, kaiha

protruding – *kan.* nabudlot, nabutol

protrusion – *n.* bútol, budlot

provenance – *n.* tinikangan, ginbuhatan

proverb – *n.* darahunon, siringanon, siridnganon, kapulungan

provide care – *n., a.* asikaso, ataman, timangno, pagasikaso, pagtimangno, pagataman

provision – *n., a.* balon, pagbalon

prow – *n.* dúlong

proxy – *n.* saliwan, kasaliwan

pry – *n., a.* lukba, ligwat, paglukba, pagligwat

pry coconut meat – *n., a.* lukad, lugit, paglukad

psoriasis – *n., kan.* buti, buni, butihon

psychosis – *n.* pagkalurong

psychotic patient – *n.* luronglurong

pubes – *n.* puson

pubic hair – *n.* bulbol, burungos

public – *n.* publiko - Spanish *publico*

public auction – *n.* subasta - Spanish *subasta*

public water – *n.* tubig, agwas - Spanish *agua*

puckered – *kan.* kiripot, pirikot

puddle – *n.* lasaw

puffer fish – *n.* butiti

pull – *n., a.* bútong, hatak, pagbútong, paghatak

pull out – *n., a.* hulbot, búnot, bulnot, gabot, paghulbot, pagbúnot, pagbulnot, paggabot

pull trigger – *n., a.* kablit, pagkablit

pulse – *n.* kutob, pitig, pulso - Spanish *pulso*

pump – *n., a.* búmba, pagbumba

pump boat – *n.* pambot - American *pump boat*

punch – *n., a.* yábo, suntok, pagyabo, pagsuntok

punctuation – *n.* panigaman, panigamnan

puncture – *n., a.* burit, turok, pagburit, pagturok

punish – *n., a.* pagsirot, pagkastigo - Spanish *castigo*

punishment – *n.* sirot, kastigo - Spanish *castigo*

puppy – *n.* iró, idó

pure – *kan.* putli, púro - Spanish *puro*

purgatory – *n.* purgatoryo - Spanish *purgatorio*

purge – *v.* pagpurga – Spanish *purga*

purple yam – *n.* ubi

purpose – *n.* tuyo, hinungdan

purse – *n.* pitaka

pus – *n.* nana, búog

push – *n., a.* tulak, duso, tikwang, pagtulak, pagdusó, pagtikwang

pustule – *n.* sabak

put aside – *n., a.* tabi, pagtabi

put down – *n., a.* butang,
pagbutang
put in order – *n., a.* ayos,
pagáyos, pagtuhay
put off light – *n., a.* parong,
pagparong
put on – *n., a.* súlot, suklob,
pagsulot, pagsuklob
put on top – *n., a.* tungbaw,
patong, pagtungbaw,
pagpatong
putrid – *kan.* langsa, malangsa,
butod, mabutudbutod
python – *n.* sawá

Q:q

quake – *n., a.* linog, kimbig,
pagkimbig
quality – *n.* kalidad - Spanish
calidad
quarrel – *n., a.* away, aragway,
pagaway, pagaragway
queen – *n.* rayna - Spanish
reyna
question – *n., a.* pakiana,
pagpakiana
quick – *kan.* kalit, malaksi,
madagmit
quicken – *n., a.* bantad,
pagbantad
quickly – *kaa.* dagmit, dalían,
kadagmitan
quicksilver – *n.* asoge -
Spanish *azoque*
quiet – *kan.* mamingaw,
mahuyo
quit – *n., a.* hunong, ukoy,
paghunong, paghukoy
quite – *kan.* haros, pagka

R:r

race – *n.* lahi, kalahian
race in sport – *n., a.* parumba,
dalaganay, dadlaganay
radio – *n.* radyo - American
radio
rag – *n.* trapo, pahíd
ragged – *kan.* gisígisí, gusígusí
railing – *n.* barandilya -
Spanish *barandilla*
rain – *n.* urán
rainbow – *n.* balangaw
rainy – *kan.* maurán
raise – *n., a.* angat, alsa -
Spanish *alzar*, pagangat
rake – *n.* kagkag, kahig, kalkag
rake – *n., a.* kahig, kagkag
rampart - *n.* balawarte,
balwarte
rancid – *kan.* pánus, mapános,
karukatutang
rape – *n., a.* lugos, talo,
paglugos, pagtalo
rapids – *n.* pangas
rare – *kan.* talagsa, birilingon,
birilngon
rarely – *kaa.* ikagusa,
panalagsa
rash – *kan.* nakarangkang
rat – *n.* yatot
rattan – *n.* kauwayan
rattan strips – *n.* uway, luway
rattan fruit – *n.* kalapi
raven – *n.* kikik
ravenous – *kan.* makaon
reach – *n., a.* pagabot,
pagduhol, pagpabot,
pagpaduhol
reach the bottom – *n., a.*
tugkad, pagtugkad
read – *n., a.* basa, pagbasa

reader – *n.* mamamasa, mambarasa
readiness – *n.* andam, kaandaman
reading materials – *n.* basahon, barasahon
ready – *a., kan.* andam, listo, preparado - Spanish *preparado*
real – *kan.* ungod, tinuuray, matuod
reality – *n.* kamatuuran, tinuod, uray
realized –*kan.* ginbútan
really – *kaa.* daw, tinuuray
realm – *n.* kahadian, ginhadían
rear – *n., kan.* pútik, ulin, urhi
reason – *n., a.* katadungan, hinungdan, tungod, rason - Spanish *razon*, pagrason, panrason, pangatadungan, pahinungdan, pagpahinudan
rebuff – *n., a.* bukó, sukmat, pagbukó, pagsukmat
rebuke – *n., a.* sukmat, bukó, suson, pagsukmat
recall – *n., a.* panumdom, pagdumdom
receding forehead – *n.* dangas
receipt – *n.* resibo - Spanish *recibo*
receive – *n., a.* karawat, pagkarawat
reckless – *kan.* kimas, nakimas
recliner – *n.* papag
recognition – *n.* kahingatungdan
recognize – *n., a.* asi, pahitungod, pagasi, pagpahitungod
recollection – *n.* panumdum
recourse – *n.* rimedyo
recreation – *n.* kaliawan, kalingawan

rectify – *n., a.* tádong, pagtádong
rectum – *n.* kala, bubot
red - *n., a., kan.* pula, mapula, bagá, burahag
red bark - *n.* barok
red pepper - *n.* sili
redeem – *n., a.* tubós, lukat, tubyan, pagtubós, paglukat, pagtubyan
redeemer – *n.* manunubos
reduce – *n., a.* iban, kulang, pagiban, pagkulang
reed – *n.* tigbaw, talahib
reef – *n.* takot
refer – *n., a.* basi, pagbasi
reference – *n.* basihan, sanghiran
refresh – *n., a.* hayahay, hulagway, pagpahayahay, paghulagway
refreshing – *kan.* matugnaw, mabugnaw
refuge – *n., a.* dangupan, dalaganan, dangpanan, darangpan, pagdangop
refuse – *n., a.* ayáw, baribad, nadiri, pagdiri
regarding – *s.* sumala
register – *n., a.* parehistro - Spanish *registro*
regret – *n., a.* basol, pagbasol, maan, pagmaan,
reject – *n., a.* salikway, pagsalikway
reliant – *kan.* tapód
relapse – *n., a.* bughat, paghibughat
relative – *n.* kaurupdan, paryinte - Spanish *pariente*
relax – *n., a.* hayahay, hulagway, pahuway, pahayahay, pagpahuway

relaxation – *n.* pamahuway,
pahuwayan, panhulagway
relay – *n., a.* tugon, pagtugon,
pagpatugon
release – *n., a.* ariya, búliw,
pagariya, pagbúliw
reliable – *kan.* tultol,
matatapuran
relief – *n.* bulig, tambulig,
rimedyo - Spanish *remedio*
reliever – *n.* saliwan
religion – *n.* tulúohan,
relihiyon - Spanish *religion*
religious festival – *n.* patron
reluctance – *n.* alangalang,
ruhaduha, kahulop
reluctant – *kan.* palabilabi,
nagaalangalang, sarahuon
rely – *n., a.* tápod, pagtápod
remain – *n., a.* bilin, pagbilin,
pagpabilin
remedy – *n., a.* tambal, bulong,
rimedyo - Spanish *remedio*
remember – *n., a.* tigaman,
dumdom, pagtigaman,
pagdumdom, panumdom
remembrance – *n.* tigamanan,
tigamnan, hinumduman,
rekwerdo - Spanish *recuerdo*
reminder – *n.* tigaman
remnant – *n.* tabigi
remote control - *n.* kontrol -
Englsih *control*
removable – *kan.* kuhakuha
remove – *n., a.* kuha, tanggal,
pagkuha, pagtanggal
rent – *n., a.* pliti, pagpliti
rental - *n., kan.* pliti, paplitihan
repair – *n., a.* ayad, ayos,
pagayad, pagayos
repay – *n., a.* balos, bayad,
pagbalos

repeat – *n., a.* liwat, utro -
Spanish *otro*, pagliwat, pagutro
repeatedly – *kaa.* urúuto
repent – *n., a.* basol, pagbasol,
maan, pagmaan
repent sins – *kah.* Simbako!,
expression of regret
repentance – *n.* pagbasol
repetition – *n.* uruutro
replenish – *n., a.* dugang,
ayaw, pagdugang, pagáyaw
reprimand – *n., a.* saway, isóg,
sina
request – *n., a.* hangyo, araba,
alayon
requirement – *n.* tutumanon,
turumanon
rescue – *n., a.* tabang, bulig
research – *n., a.* hikay, hinikay,
paghikay
reside – *n., a.* puyo, ukóy,
pagpuyo, pagukoy
residence – *n.* puyuanan,
púynan, urukyan, risidensya -
Spanish *residencia*
resident – *n.* tagbalay, risidente
- Spanish *residente*
resignation – *n., a. kah.* buliw,
pagbuliw, bahala na!
resilient – *kan.* mailob,
mabaliknon
resin – *n.* tagok, dapadapo,
sahumeryo
resolve – *n., a.* bisog,
limbasog, panlimbasog
resonate – *n., a.* aningal,
paganingal
resourceful – *kan.* mauyatom,
matinguhaon
resourcefulness – *n.*
kamauyatom, tinguha
respect – *n., a.* tahod,
pagtahod

respected – *kan.* tinahod
respectful – *kan.* matinahuron
respond – *n., a.* balos, baton
responsiblity – *n.* tutumanon, turumanon, katungdanan
rest – *n., a.* pahuway, himurayaw, hundaray, hulagway
rest area – *n.* pahuwayan
restless – *kan.* mairas, maluyá
restlessness – *n.* iras
restrain – n., a. pugong, pagpugong
result – *n.* dangatan, kahingadtuan
result – *s.* hiunong
resurrect – *n., a.* banhaw, pagkabanhaw
resurrection – *n.* kabanhaw
retain – *n., a.* awil, pagawil, pagbilin
retaliate – *n., a.* bulós, pagbulós
retrieve – *n., a.* bawi, pagbawi
return – *n., a.* úli, paguli
return favor – *n., a.* balos, pagbalos
reunion – *n., a.* tipuntipon, kirigta, pagkaurosa, pagkatitipon, pakigkirigta
reveal – *n., a.* bunyag, buking, hataw, paghataw, pagbuking
revelation – *n., a.* bunyag, pahayag
revenge – *n., a.* dumot, bulós, pagdumot, pagbulos
reverberate – *n., a.* haráging, hagurong, pagharging, paghagurong
reverse – *kan.* bali, balisa
revise – *n., a.* liwat, utro, pagliwat, pagutro

revolution – *n., a.* aragway, paglibotlibot
reward – *n.* pahalipay
rheumatism – *n.* rayuma - Spanish *reuma*
rice coconut milk sweet delicacy – *n.* biko, sahog, sinahog, suman, kurukod
rice field – *n.* kahumayan
rice flour – *n.* tiktik, bukbok, binukbok
rice husk – *n.* upá
rice knife – *n.* sipol
rice mill – *n.* gilingan, mulinohan - Spanish *molino*
rice noodle – *n.* bihon
ricefield bird - *n.* maya
rich – *kan.* mayada, bahandianon, salapían, riko - Spanish *rico*
riddle – *n., a.* tigutigo, tigutiguay
ride – *n., a.* sakáy, pagsakay
ride bicycle – *n., a.* angkas, pagangkas
ridicule - *n., a.* tamay, singgit, intrimis, pagtamay, himurangtan, pagsinggit
rifle – *n.* pusil - Spanish *fusil*
right – *kan.* asya, tultol, túo
right turn – *kaa.* patúo
righteous – *kan.* matadong
righteousness – *n.* katadungan
rigidity – *n., kan.* tuskig, matuskig
rigor mortis – *n.* pagtikig
rim of wheel – *n.* yanta - Spanish *llanta*
ring – *n.* singsing
ring the bell – *n., a.* bagting, pagbagting
ringing in the ear – *n.* ugong, hagurong

rinse – *n., a.* bulyas, hugas, pagbulyas, paghugas
rinse rice – *n., a.* kiris, pagkiris
riot – *n., a.* aragway
ripe – *kan.* hinog
rise – *n., a.* buhát, bangon, pagbuhát, pagbangon
river – *n.* sálog
riverbank – *n.* pangpang
riverbend – *n.* tarusan
road – *n.* kalsada, karsada, dalan, agían, aragian
roast – *n., a.* sugba, pagsugba
rob – *n., a.* tikas, pagtikas
robber – *n.* tikasan
rock – *n.* bató
rock and roll – *n., a.* tuwadtuwad, lurulukso
rocky – *kan.* batúbato, kabatuan, kababtuan
roe – *n.* bihod
roll between hands – *n., a.* kirikisi, pagkirikisi
roll over – *n., a., kaa.* pulilid, karukaliding, limbaglimbag, pagpulilid
rolling over – *kaa.* purupulilid
romance – *n.* higugmaay, aring
romantic idle talk – *n.* aringaring
roof – *n.* atop
roof gutter – *n.* sayurong
room – *n.* súlod, kwarto - Spanish *cuarto*
roomy – *kan.* halúag
rooster's spur in cockfights – *n.* tadí
roots – *n.* gamot, puno
rope – *n.* higot, pisi
rosary – *n.* rosaryo, rosaryohan - Spanish *rosario*
rose – *n.* rosa - Spanish *rosa*
rotate – *n., a.* libot, paglibot

rotation - *n.* libotlibot
rotisserie whole pig – *n., a.* litson, paglitson
rotten fruit – *n., kan.* dunot, nadunot
rotten wood – *n., kan.* dumog, nadumog
rotund – *kan.* búyayon
rough blade – *kan.* mangarol, dupol
rough sea – *n.* mabalod, habagat
rough surface – *kan.* gusakgusak, gurakgusak, masapara
round – *n., kan.* lidong, malidong, lison
round smooth rock – *n.* hantakan
rub – *n., a.* bágid, hírog
rubber – *n.* guma - Spanish *goma*
rubber band – *n.* lastiko - Spanish *elastico*
rubber band flicking game – *n., a.* pitikay, lastiko
rubbing ointment – *n.* hiróg, lana, tampos
ruby color – *n.* bulagaw
rudder – *n.* timon - Spanish *timon*
rude – *kan.* bastos
rule – *n.* baláod, mando, surundon
rules – *n.* mga baláod
rumble - *n.* aragaway, aragway
rumor mongering – *n.* hurobhurob, huribhurib
run – *n., a.* dalagan, pagdalagan
run after – *n., a.* bukod, apas, pagbukod, pagapas

run aground – *n., a.* sanglad, pagsanglad
run around – *n., a.* libot, libotlibot, paglibot, palibotlibot
run away – *n., a.* layas, paglayas
run over – *n., a.* ligis, pagligis
runt – *n.* pigos
rural resident – *n., kan.* tagahuron, hurunanon
rushing sound – *n., kan.* haganas, nahaganas
rust – *n., a.* taoy, pagtaoy
rustic – *kan.* hurón, hurunanon
rusty – *kan.* tauyon

S:s

sack – *n.* sako
sacred – *kan.* sagrado - Spanish *sagrado*
sacrifice – *n., a.* halad, paumaya, pagpaumaya, sakripisyo - Spanish *sacrificio*, pagsakripisyo, paghalad
sanctuary – *n.* dalaganan, dangupan, darangpan
sad – *kan.* masulúbon, nabido
sadden – *n., a.* pangandoy, nabido
sadness – *n.* bìdo, kabiduan, kasubo, kasulúbon
safe – *kan.* sigurado
safety pin – *n.* pirdible - Spanish *imperdible*
sag – *n., a.* saghid, tawidil, pagsaghid, pagtawidil
sagging skin – *kan.* kuros, nakuros, kupos
sail – *n., a.* layag, paglayag
sailboat – *n.* paraw

sailor – *n.* manaragat
sala – *n.* ruwang
salacious – *kan.* maláway
salary – *n.* kíta, sweldo - Spanish *sueldo*
salinity – *n.* págad, kapagaran
saliva – *n.* laway
salivate – *n., a., kan.* paglawáy, malawáy
salmon – *n.* salmon - Spanish *salmon*
salt – *n.* asin, págad
salted anchovy – *n.* lawlaw
salted ground shrimp – *n.* hipon
salted mussel – *n.* bahong
salted oyster – *n.* sisí
salted sweet rice – *n.* ibos
salty – *kan.* maasin, mapágad
same – *kan.* kapariho, mismo - Spanish *mismo*
sand – *n.* baras
sandbar – *n.* mumbon, kabarasan
sandpaper – *n.* hagupit, papildeliha - Spanish *papel de lija*
sandy – *kan.* barason, masapara
sap – *n.* tagok
sapling – *n., a.* saringsing, tumos, panaringsing
sarcasm – *n.* súro
sardine – *n.* tamban, sardinas - Spanish *sardina*
sashay – *n., a.* kimbot, pagpakimbot
satiety – *n.* kaluwad, kabusogan
satisfaction – *n.* tunga, pagtunga, kuntento - Spanish *contento*

174

satisfy – *n., a.* tunga, pagtunga, pagayon, pagpatunga

Saturday – *n.* sabado - Spanish *sabado*

saucer – *n.* platito - Spanish *platillo*

sauté – *n., a.* gisa, paggisa

sautéed noodles – *n., a.* pansit, pagpansit

savage – *n., kan.* ihalas, salbahi - Spanish *salvaje*

save – *n., a.* sapod, tabáng, pagsapod, pagtabáng

save money – *n., a.* tipig, tipon, pagtipig, pagtipon

savings – *n.* tipon, tipig, tinipon, tinipigan

saviour – *n.* mananabang

saw – *n.* sirutso

say – *n., a.* luwas, hilwas, siring, tingog, pagluwas, paghilwas, pagsiring, pag tingog

saying – *n.* siringanon, siridnganon, darahunon, kapulungan

scale – *n.,* a. timbang, pagtimbang, timbangan

scallion – *n.* prisya

scam – *n., a., kan.* panguwat, naunong, nauwat

scamper – *n., a.* kaplag, pagkaplag

scar – *n., a.* ulat, piklat, pagulat, napiklat

scarab – *n.* bágang

scare – *n., a.* kahadlok, pataranta, paghadlok

scarecrow – *n.* pahoy

scary – *kan.* hiribhirib, makahiribhib, makaharadlok, makakurulba

scatchy noise – *n., a.* karasikas, nakarasikas

scatter – *n., a.* burublag, sarang, sabrang, sabrak, pagburublag, pagsarang, pagsabrnag, pagsabrak

scatterbrain – *kan.* kalamira, nakalamira

scent – *n.* hamot

scholar – *n.* magaaram, iskolar - English *scholar*

school – *n.* araman, aradman, iskwelahan - Spanish *escuela*

schoolmate – *n.* kaiskwela

science – *n.* syinsya - Spanish *ciencia*

scissors – *n., a.* gunting, paggunting

scissors-stone-paper game – *n.* salagunting

scold – *n., a.* busá, isóg, yakan, pagbusá, pagisóg, pagyakan

scoop – *n.* hungot, kabó

scoop cooked rice – *n., a.* kuhit, pagkuhit

scoop for bailing – *n., a.* limás, paglimas

scoop with palm – *n., a.* harop, pagharop

scorch – *n., a., kan.* tubód, sunóg, páso, natúbod, nasunóg, napáso

scorched rice – *n.* itip

scorching heat – *n.* mapasupasó, madagaang, maalindanga

score – *n.* iskor - English *score*

scorpion – *n.* bungad

scowl – *n., a.* kurisom, pangurisom

scrape – *n., a.* kudkod, bágid, pagkudkod, pagbágid

scratch – *n., a.* kagís, gasgas, kamras, pilas, kagis, bagis, pagkagís, paggasgas, pagkamras, napilas, pagbagis

scratch an itch – *n., a.* kalot, pagkalot, pangalot

scratch with fingernail or claw – *n., a.* kamras, pagkamras

scratching sound – *n.* ngidlis

scratchy – *kan.* makatol

scratchy noise – *n.* karasikas

scream – *n., a.* kuyahaw, guliat, pagkuyahaw, pagguliat, paggulíat, pagsuriyaw

screeching sound – *n.* agikik

screen – *n.* iskrin - English *screen*

screw — *n.* turnilyo - Spanish *tornillo*

scribble – *n., a.* bagisbagis, pagbagisbagis

script – *n.* surat, kasurat

scripture – *n.* kasuratan, kasumatan

scrotum – *n.* búyong

scrub – *n., a.* kuskos, hírog, banos

scrub floor – *n., a.* lampaso, pampaso, pagbunot

scrub skin – *n., a.* ludgod, pagludgod

scuffle – *n., a.* karamsaw, araway, aragway

scythe – *n.* garab

sea – *n.* dagat, kadagatan, kalawdan

sea cucumber – *n.* balat

sea foam – *n.* bura

sea snake – *n.* tigo

sea turtle – *n.* pawikan

sea urchin – *n.* tayom

sea weed – *n.* lato

seabound – *kaa.* ilawod

seal – *n., a.* timre, pagtimre

seam – *n.* takip

seaman – *n.* manaragat

seashell – *n.* buskay, bulalo

seashore – *n.* baybay

seasonal market – *n.* tiyangge, tabo

seat – *n.* lingkuran

sea turtle – *n.* pagong, pawikan

second thoughts - *n., a.* duhaduha, kahulop

secondhand – *kan.* sigundamano - Spanish *segunda mano*

secret – *n.* tinago, sikreto - Spanish *secreto*

secure – *kan., a.* sigurado, siguro - Spanish *seguro*, pagsiguro, pagkasigurado

security – *n.* kasiguraduhan

sedge grass – *n.* tikog

sediment – *n.* larog

see – *n., a.* kitá, bisto, pagkitá, pagbisto

seed – *n.* liso

seek help – *n., a.* dangop, pagdangop

segment – *n.* kapinit, kadugtong, kasumpay

seizure – *n.* buntog

seldom – *kaa.* talagsa, usahay, danay

select – *n., a.* pili, pagpili

self – *kan.* kalugaringon, mismo - Spanish *mismo*

self-righteous – *kan.* masuson

selfish – *kan.* halot, maimot, hangol, awaanon, lamot, hakog, makiíyaíya

selfishness – *n.* kahalutan, kalamutan, kahakugan, kahangulan

sell – *n., a.* baligya,
parabaligya, tindero – Spanish
tienda
semblance – *n.* alagidagid
semen – *n.* turá
senate – *n.* senado - Spanish
senado
senator – *n.* senador - Spanish
senador
send – *n., a.* dúlong,
pagdúlong
send errand – *n., a.* sugo,
pagsugo
send off – *n., a.* pagikan,
pagpagikan
send package – *n., a.* padará,
pagpadará
sentence – *n.* pamulong
sentiment – *n.* kaguol
sentimental – *kan.*
makahiridlaw, namimingaw
separate – *n., a.* bulag, utod,
pagbulag, pagutod
September – *n.* Sityembre -
Spanish *setiembre*
sequel – *n.* sumurunod
sequence – *n.* kadugtong,
sumurunod
sequentially – *kaa.* surunod,
sunúdsunód
serenity – *n.* kamingawan
serious – *kan.* ungod, gulpi,
grabe - Spanish *grave*
seriously – *n., kaa.* inungod
servant – *n.* surugúon, kabulig,
binatá, tinapuran
service – *n.* katungdanan,
serbisyo - Spanish *servicio*
sesame seeds – *n.* lungá
set example – *n., a.*
pananglitan, pananglit
set foot – *n., a.* tamak,
pagtamak

set free – *n., a.* buhi, búliw,
pagbuhi, pagbúliw
set the price – *n., a.* pira,
presyo – Spanish *precio*,
pagpresyo, tagpira
setback – *n.* atraso
setting sun – *n., a.* pagtunod,
katunod
settle – *n., a.* tuhay, pagtuhay,
aragtubang, areglo - Spanish
arreglar, pagareglo
settle down – *n., a., kan.*
himutang, paghimutang,
pahimutang, asintado –

Spanish *asentado*
seven – *num.* pitó, syite -
Spanish *siete*
seventeen – *num.* dyesisyete -
Spanish *diecisiete*
seventy – *num.* kapituàn,
sitenta - Spanish *setenta*
sever – *n., a.* utod, pugot,
pagutod, pagpugot
severe – *kan., kaa.* uráura,
naduro
sew – *n., a.* sursi, tahi,
pagsursi, pagtahi
sex – *n.* ikinatawo, sekso –
Spanish *sexo*
sexual intercourse – *n., a.*
putík, iyot, paghilawas,
himaga, pagputik, pagiyot,
paghimaga
shabby – *kan.* buringot,
barumbado
shack – *n.* payag, balaybalay,
malaybalay
shade – *n.* hudlom,
kahudluman, lindog
shadow – *n.* lambong
shady – *kan.* mahudlom,
madulom

shake – *n., a.* báyog, uyog, yugyog, pagbáyog, paguyog
shake head sideways – *n., a.* pilingpiling, pagpilingpiling
shaky – *kan.* kurog, nakurog
shallow – *kan.* hababaw, hibabaw
shallow waters – *n.* kahababawan, kahababwan
shame – *n.* awod, kaawod, kaarawdan, álo
shameful – *kan.* makaarawod, napaalo, nakakaalo
shameless cry – *n.* ngurahab
shape – *n.* hitsura – Spanish *hechura*
share – *n., a..* bahin, gahin, sahid, pagbahin, paggahin
share food – *n., a.* pagsaro, pagsarusaro
shark – *n.* pating
sharp – *kan.* taís, madulot, matarom
sharpen – *n., a.* báid, tahar, pagbáid, pagtahar
sharpener – *n.* bairan
sharpness – *n.* tarom, kataruman, katarman, katadman
shave head – *n., a.* kiskis, pugo, pagkiskis, pagpakiskis, pagugo, pagpapugo
shawl – *n.* panyo - Spanish *paño*
she – *han.* hiya, siya
sheath – *n.* takob
sheep – *n.* karniro - Spanish *carnero*
shell fragment – *n.* timbi
shellfish – *n.* bukawil
shelter – *n., a.* dalaganan,

pahimutangan, dangpanan darangpan, pagdangop, pagpahimutang
shenanigan – *n.* kinasabang, aringaring, yakyak
shield – *n., a.* taming, sagang, pagsagang, panagang
shill – *n., a.* manguruwat, panguwat
shine – *n., a.* inggat, sikát, paginggat, pagsikát
shine (sun) – *n., a.* sirang, sirak, pagsirang, pagsirak
shingles – *n.* balangaw
shining – *kan.* nasiga, nalamrag
shiny – *kan.* mainggat
ship – *n.* barko, bapor
shirt – *n.* kamisita - Spanish *camisa*
shiver – *n., a.* kadal, pagkadal
shoes – *n.* sapin, sapatos - Spanish *zapato*
shoo – *n., a.* tabog, pagtabog
shoot with arrow – *n., a.* pána, pagpána
short – *kan.* halipot, hilipot
short of breath – *kan.* hangos, nahangos, makapoy, mapunga
short of breath – *n., a.* punga, kapoy, hapo
short of hands – *n., a., kaa.* sugabin, puliki, garamo, pagkapuliki, pagkagaramo
short of help – *kan.* tagdal
short stick batting game – *n.* sato
short-tempered – *kan.* putong, pungtanon
shortage – *n.* puwaki, kakulangan
should – *a.* kinahanglan
shoulder – *n.* sugbong

shoulder arm – *n., a.* sagubay, sagbay, pagsagubay
shout – *n., a.* gulíat, suriyaw, susriyaw
shove – *n., a.* tikwang, duso, pagtikwang, pagduso
shovel – *n.* pála
show – *n.* kiríton
show – *n.* pasundayag
shower – *n., a.* tarahiti, tarithi, pagtarahiti, pagtarithi
show off - *n., a.* hambog, parayaw, pasikat, pasangyaw
show up – *n., a.* tambong, sipot, pakita, pagtambong
shower – *n.* tarahiti, tarithi
shower – *n., a.* karigus, parigo
shower room – *n.* karigusan, pariguan
shrewd – *kan.* switik
shrill – *n., a.* piyait, napiyait
shrimp – *n.* pasayan
shrine – *n.* panáaran
shrink – *n, a.* kupós, kuro, pagkupós, pagkuro
shrunken – *kan.* kúpos, kuro
shuffle – *n., a.* kirikisi, pagkirikisi
shut up – *n., a.* saba, hilom, tákom
shy – *kan.* awdunon
sibling - *n.* bugto, (plural) kabugtuan
sick – *kan.* masakit, duás, irapa
sickly – *kan.* masakiton, irapahon
sickness - *n.* sakit, kasakit, irapa
side – *n.* ligid, kaligiran, kilid
sideways – *kaa.* ligidligid
sieve – *n., a.* sará, pagsára
sigh – *n., a.* hiyom, paghiyom

sign – *n., a.* pirma - Spanish *firma*, pagpirma
sign of the cross – *n., a.* kudos
signal – *n.* sinyal- Spanish *señal*
signature – *n.* pirma – Spanish – *firma*, signatura - English *signature*
significance – *n.* kahulugan, hinungdan, pangahulugan
significant – *kan.* mahinungdanon
silence – *n., a.* mingaw, saba, kamingawan, pagmingaw, pagsaba, paghilom, pagtákom
silent – *kan.* mamingaw
silk – *n.* sida - Spanish *seda*
silly – *n., kan.* pusong, bungaw, salipungog
similar – *kan.* bagá, bagay, angay, alagidagid, sama, sugad, pariho - Spanish *pareja*
simmer – *n., a.* sukob, pagsukob
simple – *kan.* yano
simpleton – *n.* pusong
simultaneous – *n., a., kan.* dungan, pagdungan, durungan, pagdurungan
simultaneously – *kaa.* kadungan, durungan, dudrungan
sin – *n., a.* salá, pagsala, pakasala, pagpakasala
since – *s.* tikang
sincere – *kan.* húlos, kinasingkasing, tikos
sincerely – *kaa.* kinasingkasing
sinful – *kan.* makasasala, makasarala
sing – *n., a.* kanta, awit, pagkanta, pagawit
sing off key – *n., a.* yabag,

pagyabag, sintunado, bira - Spanish *berra,*

singer – *n.* kantor, parakanta, paragkanta, paraawit

singly – *kaa.* usahan, usaan

sink – *n., a.* lunod, paglunod

sinner – *n.* makasasala, makasarala

sip – *n., a.* higop, paghigop

siren – *n.* kataw

sister – *n.* bugto nga babayi

sister-in-law – *n.* hipag nga babayi

sit down – *n., a.* lingcod, paglingkod

sit on floor or ground – *n., a.* lunay, paglunay

sitter – *n.* mangno, magmarango

situation – *n.* kamutangan, kahimutangan, kahimtang

six - *num.* unom, sais, sayis - Spanish *seis*

sixteen - *num.* napulo kag unom, dyesisais - Spanish *dieciseis*

sixty - *num.* sisenta - Spanish sesenta

sixty - *num.* kaunuman, kaunmán

skeleton – *n.* kabukugan, kabukgan

skewer – *n., a.* tusok, tugsok, pagtusok, pagtugsok

skies – *n.* kalangitan

skill – *n.* karit, kaaraman, kaabtikan, kakaritan, kaadman, kinaadman

skillful – *kan.* maaram, makarit, maabtik

skin – *n.* panit

skin bump – *n.* bukol, hubag, bukulbukol

skin infection – *n.* katol, samad

skin irritation – *n., kan.* katol, makatol

skin scratch – *n.* pilas, kagis

skip – *n., a.* laktaw, piktaw, paglaktaw, pagpiktaw

skirt – *n.* saya

skull – *n.* alintarakan, bungo

sky – *n.* langit, kalangitan

slander – *n.* panhimuwa

slap – *n., a.* tampalo, taplong, sakma, pagsakma, pagtampalo, pagtaplong,

slap face – *n., a.* tampalo, tamplong, pagtampalo, pagtaplong

slash – *n., a.* tigbas, haras, pagtigbas, pagharas

slash-and-burn farming – *n.* kaingin

slaughter – *n., a.* ihaw, pagihaw

slaughterhouse – *n.* ihawan, irihawan

slave – *n.* uripon

sleep – *n., a.* katurog, pagkaturog

sleep late – *n., a.* piraw, pagpiraw

sleep over – *n., a.* húron, paghúron

sleep with someone – *n., a.* dirig, durog, pagdirig, pagdurog

sleepiness – *n.* kapirawan, katurugón

sleepy – *kan.* piraw, nahingaturog, pinipiraw

slice of bread – *n.* pinit

slice meat – *n., a.* gurot, paggurot

slide – *n., a.* dalusdos, luslos, huros, pagdalusdos, pagluslos, paghuros
slightly – *kaa.* antuman
slime – *n.* dalunot, lumot
slimy – *kan.* madalunot, madulas
slimy fish – *n.* parutpot, lawayan
slimy seed – *n.* santol
slingshot – *n., a.* santik, pagsantik
slip – *n., a.* balinas, dulas, hurós, pagkabalinas, pagkadulas, paghurós
slip foot – *n., a.* búlos, hibúlos, paghibúlos
slip through – *n., a.* lusot, paglusot
slippers – *n.* tsinelas
slippery – *kan.* madalunot, madulas, malumot
slipshod haircut – *n.* parakatpakat
slit eye – *n., kan.* síngkit, pikot
slobber – *n., a.* mulmol, pagmulmol
slope – *n.* bakilid
sloppy – *kan.* mayamuit
slow – *n., a.* hinay, paghinay
slow – *kan.* mahinay
slow learner – *n.* bulok
slowly – *kaa.* hinayhinay
small – *kan.* gutiay, gamay,
small bell – *n.* kampanilya
small cleaver – *n.* bolo
small intestine – *n.* tripilya
small kettle – *n.* anglit
small quantity – *kan.* guti, pirapira
small size – *kan.* guti, gutiay, gutiksoy
small swordfish – *n.* sugi

small, slimy fish – *n.* parutpot, lawayan
smart – *kan.* maaram, makarit
smarting pain – *n.* hapdos
smash – *n., a.* bunggo, bangga, pagbungo, pagbangga
smashed fruit – *kan.* taog
smegma – *n.* kapa
smell – *n., a.* báho, hamot
smelly – *kan.* mabaho
smile – *n., a., kan.* hiyom, mahiyumhiyom
smirk – *n., a.* yámid, pagyámid
smoke – *n., a.* asó, púot, pagasó, pagluon
smoke cigar or cigarette – *n., a.* dubdob, tustos
smoky – *kan.* maaso, mapúot
smooth – *kan.* mahamis
smooth coconut wine – *n.* bahalina
snack – *n.* isnak - English *snack*, miryenda - Spanish *merienda*
snag – *n., a., kan.* sangko, sáag, pagsangko, pagsaag
snake – *n.* halas
snake poisonous – *n.* agwason
snatch – *a.* pagagaw, pagtabag, pagbingwit
sneaky – *kan.* bugkuton
sneaky find food – *kan.* maharaw
sneer – *a.* yámid, panyámid
sneeze – *n., a.* sungá, singa
sniff – *n., a.* simhot, pagsimhot
sniffle – *n.* sipon
snob – *kan.* malabyaw, suplada
snore – *n., a.* hagong, paghagong
snort – *n., a.* hinggok, huthot, paghinggok, paghuthot

snot – *n.* sipon
snout – *n.* ngawingawi, nguso
snubbish – *kan.* hayhat
so – *kaa., s.* ngáyan, sanglit, salit
so that – *s.* abir, basi
soak – *n., a.* babad, hurom, pagbabad, paghurom
soak rice – *n., a.* lagtok, pagpalagtok
soap – *n., a.* sabon - Spanish *jabon*
sob – *n., a.* tangis, bakho, nguyngoy, pagtangis, pagbakho, pagnguyngoy
soft – *kan.* mahumok
soft and wilted – *kan.* luyat
soften – *n., a.* pahumok, pagpahumok
softness – *n.* kahumók, kahumokan
soil – *n.* tuna, húgaw, lamiri,
soiled – *n kan.* mahúgaw, malamiri
soldier – *n.* sundalo - Spanish *soldado*
sole – *n.* rapádapa
solely – *kaa.* gudla, lúsay, manta
solidify – *n., a.* bagtik, pagbagtik
solve – *n., a.* pagtama, pagsulbar - English *solve*
somehow – *kaa.* bagabaga, sugadsugad
somersault backward – *n., a.* baliskad, pagbaliskad
somersault forward – *n., a.* balintong, pagbalintong
sometimes – *kan.* danay, usahay, talagsa
somewhat – *kaa.* bagabaga, sugadsugad

son – *n.* anak nga lalaki
son-in-law – *n.* umagad nga lalaki
song – *n.* awit, kanta - Spanish *canto/cancion*
sonorous – *kan.* basag
soot – *n.* ariw, abó
sorrow – *n.* bìdo, kabido, subo, kasubo
sorrowful – *kan.* masulúbon, mabiduon
soul – *n.* kalag
soul mate – *n.* hinigugma, higugmaon, asawa
sound – *n., a.* tingog, tunóg, ngiras, huni, pagtingog, pagtunóg, pagngiras, paghuni
sound hollow – *n., a.* hulang, karatong, pagkaratong
sound of small bell – *n., a.* tagingting, pagtagingting
soup – *n., a.* sabaw, pagsabaw
sour – *kan.* maaslom, mapintas
sour crunchy fruit – *n.* alawihaw
sour fruit and sweet – *n.* santol
sour hardy fruit – *n.* batwan
sour succulent fruit – *n.* íba, kamyas
source – *n.* gintikangan, ginbuhatan
source of firewood – *n.* bakhawan
source of income – *n.* hiagi, pakabuhi
soursap – *n.* gwardabano
south wind – *n.* timog
souvenir – *n.* hinumduman, rekwerdo - Spanish *recuerdo*
sow – *n., a.* tanom, pagtanom
sow – *n.* anáy
soy sauce – *n.* tuyo

space – *n.* tungod, lugar -
Spanish *lugar,* kalarakan
Spaniard – *n.* katsila, kastila-
Spanish *castila*
Spanish language *n.* kinastila,
kinatsila
Spanish mackerel – *n.* tangigi
sparkle – *n., a.* inggat, ranggat,
paginggat, pagranggat
sparrow – *n.* gitgit,
balinsasayaw
sparse – *kan.* halaghag
speak – *n., a.* yakan, hilwas,
pagyakan, paghilwas
speaker – *n.* magyayakan,
magrayakan, mamumulong,
ispiker - Engsih *speaker*
spear – *n., a.* bangkaw, bulós
spearfishing – *n.* paná
speech – *n.* yinaknan,
kayakan, diskurso - Spanish
discurso
speech impairment – *n.* nguyit,
ngula
speed – *n.* tulin, laksi,
kapaspas, katulinan,
kalaksihan
speed competition – *n.*
parumba, paprumba.
paspasay, paraspasay
speedy – *kan.* matulin
spell – *n.* baráng, birtod
spend – *n., a.* gasto, paggasto -
Spanish *gastar*
spendthrift – *kan.* magasto
sperm – *n.* turá
sphere – *n.* lison
spice – *n.* haráng, panakot
spicy – *kan.* maharang
spider – *n.* báraw
spill water – *n., a.* takbo, yabo,
watakwatak, pagtakbo,
pagyabo

spin – *n., a.* tuyok, birik,
birikbirik, pagtuyok,
pagbirikbirik
spiny – *kan.* bukugon
spirit – *n.* kalag, ispirito -
Spanish *espiritu*
spit – *n., a.* lura, tupra
spite – *n., a.* tamay, pagtamay
spiteful – *kan.* matamay,
matapubre, hayhat
splash – *n., a.* lasurbo, yabo
splatter – *n., a.* tabsik, tapsik,
pagtapsik, pagtabsik
splinter – *n.* basuni, tiunay,
tunok
split – *n., a.* bulag, tunga,
pagbulag, pagtunga
split coconut shell – *n., a.*
bagtak, pagbagtak
split in half – *n., a.* tunga,
pagtunga
spoil – *n., a.* paura, palangga,
pagpaura
spoiled – *kan.* pikat
spoiled rice – *kan.* maamhok
spoon – *n.* kutsara - Spanish
cuchara
spoon feed – *n., a.* hungit,
pagpahungit
sporadic – *kan.* tayakutak
spouse – *n.* asawa, bana
spread – *n., a.* sarang,latag
taltag, pagsarang, paglatag,
pagtaltag
spread by rake – *n., a.* kahig,
kalkag, pagkahig, pagkalkag
spread by throwing – *n., a.*
saburak, sabrak, pagsaburak
spread legs – *n., a.* sikangkang,
pagsikangkang
spread rumor – *n., a.*
hurubhurob, huribhurib,
paghurubhurob

spring – *n.* burabod, bubon, timba
spring roll – *n.* lumpya
sprinkle – *n., a.* taburos, warikwik, witik, tapsik
sprint – *n.* dalaganay, dadlaganay
sprout – *n.* ubod, saringsing, biyúos, pisót
squabble – *n.* aragaw, aragaway, aragway, puniti
squash – *n.* karubasa
squat – *n., a.* pungko, luob, pagpungko, pagluob
squeaky – *n., kan.* ragaak, naragaak
squeeze – *n., a.* pidlit, ipit, piit, pagpidlit,pugá, pagpiit squeeze by hand – *n., a.* pugá, pidlit, pagpugá, pagpidlit
squeeze out – *n., a.* busni, pagbusni
squeezing sound – *n., a.* lapirit, paglapirit, nalipirit
squid – *n.* núos
squint – *n., a.* duling, libát, pagkaduling, pagkalíbat
squinting – *kan.* naduduling, nalilibat
squirt – *n., a.* pigsot, sirit, pagpigsot, pasirit
stab – *n., a.* bunó, pagbunó
stack – *n., a.* patong, pagpatong
stage – *n.* intablado - Spanish *tablado*
stagnant – *n., a., kan.* biaw, nabiaw, pagbiaw
stain – *n., a.* alop, dukit, húgaw, pagalop, pagdukit, paghúgaw
stair – *n.* balitang, hagdan
staircase – *n.* hagdanan

stale – *n., kan.* pánus, mapános, butod
stale bread – *kan.* pangkag
stale fish – *n.* butod
stall engine – *a.* hunong, tirik, abiriya
stamp – *n., a.* timre - Spanish *timbrar*, pagtimre
stand – *n., a.* tukdaw, tindog, pagtukdaw, pagtindog
stand on platform – *n., a.* tungtong, pagtungtong
stand on water bottom – *n., a.* tugkad, sungkad, pagtugkad, pagsungkad
stand straight – *n., a.* tiso, tadong, pagtiso, pagtadong
stand up – *n., a.* buhát, tindog, pagbuhát, pagtindog
star – *n.* bitúon
star apple – *n.* atis
star fruit – *n.* balimbin, malimbin
starch – *n.* gawgaw
starchy – *kan.* matari
stare – *n., a.* buslong, tutok, titig, pagtutok, pagtitig, pagbuslong
start – *n., a., s.* tikáng, pagtikáng, tíkang
start engine – *n., a.* bira, pagbira
starting point – *n.* tíkang, katikangan, tinikangan
startle – *n., a.* kalas, pakalas, pagkalas
starvation – *n.* gútom, kagutom, katgutom
starve – *n.,a.* gutóm, paggutom
state of confusion – *n.* kagupong
state of health – *n.* kalawasan

statement – *n.* pahayag, pamulong, hinilwas
statue – *n.* istatuwa - Spanish *estatua*
stature – *n.* tindog, dungog, kadungganan
stay – *n., a.* ukóy, puruko, pagukóy, pagpuruko
steadfast – *kan.* pirme – Spanish *firme*
steal – *n., a.* kawat, pangawat, pagkawat,
steal food – *n., a.* haraw, pagharaw
steam – *n., kan.* utbo
steam therapy – *n.* túob
steamboat – *n.* bapor - Spanish *vapor*
steamed rice cake – *n.* puto
steamed rice in palm leaf – *n.* pusó
steel – *n.* puthaw, asero - Spanish *acero*
steering wheel – *n.* timon - Spanish timon
stench – *n.* alisngaw, baho
stench of urine – *n., kan.* angso, maangso
step – *n., a.* pitad, pagpitad
step carved on trees – *n., a.* lublob, paglublob
stepchild – *n.* anak ha gawas
step hard on surface – *n., a.* sagudsod, pagsagudsod
step on – *n., a.* tapak, tunob, pagtapak, pagtunob
step quick – *n., a.* pitig, napitig, pagpitig
sterile – *kan.* baog
stern – *n.* ulin
stevedore – *n.* hurnal
stick – *n., a.* pilit, dukot, pagpilit, pagdukot

stick with pointed object – *n., a.* tusok, tugsok, pagtusok, pagtugsok
sticky – *kan.* dikit, dukot, madukot, mapilit
sticky rice – *n.* pilit
stiff – *kan.* matuskig, mabaskog, natikig
stiffen – *n., a.* tuskig, tikig pagtuskig, pagtikig
stiffness – *n.* kabaskugan, katuskigan, pagtikig
stifling – *kan.* búot
stifling humid air – *n., kan.* alisngaw, maalisngaw, maalinsoob
stilt – *n., a.* kadang. pagkadang
stinginess – *n.* imot, kuripot
stinging jellyfish – *n.* salabay
stingray – *n.* pagi, punsúan
stingy – *kan.* barat, pispis, kuripot, halot, maimot
stinky – *kan.* mabaho, naalisngaw
stir – *n., a.* kirikisi, ukay, sakot, timpla, halo, pagkirikisi, pagukay, pagsakot, pagtimpla, paghálo
stitch – *n., a.* sursi, pagsursi
stoic – *adj.* malimbasog
stomach – *n.* tungol
stomachache – *n.* kabag, suruksurok
stone – *n., a.* bató, pagbató
stone grinder – *n.* giling, bairan, garingan
stone mill – *n.* garingan
stone scrub – *n.* ludgod
stone wall – *n.* kuta – Spanish *coto*
stop – *n., a.* ukóy, hunong, lugar, pára - Spanish *parar,*

pagukoy, paghunong, pagtirik, pagabiriya

stop and go – *kaa.* ukúyukóy

store – *n.* baligyaan, tindahan – Spanish *tienda*

storm – *n.* madlos, bagyo

stormy – *kan.* madlos

story – *n.* sumat, susumaton, surumaton, istorya - Spanish *historia*

stout – *kan.* buntol, búyayon

stove – *n.* abuhan, kalan

straight – *kan.* tadóng, matadong

straight ahead – *kaa.* dayon, katadungan, diretso - Spanish *derecho*

straighten up – *n., a.* tádong, tigdong, pagtadong, pagtindog

strain – *n., a.* sára, pagsára,

strainer – *n.* sará, sira

strange – *adj.* urusahon

stranger – *n.* langyaw, banyaga, dayuhan

strangulate – *n., a.* pitlok, pagpitlok

straw mat - *n.* banig

street – *n.* kalsada, karsada, kalye - Spanish *calle*

street child - *n.* bugoy, bangaw

street smart – *kan.* switik

strength - *n.* kusóg

stressful – *kan.* makulba, makalilisang

stretch – *n., a.* unat, pagunat

strict – *kan.* masungit, istrikto – Spanish *estricto*

stride – *n., a.* bakang, pagbakang

string – *n.* higot, hiludibila, lubid

stroll – *n., a.* lakatlakat, pasyada, pamasyada

strong – *kan.* makusog, kusugan, kusgan

strong current – *kan.* masulog

stubborn – *kan.* sarawayon, palabilabi, sarahuon

stuck – *n., a.* sangit, pagsangit

stuck fishbone in the throat – *kan.* nabukog

stuck in mud – *kan.* natalnod

stuck as splinter – *kan.* naungot

student – *n.* magtutúon, istudyante - Spanish *estudiante*

study – *n., a.* arám, tuón, pagarám, pagtuón

study room – *n.* basahan

stumble – *n., a.* salaki, pakdol, napakulob, natumba, nasalaki, tukmod, natukmod

stupid – *kan.* paog, paugpaog, bungaw, tunto - Spanish *tonto*, salipungog

stupidity – *n.* kapaugan

sturdiness – *n.* kadígon, karígon

sturdy – *kan.* madígon, marígon

sty – *n.* síngit

subjugate – *n., a.* suhito - Spanish *sujeto*, pagsuhito

submerge – *n., a.* lurop, tiksop, tulnob, paglurop

substance – *n.* sustansya – Spanish *sustancia*

substitute – *n., a.* líwan, saliwan, kasaliwan

subtrahend – *n.* kaíban, kabawas

subtract – *n., a.* iban, bawas, pagiban, pagbawas

subtraction – *n.* pangiban, pagiban

succeed – *n., a.* sangpot, talwas, pagsangpot, pagtalwas
success – *n.* katalwasan, kasangputan
suck – *n., a.* súso, supsop, mulmol, tsupa - Spanish *chupa*, pagsúso, pagsupsop, pagmulmol, pagtsupa
suck in belly – *n., a.* hiyak paghiyak
sucker – *n.* huthot, supsop
sudden – *kan., kaa.* tigda, kalit, dalikyat
sue – *n., a.* kiha, pagkiha
suffer – *n., a.* antos, pagantos
suffering – *n.* antos, nagaantos, kasakit, kakurian
suffice – *a., kaa.* sadang
sufficiency – *n.* sadang, kasadangan
suffocating – *n., kan.* búot, alimuot
suffocating hot – *kan.* maalinsuob, maalindanga
suffocating odor – *kan.* masungotsugar – *n.* kalamay, asukar - Spanish *azucar*
sugar cane – *n.* tubó
suicide – *n., a.* unay, pakamatay, pagunay, pagpakamatay
sulk – *n., a.* murusot, kurisom, pagmurusot, pangurisom
sultry – *adj.* mapasó, maalindanga, maalinsúob
sum – *n., a.* suma, pagsuma
summarize – *n., a.* suma, pagsuma, susumahon
summit – *n.* tuktok, talimpukayan, kasagsagan
summon with hand – *n., a.* kampay, pagkampay
sun – *n.* adlaw

sun-drying harvested rice - *n., a.* binlad, pagbinlad
Sunday – *n.* domingo - Spanish *domingo*
sunflower seed – *n.* sandiya
sunglare – *n.* silaw
sunny – *kan.* maadlaw, masirak
sunray – *n.* sidlit
sunrise – *n., a.* sirang, pagsirang, pagpunias
sunset – *n., a.* katunod, pagkatunod katunuran, katundan
sunshine – *n.* sirak
superficial – *kan.* harapaw
superstition – *n.* diwata, tuluuhan
supine – *n., a., kan.* huyang, paghuyayag, mahuyang
supper – *n.* pangiklop, panihapon
supple – *kan.* mahumok
suppleness – *n.* humok, kahumukan
supplication – *n.* pangamuyo, panginyupo
support – *n., a.* sandigan, tukod, bangil, pagsandig, pagtukod, pagbangil
suppurate – *n., a.* nana, pagnana
sure – *kan.* piho, sigurado, syimpre - Spanish *siempre*
surely – *kaa.* gud, alang, agod, manggod
surf – *n.* bura han balod
surf from prow – *n.* sibid
surface – *n., a.* harapaw, bawbaw, paghataw
surgeon – *n.* manunudlis, parabusbos, paragbusbos

surname – *n.* apelyido -
Spanish *apellido*
surplus – *n.* subra, apaw,
sapaw
surprise – *kah.* Agidaw!
surprise – *n., a.* kalas, hipausa,
pagpakalas
surround – *n., a.* libot, palibot,
paluyo, paglibot
surrounding - *n.* libong,
kaligiran, ligidligiron
suspect – *n., a.* tahap,
pagtahap
suspicion – *n.* tahap,
tahaptahap
swagger – *n.* pamalod
pamahungpahong,
swallow – *n., a.* tulon, lámoy,
pagtulon, paglámoy
swallow – *n.* balinsasayaw
swamp – *n.* katubigan,
kahanangan
swayed – *a., kan.* padára
swear – *n., a.* sumpa, sáad,
pagsumpa, pagsáad
sweat – *n., a.* balhas,
pagbalhas
sweat rash – *n.* hulashulas
sweaty – *kan.* balhason
sweep – *n., a.* siphid,
pagsiphid, paniphid
sweep away – *n., a.* anod,
anas, naanod, naanas,
paganod, paganas
sweet – *kan.* matámis
sweet potato – *n.* kamoti –
Mexican *camote*
sweet rice coconut delicacy –
n. biko, sahog, kurukod,
suman
sweetheart - *n.* higugmáon,
hinigugma, pinalangga,
kunsuylo - Spanish *consuelo*

sweetness – *n.* tamís,
katámisan
swell – *n.* humatol, balod
swelling – *n., a.* bukol, bútol,
hubag, hupong, panhupong,
paghubag
swept – *kan.* sinaphid, siniphid
swiftly – *kaa.* paspas,
kadagmitan
swim – *n., a.* langoy,
paglangoy
swim backstroke – *n., a.*
ulalay, pagulalay
swimmer's ear – *n.* lunggan
swindle – *n., a.* paglurong,
panguwat, pauwat
swindler – *n.* manguruwat
swing – *n., a.* abyog, labyog,
yugyog, pagabyog, paglabyog,
pagyugyog
swipe – *n., a.* sabod, saping,
pag sabod, pagsaping
switch – *n., a.* balyo, pagbalyo,
suwits – English *switch*,
pagsuwits
switch off – *n., a.* parong,
pagparong
switch on – *n., a.* palága,
pasiga, pagpalága, pagpasiga
sword – *n., a.* ispada,
pagispada
swordfish – *n.* malasugi
sycophant – *n.* huthot, supsop
sympathetic expression – *kah.*
intawon!, kairo man!
susmariyosep!
sympathize – *n., a.* paíd,
pagpaíd
sympathy – *n.* duyog, kaluoy,
pagduyog, pagkaluoy
synchronize – *n., a.* kadungan,
dungan, pagdungan

T:t

Table – *n*. lamisa - Spanish *mesa*
tablet chocolate – *n*. tabliya
tail – *n*. ikog
tailor – *n., a.* tahi, mananahi, manarahi, sastri - Spanish *sastre*, pagtahi
take – *n., a.* bitbit, dará, kuha, pagbitbit, pagdará, pagkuha
take advantage – *n., a.* singabot, patakas, pagsingabot, pagpatakas
take an oath – *n., a.* sumpa, saad, pagsumpa, pagsaad
take away –*n., a.* bawas, kulang, pagbawas, pagkulang
take bath or shower – *n., a.* karigo, parigo, pagkarigo
take communion – *n., a.* kumulgar - Spanish *comulgar*, pagkumulgar
take down – *n., a.* tanggal, bunkag, pagtanggal, pagbungkag
take easy – *n., a.* hayahay, hulagway, paghulagway, pahayahay
take off shoe – *n., a.* hulso, paghulso
take off hat – *n., a.* tuklas, pagtuklas
take off hanging clothes – *n., a.* bulkas, hilkas, pagbulkas, paghilkas
take refuge – *n., a.* dangop, pagdangop
take side – *n., a.* ugop, pagugop
take steps – *n., a.* pitad, pagpitad

take test – *n., a.* iksamen, pagiksamen,pagpaiksamen
taken – *kan.* kuha, nakuna
tail – *n., a.* ikog, tawidil, pagtawidil
tailor – *n*. mananahi, manarahi
talisman – *n*. antinganting, saot
talk – *n., a.* yakan, yawyaw, himangraw, pagyakan, paghimangraw
talk incoherently – *n., a.* yakimbot, yawyaw, kinasabang, pagbagulbol, pagyawyaw
talkative – *kan.* mayakan, mayakimbot, yakimbutan, mayawyaw, mayawit
tall – *kan.* hataas, hitaas
tall and slender – *kan.* lanyug
tamarind – *n*. tamarindo, sambalagi
tangerine – *n*. aranghita
tangle – *n., a.* sangit, pagsangit
tantrums – *n., a.* busyo, binubusyo, pagbusyo
tap – *n.,a.* kubit, sagmak, sakma, pagkubit, pagsakma, pagsagmak
tardy – *kan.* urhi, atrasado, Spanish atrasado
taro - *n*. gaway
taro delicacy - *n*. lidgid, iraid, sagmani
taro leaves - *n*. badyang, láing
tart - *n., kan.* saplod, masaplod
tart coconut wine - *n*. bahal
taste – *n., a.* tilaw, tagamtam, rasa, karasá, pagtilaw, kagustuhan
tasteful, tasty – *n*. marasa, matagamtam
tattered – *kan.* gisígisí

tattoo – *n.* yunal
taxi – *n.* taksi - English taxi
taxicab – *n.* taksi
teach – *n., a.* tutdo, pagtutdo
teacher – *n.* magturutdo,
manunutdo, titser - English
teacher
teachings – *n.* panutduan,
tinunan
tear – *n., a.* gísi, piksi, paggísi,
pagpiksi
tears – *n.* luha
tease – *n., a.* singgit, unggit,
sunglog, pagsinggit,
pagsunglog
teaser – *n.* masinggit, maunggit
technique – *n.* kahímo
teeth particles – *n.* tinga, kiki
television – *n.* tebe, telebisyon
- American *television*
tell – *n., a.* sumat, hisgot,
saysay, pagsumat, paghisgot,
pagsaysay
temper tantrums – *n.* busyo
temporary – *kan.* lumalabay
tempt – *n., a.* tukso, súlay,
pagtukso, pagsúlay
ten – *num.* napúlô, dyes -
Spanish *diez*
tenacious – *kan.* madígon,
matatag, mabaskog
tenacity – *n.* baskog, tatag,
kadígon, kabaskog, katatagan
tendency – *n., kaa.* hilig, maki,
pagka
term – *n.* pulong, termino
termite – *n.* ánay
terrified – *kan.* narimadima,
naugmaran, nahadlokan
terrify – *n., a.* hadlok, ugmad,
rimadima, paghadlok,
pagugmad, pagrimadima

test – *n., a.* suri, iksamen -
Spanish *examen*, pagsuri,
pagiksamen
testicle - *n.* lisík, itlog
thank – *n., a.* salamat,
pasalamat, pagpasalamat
that – *s., han.* ámo, iton, it
the – *tud.* nga, hi, si
theater – *n.* kirítan, sinehan –
English *cinema*
theft – *n.* panikas, pangawat
their – *han.* ira
theirs – *han.* ira, haira
then – *kaa., s.* kataliwan,
niyan, sanglit, salit, intonsis -
Spanish *entonces*
thence – *s.* salit, sanglit
there – *han., kaa.* aada, dida,
didto, ngada, ngadto
therefore – *s.* sanglit, salit,
intonsis - Spanish *entonces*
these – *han.* inin, hinin, sinin
thick – *kan.* bahol, madakmol
thick skin dirt – *n.* buring,
kagíd
thick syrup – *kan.* hútok
thick woven mat – *n.* bariw
thicken as liquid – *n., a.*
bagtik, pagbagtik
thickness – *n.* kadakmolan
thief – *n.* kawatan, tikasan
thigh – *n.* páa
thin – *kan.* magasá, manipis,
gamay
thin out – *n., a.* pánas, ibas
pagpánas, pagibas
thing – *n.* butang
think – *n., a.* hunahuna,
panhunahuna, paghunahuna,
pagpinsar - Spanish *pensar*
thinly spread – *kan.* halaghag
thirst – *n., a.* uhaw, hibol,
mauhaw, pagkauhaw

thirsty – *kan.* hinihibol, inuuhaw
thirteen – *num.* trese - Spanish trece
thirty – *num.* katuluán
this – *han.* ini, hini, sini
thorn – *n.* tunok
thorny – *kan.* tunukon
thousand – *num.* yukót, mil - Spanish *mil*
thread – *n.* inulang
thread needle – *n., a.* tanod, pagtanod
three – *num.* tuló, tres - Spanish *tres*
thresh harvested rice – *n., a.* giok, paggiok
throat – *n.* bútol, langaglangag, tutulunan, turunlan
throb – *n., a.* putok, pagputok
through – *s.* lapos
through and through – *kaa.* lapuslapos
throw – *n., a.* lábay, labog, pilak, itsa, paglábay, paglabog, pagpilak, pagitsa
throw spear – *n., a.* bangkaw, pagbangkaw
throw stone – *n., a.* lábay, batak, paglábay, pagbatak
throw up – *n., a.* suká, pagsuka
throw water – *n., a.* takbo, yabó, pagtakbo, pagyabó
thrust – *n., a.* bundol, kido, kiyod, pagbundol, pagkido, pagkiyod
thumb – *n.* tamuragko
thunder – *n.* dalugdog
thunderstorm – *n.* kikidlat ngan daluglog, bunok, darudalugdog, nagbubunok
Thursday – *n.* huwebes - Spanish *jueves*

tick – *n.* tungaw
tickle – *n., a.* girikgitik, gitikgitik, paggirikgitik, paggitikgitik
ticklish – *kan.* magirok, girikgitikon, gitikgitikon
tidal bore – *n.* sugpo
tidy – *kan.* maayos, mahamis
tie a bundle – *n., a.* butok, pagbutok
tie down – *n., a.* gapos, gáod, paggapos, paggáod
tie with string – *n., a.* higot, paghigot
tight – *kan.* húgot, húot, kipot
tight fitting – *kan.* lutop
tighten – *n., a.* hugót, pahuót, paghugót, pagpahuót
tilt – *n., a., kan.* pagkiling, nakiling
time – *n.* panahon, takna, tyempo, oras - Spanish *hora*
time of creation – *n.* katikangan, tinikangan
timid – *kan.* awdunon
tin can – *n.* lata - Spanish *lata*
tingling sensation – *n.* girok
tinnitus – *n.* hagurong, ugong
tiny – *kan.* gutiksoy
tiny bumps – *n.* lisuliso
tiny mud crab – *n.* kayamas
tip – *n.* tumoy
tiptoe – *n.* ikid
tire – *n.* guma, Spanish *goma*
tired – *kan.* mabutlaw, maguol, mahawol, makapoy, kapagalan
tiredness – *n.* guol, kapoy, butlaw, hawol
tireless effort - *n.* paniguro
title – *n.* tawag
titular – *kan.* hangaran
to – *kat.* ha, sa, kan, pa
tobacco pipe – *n.* hunsoy

191

toddler – *n.* puya, lugtok, lumatod, mutato

toil – *n.* buruhaton, trabaho, obra - Spanish *obra*

toilet – *n.* uruhan, kasilyas, kubita - Spanish *cubeta*

toilet paper – *n.* ulí

tomato – *n.* kamatis

tomb – *n.* pantyon, lubungan, linubngan

tomboy – *n.* palakínon, tumboy – English *tomboy*

tomorrow – *n., kaa.* buwas

tong – *n.* kimpit

tongue – *n.* díla

too much – *kaa.* uráura

tool – *n.* gamit, garamiton

tool sharpener – *n.* bairan

tooth – *n.* ngípon

toothbrush – *n., a.* tutbras - English *toothbrush*, sipelyo - Spanish *cepillo de dientes*

toothless – *kan.* sulam, ngihab

toothy smile – *n., a.* ngisí

top – *n.* sagudida, bawbaw

topical medication - *n.* hiróg

torch – *n.* súlo, suga

torn – *kan.* gisí, gusí

tornado - *n.* buhawi, ipoipo, alipuros

torrent – *n., kan.* sulog, buhos, masulog, nabuhos

torrential rain – *n., a.* bunok, pagbunok

torso – *n.* lawas

tortoise – *n.* baó, hangag

toss – *n., a.* pilak, itsa, labog, pagpilak, pagitsa, paglabog

total, totality – *n.* búgos, lubos, húlos

touch – *n., a.* tubil, labot, kubit, pagtubil, paglabot, pagkubit

tough – *kan.* mabaskog, matíga, matigás, matatag, madígon

toughness – *n.* kamatigás, kadígon, kadigunan, katatagan

tow – *n., a.* tugway, pagtugway, pagbutong, pagrimolki - Spanish *remolque*

towards – *kat., kaa.* ngadto, pakadto, pa, tipakadto, tipá

towards foot – *kaa.* tiilan, patiilan

towards head – *kaa.* uluhan, pauluhan

towards the left – *kaa.* pawala

towards the right – *kaa.* patúo

towards the sea – *kaa.* ilawod, palawod

towards upstream – *kaa.* pasuba

towel – *n.* tuwalya – Spanish *toalla*

tower – *n.* lantawan

town – *n.* bungto

town dweller – *n.* bungtuhanon

town fiesta – *n.* patron

toxic – *kan.* makahihilo

toy – *n.* mulayan, uyagan

trace – *n. a.* subay, subaybay, pagsubaybay

trace a sketch – *n., a.* lutop, palutop, pagpalutop

tracing – *n.* ági, bagis, badlis, subay

trade – *n., a.* palit, baligya, palitan, pagpalit, pagbaligya

tradition – *n.* binatasan, nahiaraan, kinabatasan, kabatasanan

traditional water splashing – *n.* kastulindas (St. John the Baptist feast) trail, trailway – *n*. aragian, dalan

traitor – *n*. lingo, traydor - Spanish *traidor*

traitorous – *kan*. malingo

transfer – *n*., *a*. balhin, pagbalhin

transient – *kan*. lumalabay

translate – *n*., *a*. hulóg, paghulóg

translation – *n*. kahulugan, pangahulogan

transparency – *n*. silhag

transparent – *kan*. masilhag, nalutop

trap – *n*., *a*. lítag, paglítag

trapped water in the ear - *n*. lunggan

trash – *n*. basura

trash bin – *n*. basurahan

travel – *n*., *a*. lakaton, sakayón, nabigar - Spanish *navigar*, biyahe - Spanish *viaje*, paglalakaton, pag nabigar, pagbiyahe

travel foreign lands – *n*., *a*. langyaw, paglangyaw, pagpalangyaw

travesty – *n*. pahimuwa

treacherous – *kan*. traydor, malingo, manunulay

treat medically – *n*., *a*. tambal, bulong, pagtambal, pagbulong

treat somebody – *n*., *a*. tahod, tratar - Spanish *tratar*, pagtahod, pagtratar

tree fairies – *n*. kahuynon

tree leaves and clippings - *n*. sighot, siot

tree sour fruit – *n*. santol

trek – *n*., *a*. baktas, pagbaktas

tremble – *n*., *a*. kúrog, kadal, pagkurog, pagkadal

tremors – *n*. kuróg, linog

trend – *n*., *a*. uso, nauso, paguso

trepidation – *n*. hadlok, kahadlok

trick – *n*., *a*. intrimis, panguwat, laksi

trickle – *n*., *a*., *kan*. turuturo, talaita, pagturuturo, pagtalaita, tinalaita

trip – *n*., *a*. salaki,tumba, pagkasalaki, pagkatumba

trip – *n*., *a*. lalakaton, biyahe – Spanish *viaje*, paglalakaton, pagbiyahe

trip one intentionally – *n*., *a*. sapikí, pagsapikí

triumph – *n*., *a*. daog, pagdaog

triumphant – *kan*. daugan

tropical tree – *n*. lawaan

trouble – *n*. samok, lungot, labad, piruwisyo - Spanish *perjuicio*

troublesome – *kan*. malabad, malungot, masamok

trousers – *n*. saruwal

true – *kan*. tuód, ungod

truly – *kaa*. inungod, pagka

trump up – *n*., *a*. himuhimo, paghimuhimo

trumpet – *n*. turutot

trunk – *n*. baol, púno

trust – *n*., *a*. tápod, pagtapod

trustworthy – *kan*. tapuran, matinumanon

truth – *n*. kamatuúran, katutungaydan

truthful – *kan*. tinúod, matúod

try – *n*., *a*. suway, tisting – English *testing*, pagsuway

try hard – *n*., *a*. himakuri, paghimakuri

tub – *n*. batya

tuba gatherer – *n.* mananangot, manaranggot, mananggiti
tube – *n.* túbo - Spanish *tubo*
tuberculosis – *n.* tibi, TB
tuber – *n.* palawan, gaway, talyan
Tuesday – *n.* martes - Spanish *martes*
tugboat – *n., a.* rimulki, pagrimulki -Spanish *remolquer*
tumble – *n., a.* balintong, baliskad, pagbalintong, pagbaliskad
tumbler – *n.* hungot, baso – Spanish *vaso*
tumor – *n.* bukol, tumor - Spanish tumor
tuna fish – *n.* barilis
tune – *n.* tunóg
turbid – *kan.* malubog
turbidity – *n.* lubog
turbulence – *n.* alipuros
turd – *n.* tubol
turkey – *n.* pabo - Spanish *pavo*
turmeric – *n.* dulaw
turn a page – *n., a.* pakli, pagpakli
turn a wheel – *n., a.* waring, pagwaring
turn around – *n., a.* talikod, birik, balik, pagtalikod, pagbirik, pagbalik
turn at corner – *n., a.* liko, pagliko
turn upside down – *n., a.* taób, balikad, pagbalikad, pagtaób
turtle – *n.* pagong, baó, pawikan, hangag
turtle dove – *n.* bálod
TV – *n.* tebe, telebisyon
TV anchorman – *n.* paragsamwak

twelve – *num.* dose - Spanish doce
twenty – *num.* karuhaan, baynte - Spanish veinte
twerk – *n., a.* kido, kiyod, pagkido, pagkiyod
twilled cotton pants – *n.* maong
twine – *n.* lubid, linubid, pisi, higot
twinkle – *n., a.* pisokpisok, pagpisokpisok
twist – *n., a.* birikis, pagbirikis
twist strings – *n., a.* lubid, talunay, paglubid, pagtalunay
twisted – *kan.* birikis, nabirikis, linubid
two – *num.* duhá, dos - Spanish dos
two-fist stone-paper-scissor game – *n., a.* salagunting, pagsalagunting
typhoid fever – *n.* tipos
typhoon – *n.* bagyo

U :u

ugliness – *n.* raksot, karaksutan
ugly – *kan.* maraksot
umbilicus – *n.* pusod
umbrella – *n., a.* payong, pagpayong
umbrella-like mushroom – *n.* ligbos
unbalanced – *kan.* pihing, hiwi
unbelievably – *kaa.* harumamay, kaurusahon
uncircumcised – *kan.* pisót, piyós, supot, huló
uncivilized – *kan.* barumbado, ihalas
uncle – *n.* batá, tata, tatang

uncommon – *kan.* birilingon,
birilngon, panalagsa
uncooked – *kan.* hilaw
uncooked meal – *n.* lutúon
uncover – *n., a.* tukas,
pagtukas
under – *kat.* ilarom, sirung,
ubós
underpass – *n.* suhuton
understand – *n., a.* paìd,
santop, sabot, intyinde -
Spanish *entender*
understanding – *kan.*
mahumla, napaid
uneven – *kan.* angihas,
pilidong, hiwi
unfold – *n., a.* buklad, bukas,
pagbuklad, pagbukas
unforgiving – *kan.* madumot
unfortunate – *kan.* dimalas
unfurl – *n., a.* buklad,
pagbuklad
ungrateful - *kan.* bungalos
unhung – *n., a.* bulkas, hilkas,
pagbulkas, paghilkas
unhusked rice – *n.* humay,
tipasi
unique – *adj.* waray sugad
unite – *n., a.* urusa, pagurusa
unity – *n.* kaurusahan,
pagkaurusa
universe – *n.* kalarakan
unkempt – *kan.*
nagpaparagpag
unlike – *kan.* ibá
unlucky – *kan.* buwisit,
dimalas
unmarried man – *n.* ulitawo
unmarried woman – *n.* daraga
unproductive time – *n.*
lakwatsa
unquenchable as thirst – *kan.*
mahibulong, mahiblong

unravel – *n., a.* bákad, badbad,
rantas, pagbákad, pagbadbad,
pagrantas
unreplenished – *kan.* ubúsúbos
unripe – *kan.* hilaw, lahing
unsalted – *kan.* matábang
unsanitary – *kan.* amóg,
mahugaw, kaamog
unsavory – *kan.* matábang
unsightly – *n., kan.* raksot,
maraksot, maraot, mangílad
unstable – *kan.* tikwugon,
maluyá, matiwugtiwog
unsteady – *kan.* tikwugon,
maluyá, matiwugtiwog
unsteady gait – *n.* ingka
untangle – *n., a.* badbad,
bákad, pagbákad, pagbadbad
untie – *n., a.* hubad, paghubad
until – *kat., s.* hangtod, tubtob,
ngada, hasta - Spanish *hasta*
untruthful – *kan.* buwá
on, diri matuod
unusual – *kan.* kakaiba
unwashed clothes - *kan.*
buringon
unwind – *n., a.* bakad,
pagbakad
unyielding – *kan., a.* pakipot
upland – *n.* sagka, sugka
upon – *kat., s.* bawbaw,
tungod, pag
upper level – *n.* igbaw
uproar – *n.* alburoto
uproot – *n., a.* gabot, paggabot
upset – *a., kan.* ngalas, bigit
upside down – *n., kan.* tuwad,
natuwad
upstream – *n., a.* suba, pasuba,
pagpasuba
upward incline – *n., kan.*
bangad, nabangad
urge – *n., a.* tukso, surugsurog

195

urinary bladder – *n.* pantog
urinate – *n., a.* ihi, pagihi
urine – *n.* ihi
us – *han.* am, amon, namon,
at, aton
usage – *n.* kagamitan, pulos,
kapulsanan
use – *n., a.* gamit, pulos,
paggamit, pagpulos
use bamboo torch – *n., a.* súlo,
pagsulo
use cement as mortar – *n., a.*
simento, pagsimento
usefulness – *n.* gamit,
kagamitan, uso - Spanish *uso*
useless – *kan.* kawang,
kanugon, waray gamit
uterus – *n.* matris – Spanish
matriz
utility – *n.* kagamitan
utilize - *a.* gamit, pulos
utter – *n., a.* hilwas, luwas,
yakan, siring, paghilwas,
pagluwas, pagsiring

V:v

V-shaped fishing contraption –
n. sudsod
vacant – *kan.* bakante -
Spanish vacante, basiyo -
Spanish *vacio*
vacation – *n.* bakasyon -
Spanish *vacacion*
vaccinate – *n., a.* bakuna -
Spanish *vacuna,* pagbakuna,
pagpabakuna
vaccine – *n.* bakuna, baksin –
English *vaccine*
vagabond – *n.* latagaw
vagina – *n.* pútik, puday, pipi
Valsalva maneuver – *n., a.*
utók, undo, pagutók, pagundo

value – *n., a.* pulos, pira, balor
- Spanish *valor*
vanquish – *n., a.* daog,
pagdaog
vapor – *n.* utbo, alingasaw
variety – *n., kan.* dirudilain,
durudilain, magkadirudilain
vast ocean – *n.* kalawuran,
kalawdan
vegetable – *n.* utanon,
tanaman
vegetable dish – *n.* utan
vegetable patch – *n.*
katanuman, katanman,
tanaman
vegetable pear – *n.* sayote –
Mexican *chayote*
vegetable sprout – *n.* ugbos,
saringsing
vegetation – *n.* tanaman,
kabanwaan
vehicle – *n.* sakayán, sarakyan
veil – *n.* panyo
vengeful – *kan.* madumot,
pungtanon
verification – *n.* kasayuran
verify – *n., a.* sayod, pagsayod,
panginsayod
very – *kaa.* duro, masyado,
pagka, mismo - Spanish *mismo*
vessel – *n.* barko - Spanish
barco
viand – *n.* surá
vibrant – *kan.* maribhong
vice – *n.* bisyo
victorious – *kan.* daugan,
madaóg
victory – *n.* daóg, daugan
vie – *n., a.* aarig, aragaw,
pagaarig, pagaragaw
view – *n., a.* dungaw, tanaw,
pagdungaw, pagtanaw

view point - *n*. dungawan, tanawan

village – *n*. hurón, baryo - Spanish *barrio*

vine – *n*. balagon

vine-like parasitic plant - *n*. palaypay

vinegar – *n*. suoy

violate – *n., a*. supak, talo, pagsupak, pagtalo

violation – *n*. supak

violet – *n*. aplod, sampaga, tagimpusuon

violin – *n*. ngitngit, byulin - Spanish *violin*

virgin – *n*. daraga, daragita, birhen - Spanish *virgin*

virtue – *n*. birtod - Spanish *virtud*

virulence – *n*. lará, kalará, kamalára

virulent – *kan*. malára

virus – *n*. bayrus, English *virus*

visit – *n., a*. dúaw, dayo, bisita - Spanish *visita*, pagdúaw, pagdayo, pagbisita

visitor – *n*. dayuhan, bisita – Spanish *visita*

vitamin – *n*. bitamina - Spanish *vitamina*

vocabulary – *n*. kahulugan, kapulungan, purulungan, pangahulugan

voice – *n*. tingog, boses - Spanish *voces*

volcano – *n*. bulkan - Spanish *volcan*

vomit – *n., a*. suká, pagsuká

vomitus – *n*. súka

voracious – *kan*. makaon

vote – *n., a*. buto, pagbuto

voter – *n*. botante - Spanish *votante*

vowel – *n*. patunog

vulgar – *kan*. maláway, mangirhat, mangilad

vulture – *n*. siwak

W:w

wafer – *n*. apa

wager – *n*. pusta, taón, pustahan

waist – *n*. háwak, baláwang, baywang

wait – *n., a*. hulat, langanlangan, paghulat, paglanganlnagn

wake – *n*. lamay, taguminatay

wake up – *n., a*. pagmatá, buhat, bangon

wake up suddenly – *n., a*. bungkaras, pagbungkaras

walk – *n., a*. lakat, paglakat

walk fast – *n., a*. padog, pagpadog, napadog

walk in mud – *n., a*. sugbo, pagsugbo

walk leisurely – *n., a*. pasyada, lakwatsa, pamasyada, paglakwatsa

walk on narrow plank – *n., a*. latay, paglatay

walk with stilts – *n., a*. kadang, pagkadang

walk wobbly – *n., a*. ingka, pagingka

walking poles – *n*. kadang

wall – *n*. bungbong

waltz – *n*. balsi - Spanish vals

wander – *n., a*. laag, lakatlakat, paglaag

wanderer – *n.* latagaw
want – *n., a.* karuyag, gusto–
Spanish *gustar*, pagkaruyag,
paggusto
wanting – *kan.*
makinahanglanon,
maruruyagon
war – *n.* gubot, saramok,
aragway, gira - Spanish *guerra*
Waray speaker – *n.*
waraywaray, waraynon
warehouse – *n.* budiga -
Spanish *bodega*
warm – *kan.* mapaso
warn – *n., a.* pasabot,
pahimangno, waydong
pagpasabot, pagwaydong
pagpahimangno
warning – *n.* pahimangno,
pahibaro, waydong, abiso -
Spanish *aviso*
wash – *n., a.* hugas, paghugas
wash basin - *n.* batya,
palanggana - Spanish
palangana
wash body – *n., a.* labar,
paglabar – Spanish *lavar*
wash face – *n., a.* hirámos,
paghirámos, panhiramus
wash feet – *n., a.* himsaw,
paghimsaw, panhimsaw,
pamusa, pagtalimsaw
wash hand – *n., a.* hunaw,
paghunaw, panhunaw
wash laundry – *n., a.* laba,
paglaba, panlaba
washerwoman – *n.* paraglaba,
parapanlaba, labandera -
Spanish *lavandera*
wasp – *n.* lapinig
waste – *n., a.* basura, karag,
pagkarag, paglabog,
pagwagtang, pagbasura

waste time – *n., a.* bagisbagis,
langanlangan, hulathulat
wasted – *kan.* hubog
wasteful – *kan.* kanugon,
makarag, magasto
watch – *n.* orasan, relo -
Spanish *reloj*
watch – *n., a.* bantay, ikmat,
mangno, kitakita, pagbantay,
pagikmat, pagmangno,
pagkitakita
watch intently – *n., a.* titig,
tutok, pagtitig, pagtutok
watchman – *n.* bantay,
mangno, paramangno
water – *n.* túbig
water buffalo - *n.* karabaw
water plants – *n., a.* bisibis,
tubíg, pagtubíg, pagbisibis
water scoop – *n.* hungot, kabó
- Spanish *cubo*
water snail – *n.* susó
water spout – *n.* buhawi,
ipoipo
watercress – *n.* tangkong,
kangkong
waterfall – *n.* palanas
watermelon – *n.* pakwan
wave – *n.* balód, humatol
waver – *n., a.* alangalang,
kahulop, ruhaduha, duhaduha,
pagalangalang
way – *n.* agian, aragian, dalan
we – *han.* kami, kitá
weak – *kan.* malúya, lupaypay
weakness – *n.* luya
wealth – *n.* bahandi, karikuhan
– Spanish *rico*
wealthy – *kan.* mayada,
salapían, bahandianon
weapon – *n.* panngaway,
armas - Spanish *arma*
wear – *n., a.* súlot, pagsúlot

wear cutlass – *n., a.* taklos,
pagtaklos
wear in reverse – *n., a.* balisa,
pagbalisa
wear out – *n., a.* ibas, pagibas
weather – *n.* panahon
weave – *n., a.* lára, paglára,
panlara
weave pattern – *n., a.* sinamay,
pagsinamay
wed – *n., a.* kasal, pangasal,
pankasal
wedding dance – *n.* paado
Wednesday – *n.* Miyerkules -
Spanish *miercoles*
week - *n.* simana - Spanish
semana
weigh – *n., a.* timbang,
patimbang, pagtimbang,
pagpatimbang
weighing scale – *n.* timbangan
weight – *n.* búgat, timbang
welcome – *n., a.* paabot,
pagpaabot
well – *n.* timba, bubon
wellness - *n.* kaupayan
west – *n.* katunuran, katundan
west wind – *n.* habagat
wet – *n., a., kan.* hulós,
humog; mahulos, paghulos,
paghumog
wet and dirty – *kan.* mayamuit
whale – *n.* bungansiso
wharf – *n.* pantalan, duungan,
duruungan, mulye – Spanish
muelle
what – *han.* áno
whatever – *han.* magin,
magínano, bísano
wheat – *n.* trigo – Spanish *trigo*
wheat flour – *n.* arina -
Spanish *harina*

wheel – *n., a.* kaliding,
gulong, yanta, pagkaliding
wheelbarrow – *n.* karitilya
whelk – *n.* bukawil
when – *han.* kakáno (past
query), sáno (future query)
when – *s.* pag
whenever – *kaa.* bisansáno
where – *han.* háin
where – *han., kaa., s.* háin,
diin
wherever – *kaa.* bisandiin
whether – *s.* pananglitan
which – *han.* ámo, áno while
– *s.* samtang, myentras -
Spanish *mientras*
whine – *n., a.* aringit,
pagaringit
whip – *n., a.* latob, latigo -
Spanish *latigo*
whirlpool – *n.* alibundan
whisper – *n., a.* huring,
paghuring
whistle – *n., a.* taghoy, supliti,
sirbato - Spanish *silbato*,
pagtaghoy, pagsulpiti,
pagsirbato
white – *n., kan.* buság,
mabusag
white flower - *n., kan.*
sampaka, marol, sampagita
Jasminum sambac
whiten – *n., a.* busag,
pagbusag, pagpabusag
whitish skin fungal infection –
n. alápap
who – *han.* híno, síno
whoever – *han.* maginhino
whole – *n.* búgos, lubos
wholehearted – *kan.* húlos
wholeheartedly – *kaa.*
kinasingkasing
whom – *s.* kankanay

199

whomever - *han.* maginhino
whose – *han., s.* kanay
why - *kaa.* káyano
wick - *n.* pabilo, hiludibila -
Spanish *hilo de vela*
wide - *kan.* halapad, hilapad
wide brim hat - *n.* sadok
wide-open – *kan.* huwang,
kahaluagan
widow, widower – *n.* balo
width – *n.* lápad, kahaluag
wife – *n.* asawa
wild – *kan.* layaw, ihalas,
barumbado, salbahi - Spanish
salvaje
wild duck – *n.* gamaw wild
forest – *n.* kakahuyan,
kabagwakan
will – *n., a.* buót, tuig,
tagubilin, larang, kaburúton,
pagbuót, paglarang, pagtuig
willpower – *n.* kaladngan
wilt – *n., a., kan.* laya, luyat,
nalaya, paglaya
win – *n., a.* daog, sangpot,
pagdaog, pagsangpot
wind – *n.* hangin
wind around – *n., a.* alikos,
pagalikos
wind gust – *n.* huyop, madlos
wind-stripped – *a., kan.*
barikas, barikasan
winded – *kan.* makapoy,
nahangos
window – *n.* dungawan,
tanawan, bintana - Spanish
ventana
window panel – *n.* sada
windy – *kan.* mahangin
wing – *n.* pakó
wink – *n., a.* kiró, pagkiró
winner – *n., kan.* daugan,
madaóg

winning – *n.* daóg
winnow – *n., a.* tahop,
pagtahop
wipe – *n., a.* pahíd, lahid,
trapo, punas; páhid, pamahid
wire – *n.* alamre - Spanish
alambre
wish – *n., a.* hingyap, ungara,
hangaron
wishful thought – *kah.* iraira
wishfully – *kaa.* kunta, unta
witch – *n.* aswang, wakwak
witch doctor – *n.* tambalan
with – *kat.* upod, hin, sin
withdraw money – *n., a.*
kubra, pagkubra
wither – *n., a., kan.* laya,
pagkalaya, nalaya
within – *kat.* súlod
without interruption – *kaa.*
sigidas - Spanish *seguida*
witness – *n., a.* sayod, kitá,
saksi, testigo - Spanish *testigo*,
pagsayod, pagkita, pagsaksi
wobble – *n., a.* ingka,
kilingkiling, tiwugtiwog,
pagkilingkiling, pagingka
wobbly – *kan.* tikwugon,
maluyá, makiwa,
matiwugtiwog
wok – *n.* karaha
woman – *n.* babayi, daraga
womanizer – *n.* babayero
womb – *n.* matris – Spanish
matriz
wonder – *n., a.* úsa, pausa,
pahiusa
wonderful – *kan.* urusahon
woo – *n., a.* panguyab,
pangunsuylo
woo with music – *n., a.*
harana, pagharana
wood – *n.* kahoy

wood carving – *n.* tingib, tinigib
wood worm – *n.* tamilok
wooden image – *n.* santos - Spanish *santo*
wooden mortar – *n.* lusong
wooden pestle – *n.* bayó
wooden planks – *n.* tabla
wooden sandal – *n.* bakya
wooden vertical support – *n.* harigi
woodland – *n.* kakahuyan
word – *n.* pulong, ngaran, yakan
words of wisdom – *n.* siringanon, siridnganon, darahunon
work – *n., a.* búhat, buruhaton, ubra -Spanish *obra*, trabaho - Spanish *trabajo*, pagbúhat, pagubra, pagtrabaho
work together – *n., a.* burublig, bublig, pagburublig
workaholic – *kan.* maduruto
worker – *n.* trabahador - Spanish *trabajador,* obriro – Spanish *obrero*
working hard – *a.* pagsiguro, paniguro
workshop – *n.* talyer – Spanish *taller*
world – *n.* kalibutan
worldly – *kan.* kinalibutanon
worm – *n.* ulod, watí
worn-out - *kan.* panás, napánas
worried – *kan.* nabaraka, naringgal, kinukulba
worrisome – *kan.* karinggalan, makakarulba, kabarakan
worry – *n., a.* baraka, ringgal, kabaraka, karinggal, kulba, pagkulba, pagbaraka, pagringgal
worsening – *kan.* naduroy, pagduroy
worship – *n., a.* singba, ampo, dayig, pagsingba, pagampo, pagdayid
worth – *n., a.* pulos, pagpulos
wound – *n., a.* samad, pagsamad
woven bamboo slats – *n.* amakan
woven color pattern – *n., kan.* sinamay
wrap – *n., a.* putos, pagputos
wrath – *n., a.* ngalas, kangaralson
wrestle – *n., a.* dulóng, sunggo, sari
wrinkle – *n., a., kan.* kuros, kurumos, kupos, pagkuros, pagkurumos, pagkupos
write – *n., a.* surát, badlis, pagsurat, pagbadlis

X:x
xerox – *n., a.* seroks, pagseroks
X-ray – *n., a.* Iks-re
xylophone – *n.* silopon – English *xylophone*

Y:y
yard – *n.* libong, kaligiran
yarn – *n.* inulang
yawn – *n., a.* huyam, paghuyam

year – *n.* tuig
yearly thanksgiving feast – *n.*
patron, piyesta - Spanish *fiesta*
yell – *n., a.* gulíat, suriyaw,
kuyahaw, paggulíat,
pagsuriyaw, pagkuyahaw
yellow color – *n., kan.* dulaw,
bulaw, darág
yellow fin tuna – *n.* barilis
yellowish – *kan.* madulaw
yes – *n.* oo
yesterday – *n.* kakulop
yesterday a day before – *n.*
kasangkulop
yesteryears – *n.* kasanhi
yet – *kaa.* pa
you (plural) – *han.* kamo
you (singular) – *han.* ikaw
young – *kan.* báta,batánon
young chicken – *n.* siwo young
coconut – *n.* silot
young water buffalo (carabao)
– *n.* nati
younger – *kan.* manghod,
barubata
younger sibling – *n.* manghod
youngest child - *n.* pudo
your – *han.* imo, im, nimo
youth – *n., kan.* kabataan,
batánon

zigzag pattern – *kan.*
giringgiting
zipper – *n.* siper - American
zipper
zit – *n.* púnggod
zodiac – *n.* sodyak, English
zodiac
zonked – *adj.* hubog
zone – *n.* barangay, purok
zoo – *n.* kamanampanan
zuckini – *n.* patula

Z:z

zany – *kan.* salipungog, paog,
pusong
zenith – *n.* kasagsagan
zero – *num.* waray, sero,
Spanish *cero*
zest – *n.* pagkamalipayon
zigzag – *n., a.* likoliko,
palikoliko

Legend:

n – ngaran
han – hangaran
kan – kangaran
a – agi
kaa – kaagi
s – sumpay
kat – katungod
kah – kahiusa
tud – tudlok
num - numero